Getting Through

Getting Through

The Pleasures and Perils of Cross-Cultural Communication

Roger Kreuz and Richard Roberts

The MIT Press
Cambridge, Massachusetts
London, England

Illustrations by Enkhtur Bayarsaikhan

This book was set in ITC Stone Sans Std and ITC Stone Serif Std by Toppan Best-set Premedia Limited. Printed and bound in the United States of America.

Library of Congress Cataloging-in-Publication Data

Names: Kreuz, Roger J. author. | Roberts, Richard (Richard Miller), 1959-
Title: Getting through : the pleasures and perils of cross-cultural communication / Roger J. Kreuz and Richard M. Roberts.
Description: Cambridge, MA : The MIT Press, [2017] | Includes bibliographical references and index.
Identifiers: LCCN 2016047095 | ISBN 9780262036313 (hardcover : alk. paper)
Subjects: LCSH: Intercultural communication. | Pragmatics.
Classification: LCC P94.6 K74 2017 | DDC 302.23--dc23 LC record available at https://lccn.loc.gov/2016047095

10 9 8 7 6 5 4 3 2 1

This book is dedicated to those who serve their countries abroad.

Illustrations by Enkhtur Bayarsaikhan

Contents

Preface

If you talk to a man in a language he understands, that goes to his head. If you talk to him in his language, that goes to his heart.

—Nelson Mandela

There are only two things I can't stand in this world: people who are intolerant of other people's cultures—and the Dutch.

—Michael Caine as Nigel Powers in *Goldmember* (2002)

We live in contentious times. It's heartbreaking to see in the news so much intolerance, hatred, and fear of those perceived to be different from ourselves. But we believe that the more we understand about how people use language to communicate, the more we can avoid conflict with each other.

In this book, we explore cross-cultural communication through the lens of pragmatics. In other words, we review the scientific work on how language is used socially around the world. Our goal is not to cover every topic in this field but rather to highlight how people from different cultural backgrounds use language. In some cases, we point out linguistic similarities among cultures. In other cases, we point out differences. But just because language use differs, that doesn't mean people differ.

As Maya Angelou wrote so eloquently in her poem "Human Family," "We are more alike, my friends, than we are unalike."

We believe that cultural differences are a matter of degree, not of kind. In fact, it's not possible to define culture in such a way that clear distinctions can be made between what are, and what are not, separate cultures. In the United States, we are bogged down in a series of so-called culture wars: blue states and red states; men and women; young and old; the one percent and the ninety-nine percent; black and white; gay and straight; dog people and cat people. Members of these groups, among many others, have been described as being culturally distinct. But, for example, when men and women talk to each other in the United States, are they speaking cross-culturally? That claim has been made.[1]

Consider the following definition of culture:

... that complex whole which includes knowledge, belief, art, morals, law, custom and other capabilities and habits acquired by man as a member of a society.[2]

Based on a definition like this, any country or region could be described as consisting of one culture or as consisting of many. It's a matter of degree, and of how fine-grained you want your perspective to be. The economist John Powelson wrote, "Strictly speaking, there is no such thing as 'cross-cultural' communication. Any communication at all depends on the sharing of *some* subcultures."[3] In other words, if all communication is cross-cultural at some level, then distinguishing between what is *inter*cultural and what is *intra*cultural becomes a fool's errand. That said, people do live in different countries, do speak different languages, and do perceive themselves to be part of different cultures. We respect and celebrate this diversity.

Throughout the book, we have tried to neither overstate nor understate the influence of cultural differences. In the research we have included, we wanted the authors of the studies to speak for themselves. If they call their work cross-cultural, then we do too. If they don't, then we don't. And as cognitive scientists, we tend to cast the net rather broadly, drawing on research from anthropology, education, linguistics, philosophy, psychology, and sociology.

We have organized the book into seven chapters, each one focusing on different facets of cross-cultural pragmatics. In chapter 1, we look at some fundamentals that underlie all communication, such as empathy, intention, and attribution. In chapter 2, we introduce concepts that form the foundation on which the study of pragmatics has been built. In chapter 3, we consider how language is used to accomplish communicative goals. In chapter 4, we explore cross-cultural issues related to broad topics such as humor, profanity, and small talk. In chapter 5, we discuss some of the mechanics of language, such as the ways in which people interrupt, hedge, and use personal space. In chapter 6, we look at specific speech acts such as invitations, complaints, and apologies. And in the final chapter, we consider new forms of communication and some of the problems they facilitate, such as flaming, shaming, and trolling. We also take a look at cross-cultural issues related to Sign language and so-called secret languages. We close by discussing ways in which one can develop better pragmatic competence.

In writing this book, we have drawn on real-world examples taken from the news, books, movies, and our own experiences living, working, and traveling abroad. Enkhtur Bayarsaikhan, a talented Mongolian artist, sketched some of these situations for us. We hope these anecdotes will illustrate some of the pleasures and perils of cross-cultural communication.

It would be impossible to describe all the places where language and culture intersect. We have chosen topics that highlight important issues to keep in mind, whether you are teaching or studying a foreign language, living or traveling abroad, or just want to know more about how people use language. When you reach the end of the book, we hope you will have gained a keener appreciation for how communicative problems can arise—at any time or any place with anyone—and, even more important, how to anticipate and prevent such misunderstandings. And not just with the Dutch.

Roger Kreuz
Richard Roberts
Seaside, Oregon
July 2016

Acknowledgments

Roger would like to thank Josef Meiering and Cilli Böggering Meiering, who inspired him to launch this project. He is also grateful for the continued support of Captain Tom Nenon and all hands in Scates Hall. His crewmates Jason Braasch, Bob Cohen, Stephanie Huette, and Deb Tollefsen listened with unfailing good humor to his long-winded tales from the sea.

Richard would like to thank his shipmates at the US Embassy in Seoul, including cruise director Choi Eun Kyong, who made sure there was never a dull moment, and ship's navigator An Sun-Nam, who charted a course for Richard's discussion of language and culture throughout Korea. First mates Ha Joo-Heon and Jeff Lee helped with our discussion of age in Korea and texting conventions, respectively. And thanks to Yoshi-hiro Kitagawa, who charted the course to Odaiba. Fellow buccaneers Victoria Augustine, Sunny Chang, Cho Geon Hyeon, George "Champagne" Dolan, Eunice Ha, Hong Su Yean, Sylbeth Kennedy, Kim Sung Sig, Lee Young Kum, Greg Morgan, Park Hongduck, Jason Thornton, Mark Seaman, Keunhyun Shin, Woo Seung Hyun, Vanessa Zenji, Alex Hardin and Shuta Kobayashi were delightful company in the galley. Richard's conversations with them helped him think more deeply about these issues, and he will always remember their adventures together on the high seas.

Roger and Richard are very grateful for the continued support of Phil Laughlin, Chris Eyer, Susan Mai, Susan Clark, Judy Feldmann, and the rest of the crew at the MIT Press. We also thank William Henry for his astute copyediting. The comments of three anonymous reviewers on the project's proposal helped the authors to find their bearings. We salute Enkhtur Bayarsaikhan for illustrating our examples so swimmingly. And thanks to the sharp eyes of Susan Fitzgerald, Gina Caucci, and Alexei Kral in the crow's nest, a number of editorial icebergs were spotted and avoided.

Because Richard works for the US Department of State, he would like to make clear that the contents of the book are his opinions and not those of the US government.

About the Authors

Roger Kreuz has been a professor of psychology for nearly thirty years. After studying psychology and linguistics at the University of Toledo, he earned his master's and doctoral degrees at Princeton University and was a postdoctoral researcher at Duke University. He has conducted research and published on topics in the psychology of language, primarily in the areas of text and discourse processing and figurative language. His research has been funded by the National Science Foundation and the Office of Naval Research. He has coedited two books: *Empirical Approaches to Literature and Aesthetics* and *Social and Cognitive Approaches to Interpersonal Communication*. He currently serves as an associate dean in the College of Arts and Sciences at the University of Memphis.

Richard Roberts's educational background spans the speech and hearing sciences, clinical psychology, and experimental psychology. After earning his doctorate at the University of Memphis, he was a postdoctoral researcher at the National Center for Health Statistics. He spent twelve years teaching psychology in Europe and Asia with the University of Maryland University College. During that time, he achieved varying degrees of proficiency in

German, Portuguese, and Japanese. Since 2006 he has been a US diplomat, serving at embassies in Niger, Japan, South Korea, and Mongolia. He has also studied French, Japanese, and Korean at the US Department of State's Foreign Service Institute. He is currently the public affairs officer for the US Consulate General in Naha, Okinawa, Japan.

Together, Roger and Richard have published research articles and book chapters on discourse processing and pragmatics. They are also the authors of *Becoming Fluent: How Cognitive Science Can Help Adults Learn a Foreign Language* (MIT Press, 2015).

About the Illustrator

Enkhtur Bayarsaikhan is a character designer and 3-D artist who resides in Ulaanbaatar, Mongolia. He has illustrated a series of children's educational books and posters and created company logos and television commercials. His work has won several awards.

Prologue: Setting Sail

Think of a language as being like a ship. The sounds and words are the hull. They provide the foundation and keep the ship afloat. The grammar is the rudder, which allows you to steer the ship. Rhetorical flourishes, like metaphors and idioms, are the superstructure that gives the ship its distinctive shape. But whether your vessel is a dinghy or an aircraft carrier, if you don't know how to navigate, you'll always stay in port. That's where pragmatics comes in. Because pragmatics is how language is used, it can be thought of as the navigational equipment on a ship that takes you where you want to go. There's no reason to build a ship without also developing the skills to navigate in open water. With an understanding of pragmatics, you can set sail for foreign shores and exotic locales. And once you get there, you can maneuver around the unfamiliar reefs and shoals, unafraid of rough seas or the swells of an oncoming storm. Our mission is to help you get your sea legs.

1   Culture and Its Consequences

The Road to Communication Failure Is Paved with Good Intentions

There is a paradox inherent in cross-cultural communication. No one sets out to misunderstand or to be misunderstood. Yet it happens frequently. In fact, highlighting cultural misfires is something of a cottage industry in Hollywood, hence the ever-reliable "fish-out-of-water" story line. And although it's doubtful anyone would have gone to see a movie called *Found in Translation*, no one sets out to become lost. So it is important to understand why even the most culturally sensitive among us can still end up saying the wrong thing, or can be misunderstood as having said the wrong thing, or mistakenly believe others have said the wrong thing.

A knee-jerk reaction to problems in cross-cultural communication is to blame a communicative failure on the peculiarities of a language, culture, or the people who share them. But as the saying goes, "It's a poor craftsman who blames his tools." Misdirected finger-pointing can lead to the stereotyping of individuals or their language and culture.

One way to avoid stereotyping is to remember that the cognitive processes that underlie communication are, for all intents and purposes, the same whether you are talking to your best friend or to a stranger from another country.[1] The same kinds of communicative problems a person faces in a cross-cultural setting arise even among conversational participants who share a language or a cultural background.

Although cultural differences in and of themselves do not cause a communication breakdown, they do raise the stakes when a breakdown occurs. The real culprit of cross-cultural communication failures is when differences in language use go unrecognized, unheeded, or unacknowledged. For example, if people don't recognize when culture is exerting an influence on the ways in which they are using language, they may make faulty attributions about the other person's intentions.[2]

The British philosopher Paul Grice believed that for any two people to have a successful conversation, each had to assume the other was trying to cooperate.[3] In other words, if I believe you are trying to be understood, I will try to understand you—and vice versa. For Grice, the best way to show conversational cooperation was to tell the truth, not to say too much or too little, to be relevant, and to speak as unambiguously as possible—which all sounds quite reasonable. If we strictly followed these conversational *maxims* (as Grice called them), we might expect to have fewer misunderstandings. But as you've probably guessed, we don't always do this. People don't always tell the truth, sometimes say too much or too little, are not relevant, and don't speak as clearly as they otherwise could.[4]

According to Grice, conversations will not be derailed if the participants make what he called a *conversational implicature*. An implicature is an assumption or inference that someone makes based on what was just said. For example, if I say, "Last night I went to the library to study and lost my wallet," you might infer that I lost my wallet in the library—although that might not be true, since I didn't say where I lost my wallet.

Although it's easy to say something in such a way that the other person makes the wrong inference (for example, by saying "I ate some of the cereal" when in fact you polished off the entire box), drawing inferences usually allows conversation to flow smoothly. Just imagine what would happen if every time you needed to infer something in a conversation you stopped to verify your assumptions with the other person.

Making the right conversational implicature isn't foolproof even within one's own culture. Certainly it's possible for friends to misunderstand each other, or to jump to the wrong conclusion, or to take offense at something that wasn't meant in a negative way. The issue, then, is not whether or not people in other cultures make inferences; we all do. The challenge is to figure out what kinds of inferences are appropriate given what was just said. This is much harder to do if you don't fully understand the other person's background or culture.

Why Did She Say It Like That?

I speak Spanish to God, Italian to women, French to men, and German to my horse.

—Attributed to the Holy Roman Emperor Charles V

When Richard was living in Heidelberg, he was dining at a restaurant, and although he was speaking English to his friend, he ordered the food in German. The server seemed surprised, and she asked him nicely how long he had lived in Germany. Richard responded, "On and off for about three years." She replied in a very friendly tone, "Your German should be a lot better."

But Richard wasn't offended; he was used to comments like these. Once, when introducing himself, the person he was meeting made a face and replied, "What an old-fashioned name! Germans don't name their children Richard anymore." (In case you are wondering, this person's name was Eugen, which made Richard feel a little better.)

Similarly, very early one Sunday morning when Richard was leaving a nightclub in an industrial part of Stuttgart, he crossed against a stoplight. From seemingly out of nowhere, a woman yelled at him in German, "That is no example for children!"

What's going on here? In each case, the statement was undoubtedly true: Richard's German could have been better, the popularity of the name Richard has declined in recent years, and any children hanging out in the warehouse district at 4 a.m. would certainly have been led astray. But why were these speakers seemingly so rude?

Conversational participants have many choices in how they convey meaning, and they are aware that others also have choices. Consequently both parties in a conversation must repeatedly answer the question "Why did the other person say it that way?" The answer will fall into one of two categories. We can attribute the choice to *internal*, personal characteristics of the speaker (he's a funny guy). Or we can attribute the choice to something that is *external* to the person (he's trying to lighten the mood). It's also possible that both could be true (he's trying to lighten the mood because he's a funny guy).[5]

However, there is a bias when it comes to which kind of attribution we are likely to make. Psychologists have shown that when it comes to other people, we tend to make internal, dispositional attributions about their behavior. But when it comes to ourselves, we often explain our own behavior in external, situational terms.[6] Imagine walking down the street and seeing a homeless person. Not knowing the person, you might attribute her homelessness to being lazy or not wanting to work. But if you asked her why she is homeless, she will probably tell you about the situational factors that led to her becoming homeless.

This bias toward making dispositional attributions about the behavior of other people also holds true when we infer reasons for another's conversational choices. And it can be especially harmful in cross-cultural situations if we egotistically assume that the other person said something for the same reasons that we would have.[7] In other words, we often believe that others make the same conversational choices we do. Then we take this problematic assumption one step further. We infer that their choice reflects their personality and not their language or culture. For example, because German is considered a more direct language than English, Britons may perceive Germans who are merely speaking normally as being intentionally rude. Likewise, Germans may feel that the less-direct conversational choices of the British reflect an inherent deviousness.[8]

Obviously, when Germans speak to each other, they don't perceive each other as being particularly rude. In the same way, the British don't think of each other as being particularly sneaky just by speaking English. An erroneous attribution is made, however, when the answer to the question "Why did she say it like that?" is "*I* would only have said it that way to be rude (or sneaky), so *she* must be being rude (or sneaky)."

Problematic cross-cultural attributions can arise even between speakers of the same language. Once in Cambridge,

England, Richard was at dinner with a different friend (Richard likes to eat) when he dropped his fork on the floor. When the server walked by, Richard said, "Excuse me, but could you please bring me another fork?" After the server left, Richard's friend said, "That's just like you Americans, always ordering people around." Richard thought he had been polite—he had said "please," after all—so he asked his English friend how he would have done it. He said he would have waited until the server came within earshot, then he would have held up the fork and said, "Oh dear, I seem to have dropped my fork," and then wait for the server to offer to bring him a new one. Richard thought that if he tried that approach in New York, he'd be waiting a long time.

Although these are lighthearted examples, the attribution process can have international ramifications, as the tragic event in the next section illustrates.

The Case of EgyptAir 990

On October 31, 1999, EgyptAir Flight 990 lumbered into the crisp fall air over JFK Airport in Queens, New York. The Boeing 767 was beginning a routine ten-hour flight to Cairo, with 203 passengers and fourteen crewmembers aboard. Shortly after reaching its cruising altitude, the plane suddenly plummeted into the ocean, about sixty miles south of the island of Nantucket. The weather was good, and there had been no distress call from the pilots. In fact, everything about the flight seemed completely ordinary—right up until it crashed into the Atlantic.

A search by ships and planes failed to locate any survivors. Later, the wreckage of the plane was identified on the ocean floor, and within a few days, the flight data and cockpit voice recorders—the so-called black boxes—were recovered by a remotely controlled submersible operated by the US Navy.

There were two investigations of this tragedy to determine its cause. One was led by the US National Transportation Safety Board (NTSB); the other was conducted by the Egyptian Civil Aviation Authority (ECAA). The two investigations came to starkly different conclusions. The NTSB concluded that the crash was the result of deliberate actions by one of the pilots,[9] while the ECAA ruled that the crash occurred because of a mechanical failure of the plane's elevator control system.[10]

In its analysis of the cockpit voice record, the NTSB investigation zeroed in on the words and actions of the relief first officer,

Gameel Al-Batouti. He was a fifty-nine-year-old veteran of the Egyptian Air Force and had worked for EgyptAir for three years. He had nearly six thousand hours of experience flying the Boeing 767.

Al-Batouti was not supposed to be in the cockpit at that early point in the flight, but he had asked if he could relieve the command first officer shortly after takeoff. The request was granted. Shortly after the captain went to use the lavatory, Al-Batouti was recorded to have said, in Egyptian Arabic, توكلت على الله, *Tawakkaltu Ala-Allah*, or "I am putting my trust in Allah and depending on him." Subsequently this phrase was frequently translated as "I put my trust in God" or even more simply as "I rely on God." He then disengaged the plane's autopilot and repeated the phrase again. He idled the engines and changed the elevators so that the plane would begin to descend. Throughout all of this, he repeated the phrase a total of eleven times. Suddenly the voice of the captain was heard asking, "What's happening, what's happening?" He went on to exclaim, "What is this? What is this? Did you shut the engines?" During this exchange, the plane's elevators were in a split condition, suggesting that the captain and Al-Batouti were struggling with the controls but carrying out opposite actions. The last words captured by the voice recorder were spoken by the captain, saying, "Pull with me," even as the elevators remained in a split condition.[11]

Speculation about the cause of the plane's demise began immediately, with *USA Today* and several television networks reporting (incorrectly) that Al-Batouti had said, "I made my decision now. I put my faith in God's hands." This mistranslation of the first officer's words was publicly corrected in late November, but by then, for many, it scarcely mattered. The actual phrase, "I rely on God," seemed incriminating enough. These words, and especially their repetition by Al-Batouti, were the equivalent of a smoking gun in the minds of many. The first officer had committed suicide and mass murder, and his words were an explicit acknowledgment of his intentions and his guilt.

Al-Batouti's words were perceived very differently by his fellow Egyptians and by others in the Arab world. As a religious Muslim, Al-Batouti would routinely have uttered this phrase many times a day. It's customary to utter these words at the beginning of even quite mundane activities, such as turning the ignition key in a car or unlocking a door. Mahmoud el-Azzazzay, a former employee of EgyptAir, was quoted as claiming that devout Muslims probably utter the phrase "200 or more times a day."[12] Ibrahim Hooper, the director of an advocacy group in Washington, stated that "the mere utterance of this kind of phrase would in no way indicate criminal behavior or intent." He added, "If the inference was by a Christian pilot who said 'God help me,' we wouldn't even have this conversation." Vincent Cornell, a faculty member at Duke University, was reported as saying that the actual meaning of the phrase would crucially depend on the context in which it was employed.[13]

In addition, the opprobrium that a suicide would have brought to Al-Batouti's family—he had a wife and five children—should have precluded the act, as well. Family members stressed that he was not depressed at the time, as some media outlets had reported, and in fact he had everything to live for. He was looking forward to his upcoming retirement and spending time at his newly built retirement home.[14]

What really happened, and what did Al-Batouti mean when he repeated those words over and over? In truth, we will never know with absolute certainty. And this case is particularly fraught, since it involves both religion and the deaths of so many people. In this instance, Al-Batouti's words are like a Rorschach inkblot test in that they allow for multiple attributions based on context and culture. Knowing how context and culture exert an influence on communication is therefore crucial.

Best Foot Forward, but in Someone Else's Shoes

It may seem odd that this book about cross-cultural communication does not focus on any one language or culture. After all, most guides to understanding and being understood in a particular culture stress the unique features of the target language and culture. And we don't want to minimize the importance of such information. For example, it is considered extremely rude in Thailand to show someone the bottom of your shoe or foot. When Richard was in Bangkok, he went to a cabaret show that featured a Madonna impersonator. To stay in character, the impersonator gyrated and made lewd gestures while lip-synching to a Madonna song. At the height of the performance, however, "Madonna" did something most foreign audiences would not have considered particularly remarkable, let alone obscene. She sat on a chair, kicked up her legs, and held them in the air, flashing the bottom of her shoes at the crowd. The Thai audience gasped, went silent for a split second, and then erupted in loud cheers and applause. With that one culturally specific profanity, the Thai Madonna had found a way to truly shock—and delight—the crowd.

It is hardly surprising that cross-cultural experiences become fuller and richer as our understanding of the particulars of a target culture become deeper. Had Richard not known about the Thai taboo against exposing the soles of your shoes or feet,

he would have missed the significance of the gesture. So without a doubt, we highly recommend exploring the specifics of different cultures. If you are going to Thailand, learn as much Thai as you can, and be sure to acquire some knowledge that will allow you to interact with the Thai people in culturally appropriate ways.

But no language course, list of dos and don'ts, etiquette book, or travel guide could possibly capture every cross-cultural situation that might arise in Thailand or any other place. Moreover, an attempt to create a complete list would be fruitless, because norms vary within cultures as well as between them, and they change over time. Developing cross-cultural competence in any context relies on more than just learning what to do and not to do in a specific situation.

At its most basic level, effective communication between individuals from different cultures, no matter how large or small the difference, relies on the ability to take another person's perspective. Put simply, one must see the world through someone else's eyes. The ability to do this is called empathy, and it lies at the heart of cross-cultural communication (pun intended).

But before we all start singing "Kumbaya," it is important to make a distinction. The kind of empathy necessary for effective cross-cultural communication is cognitive empathy, not emotional empathy.[15] Cognitive empathy is one's ability to understand someone else's thoughts or feelings. Emotional empathy is the ability to share those thoughts and feelings. When considering other people's cognitive perspective, it might be desirable to share their emotional feelings, but it is not strictly necessary. These two types of empathy are distinct. For example, psychopaths, who by definition lack emotional empathy, are masters at understanding the motivations, thoughts, and feelings of others. In fact, their lack of emotional empathy allows them to be masters of manipulation.[16] Psychopaths understand their victims but aren't burdened by guilt or remorse when it comes to taking advantage of them. Conversely, individuals with Asperger syndrome, a mild form of autism, often show a lack of ability to take another's perspective,[17] but this deficit does not interfere with their concern for the well-being of others.

We often think about the importance of being empathic in sad or unfortunate circumstances. But when it comes to communication, the cognitive aspects of empathy are always required. For example, Richard wasn't shocked to see the bottom of the Madonna impersonator's feet, so he couldn't emotionally empathize with the Thai audience. But he could relate to what it means to be suddenly surprised by a rude gesture, so he could cognitively empathize with them as their reaction changed from surprised, to offended, to entertained. In the end, Richard was also entertained by the performance, but the pleasure he got from seeing it came from his ability to understand the crowd's response, not from sharing it.

Empathy in cross-cultural contexts works because even though cultures and languages vary from place to place, our humanity does not. In other words, no cultural variation, no matter how seemingly bizarre, is ever so alien as to fall outside the scope of human experience or emotion. This fact should allow us to empathize with anyone from Afghanistan to Zimbabwe.

The ability to bond with another person through empathy is one of the great pleasures of all communication—cross-cultural or otherwise. Shakespeare is still relevant today because we can empathize with his characters. Even the cave paintings at Lascaux speak to us across the millennia. This communal reaction is grounded in the fact that the fundamental human emotions, such as sadness, happiness, anger, and surprise, are remarkably similar around the world.[18] The ability to empathize is universal, regardless of whether or not one does so in a given situation.

But if the biological basis of emotions and the ability to empathize is so fundamental and universal, why do cross-cultural misunderstandings occur? One reason may be that we can never completely know all the ways in which another person differs— and does not differ—from ourselves. Our own values, norms, and background, coupled with a relative lack of knowledge about the other person's values, norms, and background, can get in the way. Even emotions that are universal will be displayed and interpreted based on cultural specifics. Miscommunication can occur when we assume that we have more in common than we actually do with another person. This is true regardless of how similar or different our cultural backgrounds are.

To make matters worse, we may also overestimate our ability to empathize with others. Consider this: would it be easier for you to empathize with someone whose house burned down or with someone who set fire to another person's house? If we could truly empathize with anyone at will, we should be able to take the perpetrator's perspective as easily as the victim's. But that is not usually the case. This selectivity in our ability to empathize was illustrated by the response to a remark in 2014 by Hillary Clinton in a speech on leadership in which she suggested that it was important to try to empathize with one's enemies.[19] Needless to say, not everyone agreed with her.[20]

Finally, LaRay Barna points out that miscommunication can also arise when we assume that we are more different from others than we actually are.[21] As a case in point, even assumptions about our similarities and differences are culture bound. Eiko Tai points out that Americans are more likely to assume greater cross-cultural similarities, whereas the Japanese are more likely to assume greater cross-cultural differences.[22] In either case, too much or too little credence given to cultural differences can create what Barna calls "stumbling blocks" in cross-cultural communication. Richard has known exchange students from Korea who came to the United States under the impression that American organizations are less formal and less hierarchical than Korean companies. This may be somewhat true, but when these students started their internships, they were surprised to find that they were expected to arrive at work on time, dress professionally, and follow sets of rules related to proper workplace behavior and etiquette. The expectation that US and Korean corporate cultures were more different than alike threw the interns a curve ball.

Empathy, then, is a sword that cuts both ways. It can be the means by which we understand another person, and it can be the means by which we *mis*understand another person. To gain cross-cultural competence, we must accept the duality of both trusting and mistrusting our ability to empathize.

The Granular Nature of Common Ground

In Dr. Seuss's classic children's book *Horton Hears a Who*, an elephant named Horton hears a voice coming from a tiny speck of dust.[23] Horton discovers that the speck of dust is actually a self-contained world called Whoville. Horton tries to protect Whoville when it is threatened with destruction by other animals that don't believe that an entire world could exist on a speck of dust. In the end (spoiler alert), the residents of Whoville work together to make enough noise so that the other animals can hear them. Whoville is saved.

Philosophers, authors, scientists, and others have long posited that our world, like Whoville, may be just one world along a continuum of larger and smaller worlds stretching to infinity. Our place in the universe then becomes one of "granularity," or level of detail. A good example of increasing and decreasing granularity can be seen on Google Maps. If you look at a map of an area and click on the + sign, the map you are looking at becomes more detailed, but you see less area overall. If you click on the – sign, you'll see a greater area, but with less detail.

Conversational granularity works the same way. When speaking with others, it is important to gauge how detailed you need to be. For example, let's say you have a friend named Martin. When you are talking to someone who also knows Martin, you can simply say, "I saw Martin yesterday." But let's say you are talking to Nancy, who doesn't know Martin. In this case, you will have to give Nancy a little more information, such as "I saw my friend Martin yesterday." The words "my friend" act like the "–" sign in Google Maps, making the conversation slightly more general to orient the listener.[24]

To select the right level of granularity, it is necessary to consider *common ground*, which is all the information, culture, and context you share, and *know* you share, with your conversational partner.[25] In this example, to know how detailed you should be when talking to Nancy, you need to know what she knows. You need to consider whether or not Nancy knows Martin. It doesn't matter whether you feel the same way about Martin that Nancy does, as long as you know what she knows about him.

But, of course, it's not that simple. Using common ground to establish the level of granularity in a conversation doesn't always work as planned. For example, suppose that Martin is a nurse. The first time you mention Martin, you might decide to add that fact for context, especially if it is relevant to what you are about to say, as in "My friend Martin, who is a nurse, told me I should lose ten pounds." Leaving out the part about Martin being a nurse would make him sound like a jerk ("My friend Martin told me I should lose ten pounds").

Once it has been established that you have a friend named Martin who is a nurse, you don't need to bring this fact up to Nancy again, because it is now in your common ground. In fact, doing so could signal to Nancy that you don't remember having talked to her about Martin before. This may not be too bad if you haven't talked to Nancy in a long time. But if you say, "My friend Martin, who is a nurse," each time you mention him, you may find Nancy getting irritated with you, because you keep forgetting that she knows who Martin is.

Of course, that doesn't happen with Google Maps, because the software doesn't care if you start out too detailed or not. But in a conversation, there are consequences for choosing the wrong level of granularity. Choosing the right level not only conveys the correct information but also signals that you are in tune with the other person. Inside jokes, for example, exploit shared common ground and serve to separate those "in the know" from everyone else. Choosing the wrong level can leave your conversational partner bewildered, insulted, surprised, angry, or just about any emotion you can name.

When traveling overseas, Americans are a little bit lucky with regard to granularity, because many people from other cultures know quite a bit about the United States. For example, you may not know the name of the leader of a particular country you are visiting, but it's likely the person you are talking to will know the name of the US president. But beyond this it gets tricky, because once you decide on a level of granularity, the other person makes an assumption about why you chose that level. In this example, selecting a detailed level, which assumes knowledge of the US political system, may be seen as egotistical. On the other hand, selecting too broad a level and providing more context than is needed may come across as patronizing.

The stakes are high, therefore, especially in a cross-cultural setting, where it's even more difficult to figure out just what is and is not in the common ground. The best advice is to be like Horton the Elephant. Listen carefully and never forget.

All Aboard for Entrainment

When two people need to refer to the same thing repeatedly, both parties will typically employ the same term, and they may even adopt a shorthand way of referring to it. For example, if your mechanically inclined older sister is attempting to fix your son's model train, she might ask you to pass her the *long flat-head screwdriver with the red handle* from her toolbox. It might be necessary for her to be that specific if there is an assortment of screwdrivers in the toolbox. As your sister's assistant, you need to be able to identify the one she wants from among screwdrivers with flat versus Phillips heads, those that are long and those that are short, and those with handles of various colors. On later occasions, however, your sister might just ask you to hand her the *long red screwdriver*, and eventually just the *red one*.

This process of referring and shortening is called *lexical entrainment.*[26] It's something that adults are quite good at; they figure out how much detail their conversational partner requires, and once that exchange has occurred successfully, they develop a less-cumbersome way of referring to the subject in the future.

Roger enjoys watching the process of lexical entrainment unfold during the televised quiz show *Jeopardy!* in which contestants are asked to create questions that match particular answers. To see an answer, the contestants select a category and a specific dollar amount. For example, a contestant might say, "I'd like 'Celebrity TV Bloopers of 2015' for $200." Later in the game, a contestant might refer to the category by requesting just "Celebrity TV Bloopers," and still later, the category name might be shortened to just "Bloopers." In this way, the contestants have lexically entrained on the category name, which speeds up the game.

The psychologists Robert Krauss and Sam Glucksberg studied how entrainment occurs through a series of experiments.[27] In these studies, two individuals are separated by a screen so that they can hear but not see each other. Both of them have a sheet of paper on which the same unfamiliar shapes are depicted. The pair's task is to put the strange shapes into a predetermined order. To begin, one person might say, "The first shape looks like an hourglass with legs on either side." The other participant attempts to find a shape on her sheet that corresponds to this description. The process of describing and labeling continues until all the shapes have been put in order.

In later trials of the same task, the pair spontaneously entrains by using shorter and shorter descriptions. So "looks like an hourglass with legs on each side" might be shortened to "hour-glass with legs" and then simply to "hourglass."

Adults are good at entrainment, but kids are not. Young children haven't yet developed an understanding that the world might look different to someone else, and as a result, their descriptions display an egocentric bias that short-circuits the process of entrainment. When they are asked to participate in the same matching task, their descriptions of the unfamiliar shapes are frequently idiosyncratic and not particularly helpful. If a child refers to one of the shapes as "Daddy's shirt," this may not be specific enough to allow the other child to unambiguously pick out the object in question. When asked to repeat the task across a series of trials, young children don't show much improvement in their matching accuracy.

So far, so good; but how does lexical entrainment apply to cross-cultural contexts? First, it appears that the process of lexical entrainment may be universal. It's difficult to imagine a language or culture where speakers don't refer to objects or concepts in mutually agreed-on shorthand ways when possible. However, when speakers are from different linguistic or cultural backgrounds, they may find this process to be challenging. A person from one culture may assume that the world looks the same to people from another culture, when in fact it doesn't. Alternatively, someone may assume the world looks different, when in fact it looks the same. In both cases, what appears to be a process of lexical entrainment becomes a lexical derailment.

Lexical entrainment is an example of a broader linguistic phenomenon known as *alignment*. Two participants in a conversation usually try to converge on a particular way of referring to something. For example, if you're using a word in a second language with a native speaker, and he keeps responding by employing a somewhat different term, this lack of alignment may be a cue that you're not using the word in precisely the right way.

Similarly, if a nonnative English speaker repeatedly told you that a horror movie made her *scary*, you might helpfully reply that yes, you were *scared* as well. You might even stress the word a little to call attention to it. An approach like this would be desirable, because instead of pointedly calling attention to her mistake, you are modeling correct usage. Of course, this approach may be too subtle, and the nonnative speaker may not even realize that a correction is being offered. Either way, it's important to keep in mind that while some nonnative speakers genuinely appreciate such feedback, others may find it unhelpful or even patronizing. It becomes a judgment call to determine whether corrective feedback will be noticed or is even desired.

Alignment may occur or fail to occur for a host of other reasons. For example, individuals might align for social purposes. In general, we like others who are like us, and so we may shift our behaviors, including word choice and way of speaking, to match someone else.[28] In one study, French Canadians were perceived more positively when they addressed bilingual English Canadians in a mixture of French and English or used English only.[29] It appears that the more you can align yourself with others in terms of speech style and bodily movement, the more positively you will be seen. Perhaps this is one reason why over time Americans who move to Great Britain start sounding more British, and Britons who move to the United States start sounding more American. It's natural to do this, but be careful not to align so closely that you become a "language zombie."[30] If your boss has curly hair, don't rush out and get a perm. Alignment should not become mimicry.

Sometimes, despite your best intentions, it's not possible to align. For example, one individual in a conversation may insist on referring to an unusual occurrence as a "miracle," whereas her conversational partner might repeatedly use the term "coincidence" to describe the same event. In this case, the failure to align could reflect fundamentally different views of agency: what one person interprets as divine intervention, another might see as fortuitous but essentially random. Therefore, attending carefully to alignment failures is crucial to discover why they have occurred.

Given the ubiquity of the processes of alignment and lexical entrainment, it might be surprising to learn that they can interfere with communication, cross-cultural and otherwise. Even for speakers of the same language, when friends, couples, and coworkers use lexical entrainment, they are setting up an "ingroup" versus "out-group" distinction in which the shorthand term may be baffling to outsiders.

Does lexical entrainment still happen when two speakers who don't speak the same language need to communicate? Yes, but the result is not just a new word. In such cases, the result is a unique communicative system that incorporates various features of the speakers' original languages. Over time, these new communicative systems develop into what are called pidgin languages. For example, Hawaiian Pidgin English grew from the communicative needs of immigrants from different places who came together in Hawaii to work in the sugarcane fields. With English as its base, Hawaiian Pidgin English includes elements of Hawaiian, Chinese, Portuguese, Japanese, some Philippine languages, Korean, and Spanish.

At first, the speakers of pidgins speak their native language among themselves and use the pidgin only to communicate with other groups. But in subsequent generations, pidgins stabilize into what are called *creole* languages. This means that linguistically, although still called "pidgin," Hawaiian Pidgin English should more properly be called a creole language. The U.S. Census Bureau officially recognized Hawaiian Pidgin English as a full-fledged language in 2015.[31] This should come as no surprise, however. Middle English (the precursor of the English we speak today) has been characterized by some as a creole language that started out as a pidgin between Old English and Norman French.[32]

Language learners are susceptible to thinking that they are learning new words in a language when, in fact, they are unwittingly using lexical entrainment to create idiosyncratic terms and usages. This is how we end up with hybrid languages that evolve through the gradual buildup of lexically entrained words like *el parking* for "parking lot" in Spanglish (Spanish and English), *babarikoteu* for a trench coat (Burberry coat) in Konglish (Korean and English), or *J'agree* for "I agree" (*D'accord*) in Franglais (French and English), to name but a few. Hybrid languages are true languages and are an example of two cultural and linguistic systems coming together. In a sense, modern English may really just be updated *Normglish*.

The Importance of Being Bicultural

The dream of many students of a foreign language is to become *bilingual*: to be able to use a second language as proficiently as their mother tongue. In the right environment, young children are able to achieve mastery of two or more languages without formal study. Adults can also become bilingual, of course, but for them it takes concentrated effort.[33] On the other hand, some people, through accident of birth or through conscious effort, become *bicultural*: they are able to navigate two distinct cultures without difficulty. In other words, they have mastered two different sets of social norms, manners, rituals, and traditions and are aware of the myriad factors that can affect public and private interactions. They are, in short, sensitive to the factors that affect communication in both cultures.

Can one be bicultural without being bilingual? Yes, and it happens frequently. If a couple emigrates to a new country, they may never become completely comfortable with their new home's language or culture. Their children, however, will understand that one set of social rules pertains to the family, and a different set is in effect in the world beyond the home. These children may also be bilingual, but if they assimilate rapidly to the new environment, they may end up with two cultural systems and only one language. Research suggests, however, that even without both languages, bicultural individuals exhibit "more fluency, flexibility, and novelty" in their problem-solving abilities.[34]

Can one be bilingual without being bicultural? This also happens frequently, and in fact, it is the fate of most people who learn a second language. Such individuals may be perfectly able to express themselves via the vocabulary and grammar of a second language. But that doesn't mean that they can tell (or understand) a joke, or they may unintentionally behave rudely in social settings. Many things they see and hear may simply go over their heads. Their imperfect understanding of the second language's pragmatics will impair their comprehension in ways and at times that can't be anticipated or predicted.

Obviously, it's best to be both bilingual *and* bicultural. Roger benefited from this combination firsthand during a visit with some relatives in Germany. He attended a family reunion in a small city near the Dutch border. The dialect spoken there was unfamiliar to him, but he did his best to follow along. One night, he was relaxing at a local *Biergarten* with a group of family members and their friends. The conversation turned, or so Roger thought, to the topic of traveling to neighboring towns. He was also pleased to hear the locals using a little English to help him understand. They repeatedly used the word "feets" as they mentioned other villages and towns in the vicinity. Assuming they were unaware of the correct plural of "foot," but grateful for any assistance, Roger tried to make sense of the conversation. However, it was very confusing. They were discussing going "by feets" to places that were fairly distant from each other, which seemed both impressive and also highly unlikely.

One of the family members present for this discussion possessed an unusual background. She had grown up in the area, and then she and her husband had emigrated to Canada and raised a family there. She returned to Germany frequently to visit her relatives. Crucially, she was both bilingual (German and English) and bicultural (Germany and Canada). She took one look at Roger's confused expression, thought for a moment, and smiled. She waited for a break in the conversation and then told him, "They're using the Dutch word for bicycle: it's *fiets*."

Suddenly everything fell into place. The topic of conversation had been a bicycle trip. This would have been obvious to Roger if the German word for bicycle (*Fahrrad*) had been employed at any point in the conversation. But in this border region, it was common to use Dutch terms, as well. And Roger thought that the others were throwing him a bone by using some mangled

English to help him understand, when in fact this actually led him down the wrong conversational path. It took someone who was both bilingual and bicultural to diagnose his confusion and to discover its source. If the unknown Dutch term hadn't sounded like an English word, Roger would simply have chalked it up to his deficient German vocabulary—but at least it wouldn't have been so confusing.

For the rest of the evening, Roger's guardian angel provided commentary to help him follow the conversation. An occasional one-sentence gloss, offered during a lull in the proceedings, was all that he needed to stay on track. Someone who was bilingual but not bicultural probably would have overexplained, but she was able to correctly infer what Roger didn't know, and her annotations were all that he needed.

Even for two North American speakers of English, however, there can still be some cultural differences. Roger was visiting in mid-May, and the upcoming Sunday was Pentecost. Roger's angel correctly assumed that he wouldn't be familiar with the German word for that holiday (*Pfingsten*) or the name of the following day (*Pfingstmontag*). However, rather than say "Pente-cost," she told him that the public holiday was "Whit Monday," which meant nothing to him. In hindsight, this makes sense, since *Whitsunday* is the name for Pentecost used by the Angli-can Church. This example demonstrates that even if two people almost share the same culture, there can still be a gap in their knowledge and ability to explain unfamiliar concepts. As we will see in the next chapter, pragmatic principles can help close the gap.

2 Pragmatics and Its Principles

Let's Get Pragmatic

If you're like most people, then you probably assume that the words we use have fixed and stable meanings. It certainly *seems* that way, and most of us own dictionaries, which purport to list the meanings of words in a given language. While this may be true, it's only true up to a point. As most of us have learned the hard way, to use a dictionary is to be disappointed.

Here's a little thought experiment that will illustrate our point. What does the following sentence mean?

John drinks.

Your first thought is probably that it means "John is an alcoholic." The verb *drink* is used euphemistically in English to refer to alcoholism (as in "a drinking problem"). But if you think about the sentence a bit more, you might realize that it also has a less-specific meaning. It could simply mean that someone named John is currently in the act of drinking *something*—it could be alcohol, but it could really be any liquid, for example, water from a water fountain. So now we have two possible meanings. Are there even more?

If you're stuck at this point, imagine two people who are making plans for a Fourth of July barbecue, which for many Americans would almost certainly include beer. The two planners might create a mental tally of beer drinkers among their friends, and at some point, one of them might say—you guessed it—"John drinks." In this context, the sentence would simply mean that one of the invitees, named John, does imbibe; not necessarily to excess, but he's one of the partygoers who would enjoy a frosty cold one on a warm July evening. So are we done? Does "John drinks" have three and only three meanings? Let's get even more creative.

Imagine that Martians come to Earth, and they select a hapless individual named John as a perfect specimen for the humanoid exhibition in their zoo back on Mars. Soon poor John is in a cage, next to a horned lizard from Venus and flying rodents from Titan. And after a couple of days, John doesn't look so good. At this point, one of the Martians might slap a tentacle against its forehead and say, "Oh, I forgot! John *drinks*!" In this context, our sentence would mean something like "John is a human being and therefore must ingest liquids on a regular basis to survive." Sound far-fetched? Perhaps. But the mere fact that it's *possible* means we have to include it as a *potential* meaning for the word *drinks*.

Okay, now let's open a big, fat, unabridged English dictionary and look up the verb senses of *drink*. So far, we've identified three distinct uses in our thought experiment, and we might expect to find all of them listed. Let's choose the biggest, fattest, most unabridged English dictionary there is: the *Oxford English Dictionary,* which consists of twenty magisterial volumes. In volume 4 of the *OED* (Cr–Du), you'll find sixteen distinct definitions for the verb *drink*. Some definitions are archaic but are included for historical purposes, such as "to inhale tobacco smoke" (definition 5), which seems to have gone out of style in the mid-nineteenth century. But, of course, you'll find "drinking liquid" (definition 1) and "alcoholic" (definition 11). The use of the word *drink* from our Fourth of July example (imbibes, but not necessarily to excess) can also be inferred from definition 11, which describes taking alcohol "either convivially, or to gratify an appetite." If you're a convivial drinker, you don't have a problem, right?

But what about our Martian example (requires the ingesting of liquids to survive)? You won't find that definition of *drink* in the *OED*, perhaps because it's never been used that way before (there are no forgetful alien zookeepers that we know of). A more likely reason for the nonappearance of this definition is that it's simply too narrow; the context in which it might be employed is so specific that it doesn't rise to the level of meriting a definition of its own. And this is true for all words: one can imagine new contexts that create new, or at least different, senses for how people (or Martians) employ the words they use.

And what about nonliteral usage? *Drink* can figuratively mean "to take into the mind" (as in "drink in the sunset"). What about all the ways in which words are used metaphorically? Clichéd or well-worn metaphors, like the "leg" of a chair, might appear in the dictionary (definition 12 of *leg* in the *OED*, in fact), but many possible metaphors would not. And how about verbal irony? If you say "I'm *fine!*" through clenched teeth when you're upset, does that mean that there should be a definition for "fine" that is "*not* fine"? To encompass all of this, as fat as it is, the *OED* would need to become infinite.

Consider another example:

The Smiths saw the Rocky Mountains while they were flying to California.[1]

It may not be immediately obvious, but this sentence is ambiguous. As its authors, Philip Johnson-Laird and Peter Wason point out, it's unclear who's doing the flying—the Rocky Mountains or the Smiths. Or perhaps they are all flying to California together! And we assume that the Smiths are in an airplane, not riding on the back of a giant eagle or using jetpacks. The reason that these interpretations don't spring to mind is that we also bring a great deal of world knowledge to bear when we interpret language. In the world that we all live in, mountains don't fly around, and when humans fly, they do so in airplanes. This knowledge is separate from the language, but it plays a crucial role in its interpretation.

So when we asked, "What does *John drinks* mean?" the answer really is: It depends. It depends on the context. Who is saying the words, and to whom? Why are they being said? Where and when are they being spoken? Context changes meaning, so context matters in a deep and fundamental way. And this is what *pragmatics* is all about: how context—which includes cultural and social factors—provides an overlay on the meanings of words. Outside of a particular context, words are ambiguous, as we've seen with *drink* and the traveling Smiths. But *within* a particular context, say at a water fountain, in a Martian zoo, or on a trip to California, words are rarely ambiguous.

Because dictionaries provide illustrative meanings for only common usages of words, everything else is shrugged off as an issue for pragmatics. But in real-world conversation, it's the "everything else" that matters most. In fact, the linguist Jacob Mey has pointed out that pragmatics was once referred to as a "wastebasket" for semantics (the study of meaning).[2] Making pragmatics a linguistic dumping ground is convenient for dictionary makers, but not so useful for those of us looking up the meanings of words.

Without an understanding of the role of culture, the importance of context, and the psychological processes that underlie how language is used, dictionaries and other reference materials won't be of much use. Dictionaries merely list word meanings. It takes pragmatics to arrive at a correct interpretation. In thinking about how languages work, we need to look under the hood and see how they are put together.

Reading the Dials

Languages are not random collections of cogs and gears but are instead composed of independent systems that operate together as one. Knowing how these individual systems work buys you a great deal in terms of how to use the language as a whole. Let's look at two such systems to illustrate this point.

Many of the world's languages have grammatical *gender*. This means that each noun in the language is assigned to a particular category. All the nouns in a given gender behave the same way, which is different from how the nouns in a different gender behave. Some languages, like French and Spanish, have two: masculine and feminine. Some, like Latin and German, have three: masculine, feminine, and neuter. And some have many more: Chechen has six, and Ganda (spoken in Uganda) has ten![3]

The assignment of gender can be fairly arbitrary: for example, the words for spoon, knife, and fork in German belong to each of the three different genders. The point is, once you've learned a noun's gender, you're all set. You know which articles to use, and how to modify other words as needed.

Now let's consider another, perhaps less-well-known rule system. It turns out that languages also have a preferred word order. Sentences consist of nouns and verbs and describe things like who did what to whom. An English speaker might read the sentence

The cat bit the dog

and have a pretty good idea about which animal is yelping in pain. The dog is not happy, because he is the *object* of the sentence, receiving the brunt of the verb (and a sharp set of teeth). English, therefore, can be described as an SVO language: the subject (S) normally comes first, the verb (V) follows, and the object (O) takes the final position in the sentence. Although English allows other orders in other constructions, such as the passive voice (the dog was bitten by the cat), SVO is the default.

Mandarin Chinese and Russian are also SVO languages, but many other languages do things differently. The most common order, it turns out, is SOV. To continue with our example, this would be the equivalent of "The cat the dog bit" in English. This is the preferred state of affairs in languages like Latin, Japanese, and Turkish. And VSO (Bit the cat the dog) is the normal order in Tagalog, Irish, and Tuareg (spoken in northern Africa). As it turns out, there are six possible orders of subject, verb, and object, and there is at least one language that uses each of them.[4]

The point is that word order is just like gender. Once you know it, you possess a fixed and unchanging parameter of that language. If you're trying to learn a new language, your teacher might tell you that it has two genders and an SOV word order. These two facts, all by themselves, would tell you a great deal about how that language works.

In fact, it's been suggested that when infants acquire their first language, they just have to figure out a certain set of parameters to understand the rudiments of the language's grammar. The linguist Noam Chomsky once likened this to a set of switches that can be flipped to only a couple of positions: once the settings for a given language have been sussed out, the rest of the language's grammar can be acquired much more easily.[5]

Could pragmatic features be described in the same way? It might be a bit more complex than gender assignment, but in principle, one could describe the way a given language is used on a set of pragmatic continua, as in the fictitious example of Martian below:

Martian

Direct ————————————×—— Indirect

Formal —×——————————— Informal

Hierarchical ————————————×—— Egalitarian

Verbose ————————————×— Terse

Now we're getting somewhere! At a glance, you would learn that a Martian's preferred speaking style is fairly indirect and formal. In addition, Martians don't care one way or the other about marking social status, but they value brevity greatly. If you went to Mars but didn't speak Martian, could you modify the way you speak English to be culturally sensitive—that is, indirect, formal, terse, yet egalitarian? Sure you could.

Therefore, when thinking about cross-cultural communication, it is important to recognize that the pragmatic dimensions of any given language, such as formality or directness, have their own default settings. Think about these dimensions as being pragmatic dials that are set higher or lower according to how the language is typically used. Knowing how the dials are set will allow you to communicate more effectively in that culture—regardless of the language you are speaking. It might also keep you from making erroneous attributions. For example, how someone speaks can now be attributed to how a dial is set (Martian is spoken rather indirectly) rather than to a personal characteristic (This Martian is sneaky). Thus you might avoid an interplanetary misunderstanding.

Of course, it's not as simple as that. When it comes to describing how a language is used, we can only speak in a general, relative way. It would be a mistake to describe the settings of the pragmatic dials in absolute terms. For example, one can say that, in general, Japanese is more formal than English. But one can be quite informal in Japanese, for example, at a karaoke bar, and extremely formal in English, for example, when addressing the Queen at court.

It should be clear by now that understanding the pragmatic aspects of even one's native language requires a certain level of sophistication. Moreover, there is a great deal of variability among individuals within any culture. And regardless of how the pragmatic dials are set, there are times when people intend to be rude or unpleasant. But if you have to make a judgment call, why not give the person (or Martian) the benefit of the doubt?

Culture Club

Human nature appears to be just the same, all over the world.
—Mark Twain, *The Innocents Abroad* (1869)

Making cultural generalizations is a risky enterprise at best, although there are times when it can be genuinely useful. Most of us are somewhat offended when we hear our own culture reduced to a stereotype (You know what those Americans are like). At the same time, it clearly is the case that some cultures are more similar than others. Italian and Greek cultures are more similar than Italian and Japanese cultures, for instance. This is not to say that the psyche of every Italian and Greek is in sync, but they may have more in common than they do with people living in other societies. So with these caveats in mind, let's consider three such cultural classification schemes that have been proposed (although there are many others).

Perhaps the broadest and most well-known of these general-izations is the distinction between cultures that are *collectivistic* and those that are *individualistic*.[6] The idea is that cultures exist on a continuum. The needs of the group are paramount at one end, and the needs of the individual are most important at the other. Put more simply, collectivistic cultures are "we" centered, and individualistic cultures are "I" centered. In theory, then, any culture could be assigned a specific place on this collectivistic–individualistic continuum.

In general, traditional, agrarian, and less economically and technologically advanced societies are more collectivistic. And this does make sense; if a group is just getting by, then its members must work together to survive and flourish. Societies that are more economically and technologically advanced, on the other hand, have the luxury of allowing individuals to put their wants and desires ahead of those of the group.

Speaking very broadly, we can classify Western Europe, North America, Australia, and New Zealand as part of Team Individu-alistic. Large parts of Asia, the Middle East, South America, and Africa could be considered more collectivistic. Of course, within any region there will be variability, and some countries will be closer to the midpoint of the continuum.

But we must be careful. Richard knew a Korean student who had studied English in the United States. One day Richard asked the student what had surprised him the most about living there. His answer? That Americans love their children. Richard was shocked. The student explained that he had grown up hear-ing stories about how Americans were very individualistic. He thought that when Americans turned eighteen, they left home and became completely independent. Therefore he believed that family was less important to Americans than it is to Koreans.

Clearly, then, it's dangerous to read too much into a distinction such as "individualistic" or "collectivistic."

It's also important to realize that the relationship between advancement and individualism is not a simple one. A technologically advanced country can become more collectivistic through political upheaval, as happened in Nazi Germany. Modern Japan, clearly a technologically advanced culture, is still somewhat more collectivistic than similarly technologically advanced societies in the West. And even extremely individualistic societies can become more collectivistic, at least for a time. During World War II, for example, the strongly individualistic United States accepted the necessity of rationing and high levels of conscription. Societies can also become briefly more "we" centered because of great accomplishments or historic events (think of the fall of the Berlin Wall) or tragedy (think of the period immediately after 9/11).

Viewed through this lens, many aspects of culture become easier to understand. For example, most Westerners shudder at the thought of arranged marriages, which are common in more collectivistic cultures. It's difficult for people in individualistic societies to imagine allowing others to make such a personal and consequential decision for them. But even in individualistic countries, family members can wield great influence over the choice of a partner and the success of a marriage. Marriages may not be arranged, but families are generally not irrelevant in the process of selecting a spouse.

Another way to describe broad cultural differences is to differentiate between *high-context* and *low-context* cultures. This distinction was proposed by the American anthropologist Edward Hall.[7] Once again, this dimension can be thought of as a continuum. In relatively high-context societies, many things are simply left unsaid: it is assumed that others can figure out what is intended by referring to the society's relatively homogeneous culture. So if, for example, suicide is viewed extremely unfavorably within a culture, perhaps as an act that brings great shame and dishonor to remaining family members, then references to it are likely to be highly euphemistic or elliptical—or simply not made at all.

For example, inhabitants of countries in which low-context culture predominates will typically be much more explicit in their referring expressions. Speakers in such countries have less confidence that the intentions of their utterances will be unambiguously inferred, so they tend to spell things out. A culture may be relatively low context if it has experienced a great deal of immigration from other countries. The reverse will be true in high-context countries that typically do not receive (or actively discourage) large numbers of immigrants. Likewise, since notions like humor are typically culturally bound, we might predict that an episode that was humorous in one high-context culture would not be perceived in the same way in another culture.

In general, smaller, historically more isolated countries can be thought of as being relatively high context. Greece, Ireland, and Korea might be good examples. In contrast, larger or more diversified countries like the United States and the nations of Scandinavia would be relatively low context. However, even this generalization is problematic, because a small country like Switzerland turns out to be relatively low context. In the case of Switzerland, the use of four official languages in different parts of the country may lower the degree of shared common ground at the cultural level.

Researchers have found the high- versus low-context distinction to be helpful in explaining, for example, differences in conflict resolution, the use of visual effects on web pages, and even celebrity endorsements. For example, Korean advertisers use more celebrity endorsement than US advertisers. In addition, US celebrities typically appear as themselves when they endorse products, and appeal directly to the audience. Korean celebrities, on the other hand, endorse products by playing roles, thus making their endorsement of the product more indirect. However, the findings from other studies have not always supported a high- versus low-context distinction.[8]

A third approach to classifying cultures has been put forward by the British linguist Richard Lewis.[9] He believes that the world's countries can be located somewhere on a triangular continuum with three distinct points. The points of the triangle are *linear active* (people do one thing at a time, plan step-by-step, and are fact and result oriented), *multiactive* (people multitask, plan only generally, and put feelings and relationships before facts), and *reactive* (people react to others' actions, use general principles, and are harmony oriented).

While many countries in the Lewis model fall between two of the three points, others can be found closer to each of the points. Examples of highly linear-active countries are the United States, the UK, and Germany. Highly multiactive countries are exemplified by Brazil, Chile, and Italy. And examples of highly reactive countries are China, Japan, and Vietnam. In terms of our first classification scheme, linear-active countries are, by and large, more individualistic, reactive countries are more collectivistic, and multiactive countries fall somewhere in between. The mapping is far from perfect, but it can serve as a rough guide for our purposes.

For example, because he comes from a low-context, individualistic, linear-active culture, Richard is used to relying on others to correct him when they notice he's made a mistake. That is, he is used to operating under the logic of "someone will tell me if I say something wrong." But when he works in high-context, collectivistic, reactive cultures like Mongolia, Japan, and Korea, Richard has had to learn that his local colleagues are unlikely to correct him unless he says something particularly egregious—a state of affairs that often leaves Richard quite befuddled. In these cultures, saving face is more important than accuracy. To combat this, Richard learned to ask directly, "Is this correct?" rather than to rely on others to step in and rectify any false assumptions he has made.

Anthropologists, sociologists, and others have attempted to classify the world's cultures in many other ways, but the three we have discussed here should give you some sense of both the utility and the pitfalls involved in making such distinctions, as the next story also illustrates.

Reading the Air

One Sunday afternoon when Richard was living in Tokyo, his good friend Yoshihiro asked if he'd like to have lunch with him. Always hungry, Richard readily agreed. Yoshihiro then suggested that perhaps they should go to Odaiba, which is an island in the middle of Tokyo Bay. It is a popular destination for locals and tourists, with plenty of shopping, restaurants, and even a replica of the Statue of Liberty. Although it would take more than an hour to get there, it was a lovely day, and once there the possibilities seemed endless.

On the train to Odaiba, Richard and Yoshihiro didn't talk about where they would eat, so when they arrived, Richard stopped at the first restaurant he saw. It happened to be an Italian restaurant, and knowing that Yoshihiro loved pasta, Richard asked if he wanted to eat there. His friend's reply surprised him: "Do *you* want to eat here?" Richard said it didn't really matter to him, and without answering, Yoshihiro turned and walked quickly away. All Richard could do was follow. As they weaved in and out of the crowd, they passed restaurant after restaurant. Exasperated, Richard caught up with Yoshihiro and pointed to another restaurant. "How about here?" he asked. Yoshihiro replied the same way, "Do *you* want to eat here?" Again, Richard said it didn't really matter to him, and just as before, Yoshihiro took off in a flash, zipping even more quickly through the crowd.

At this point, Richard decided that Yoshihiro must have something in mind, so he gave up looking for a restaurant and just followed him. Finally, Yoshihiro stopped. But when Richard caught up to him, he could not have been more disappointed. It was an American chain restaurant. They had traveled more than an hour to fight their way through throngs of people just to end up there. Irritated but hungry, when Yoshihiro asked, "How about here?" Richard acquiesced, and they went inside. As they passed the salad bar, Richard realized that they were heading outside onto a terrace, and when he looked up, he froze in his tracks. In front of him was one of the most spectacular views of Tokyo he had ever seen. The water below was dotted with sailboats, to the right the Rainbow Bridge spanned the bay, and directly across from them was the Tokyo skyline. It was the perfect place to eat on such a beautiful day.

After Richard had taken it all in, he looked over to see Yoshi-hiro smiling. It was clear that this had been his plan all along. But what Richard couldn't understand was why Yoshihiro hadn't said something sooner, especially at the first two restaurants. Had Richard answered, "Yes, I want to eat here," Yoshihiro told him that he would have agreed and would not have said a word about his plan.

The Japanese have an expression that they use when some-one is clueless: *kuuki yomenai* (or more easily just "KY"). This phrase can be translated literally as "can't read the air," and in the United States it might be considered equivalent to a lack of emotional intelligence. Although the concept of KY is varied and its use has changed over time, at its heart, reading the air is a way of establishing rapport and maintaining harmony.[10]

One of the themes of this book is that speakers have many choices in how they communicate. These choices come with associated costs and benefits. If the likelihood of being misun-derstood is perceived to be high, a speaker may decide on an explicit, literal approach, rather than risk a misunderstanding.[11] On the other hand, if there is a perceived benefit of speaking in a less-direct way, a speaker may risk a misunderstanding to accom-plish other interpersonal goals, such as to be humorous. Further-more, when it comes to conversational costs and benefits, it is both the speaker *and* the listener who will win or lose as a result of a conversational gambit's success or failure.[12]

Yoshihiro took the chance that Richard knew him well enough to "read the air" and let him guide them to a restaurant without explicitly saying what he was doing. He doubled down on that bet when he asked Richard very pointedly, "Do *you* want to eat here?" rather than simply spilling the beans that he had a place in mind. Clearly Yoshihiro was taking a risk that Richard would understand his intentions.

But what did Yoshihiro stand to gain by not divulging his plan? If Richard would just read the air, Yoshihiro could show that he knew him well enough to pick a restaurant that would delight him. Richard also gained because he did read the air (well, after two attempts, anyway) and showed Yoshihiro that he also knew him well enough to stop trying to force a restaurant on him. The result was that the implicit way in which Yoshihiro chose to guide Richard to the restaurant strengthened their bonds of friendship and made the day more memorable. Richard and Yoshihiro still talk about their meal in Odaiba.

Although reading the air may be more important in high-context cultures like Japan and Korea than in low-context cultures, no matter where you are, being able to read the air is the conversational equivalent of giving someone just the right present. And it means all the more because you didn't have to ask.

Saving Face

Punctuality is the politeness of kings.
—Attributed to King Louis XVIII of France

What does the word "politeness" mean? The question seems simple, but it's actually quite difficult to answer. Politeness is codified in all languages of the world. However, because there are widely varying expectations about what it means to be polite across cultures, it is virtually impossible to define politeness in such a way as to capture all senses of the word.

A more fruitful question might be: what purposes does politeness serve? One answer is that it allows people to live together more easily by creating a set of expectations that minimize discord or conflict. When people agree on how they should act in public settings, life becomes more predictable and harmonious, in theory at least. We're typically aware of the social norms we follow only when they have been violated. The Canadian sociologist Erving Goffman noted that many politeness rules are unspoken, such as our behaviors in public restrooms, a locale that has received attention from later scholars, as well.[13] Jeremy Justus, for example, described the discomfort that some men feel when someone is using a urinal next to them or even looks in their direction. The discomfiture that is experienced when a stranger isn't playing by the rules highlights the fact that such rules clearly do exist, although the rules may differ by culture.[14]

Goffman used what is called a *dramaturgical perspective* to answer questions about social behavior and norms. In *As You Like It* (act 2, scene 7), Jaques tells Duke Senior that "all the world's a stage, and all the men and women merely players ... and one man in his time plays many parts." Goffman developed this key insight of Shakespeare's into a highly influential model that set the stage for modern sociolinguistics.

Just think about all the roles that you play during the course of a day. Over a span of just a few hours, you might be a loving spouse, a doting parent, a highly competitive athlete, a dutiful employee, and a wisecracking friend. We change roles frequently and easily and are only really aware of these roles when they come into conflict. If you're always telling your friends that you aren't afraid of your boss, and they happen to run into you as you're catering to one of her whims, you experience discomfort

because your roles (obedient worker and trash-talking employee) have come into conflict. Your friends may mock you because of the mismatch between your tough talk and your subservient behavior. But it can't be helped. We have no choice but to juggle multiple roles, which are in turn reflected in our linguistic choices. You don't speak to your father the same way that you speak to your younger brother.

Goffman is also responsible for introducing the Eastern concept of *face* into Western sociological theory.[15] Face refers to maintaining one's positive self-image when interacting with other people. In the previous example, if your friends think you are a hypocrite, then you're "out of face" with them, and you might feel embarrassment or shame. Thus an important goal in social encounters is to maintain one's face. To facilitate this, cultures have developed elaborate systems and rules of etiquette, largely unspoken, which codify the expectations that others will have in a particular social situation. If everyone knows the rules and plays by the rules, then no one is out of face.

People can also employ a variety of strategies to maintain their own face and the face of others they like and care about. Goffman refers to these strategies collectively as *facework*, and a few examples may be helpful. Perhaps the easiest way to maintain face is simply to avoid situations in which a loss of face is possible. To continue with the earlier example, if you are taking your boss's suits to the dry cleaner, you might avoid the street corner where your friends hang out. And this can cut both ways: your friends may pretend not to see you out of deference to the subservient position that you must put yourself in to stay in the boss's good graces.

Another type of facework occurs when we fish for compliments. If you have reason to believe that others will respond in a positive way, then you might make an overly modest statement, relying on the goodwill of others for praise and compliments. Of course, certain dangers lurk here, as well; one possible result of fishing for compliments is discovering that there are no fish to be caught after all. The studied silence of others after your statement of modesty could cause you to lose face, so people who are friendly to you might offer some show of support to prevent your embarrassment.

Even greetings and farewells can be thought of as facework. Goffman points out that a friendly, ritualistic greeting is reassuring to both parties: it's an acknowledgment that all is well in their relationship. In a similar way, warm words when people part serve to acknowledge their continued high regard for one another.

As an example of the complex ways in which face and facework play themselves out, consider the case of teasing. This behavior certainly seems like a prototypical example of a face-threatening act, and yet such "playful provocations" occur frequently between friends and intimate partners and can actually serve to increase affiliation.[16] However, it is also the case that these face threats can lead to bullying and other antisocial outcomes. In addition, teasing invokes culturally specific norms, like traditional gender roles.[17] Clearly, who is doing the teasing, and where, and with whom, all matter a great deal.

Not surprisingly, however, the concepts of face and facework play themselves out somewhat differently in different cultures. A study of face in China, Germany, Japan, and the United States found a number of differences. German participants had more face concerns than did the Americans, for example, and the Chinese participants had more such concerns than the Japanese.[18] It seems clear, therefore, that we should avoid making any glib generalizations about Eastern or Western concepts of face; as with any construct, there are nuances that are informed by a country's history and culture. And it is important to remember that people within a culture aren't all the same. Just as it's easy to think of specific people in your own culture as relatively friendly or unfriendly, so it's also the case that a person's face needs and concerns will vary considerably, even within the same cultural and linguistic community. We will see the importance of face and facework throughout the rest of the book.

Say the Magic Word!

Goffman's work served as a starting point for the American and British anthropologists Penelope Brown and Stephen Levinson.

In their pioneering work on linguistic politeness, they endeavored to determine whether any aspects of politeness could be considered universal across the world's languages and cultures.[19] They focused in particular on three languages spoken in very different parts of the world: British (and American) English; Tzeltal, which is a Mayan language spoken by about 400,000 inhabitants of the Mexican state of Chiapas; and Tamil, a Dravidian language spoken by about 70 million people in the southeastern Indian state of Tamil Nadu, Sri Lanka, and Singapore.

Brown and Levinson's rich analysis of politeness phenomena has been extremely influential, and we draw on their work repeatedly throughout the book. We'll start by considering their theoretical perspective, in which they assert that politeness can be understood in terms of three interrelated concepts: relative power, social distance, and degree of imposition. Let's consider each of these in turn.

Relative power is easy to understand: it refers to the social standing that exists between two people. While we primarily interact with our social peers, we also have people in our lives who are "in charge" in some way. Employers, religious and political leaders, and civil authorities are people who can make us do things: get back to work, say ten Hail Marys, or fix our car's broken taillight. On the other hand, there are those whom *we* get to order around. These would include our subordinates at our place of employment or our children. They may not like it any more than we do, but in this case, we get to call the shots.

Social distance, on the other hand, is more a matter of familiarity between two people. An employee and an employer, for example, may have a close, almost intimate relationship with each other, even though they are separated by a clear difference in relative power. (Think about an administrative assistant and his boss.) Strangers, on the other hand, even if they occupy the same stratum of society, are separated by social distance.

Finally, the degree of imposition that we place on one another is important, as well. In the course of daily life, we must often ask questions, make requests, or otherwise impose on others to help us. Sometimes such requests are minor, but in other cases, they can be quite large.

Let's see how these three factors work together in some examples. Imagine a situation in which you need to borrow a quarter from your brother. You might feel perfectly comfortable in saying something like:

Hey, jerk, give me a quarter.

There's no attempt at politeness here, and none is really required. Your brother doesn't have relative power over you, and social distance is very low. And the degree of imposition is also low, since the amount of money involved is trivial.

So let's make things more interesting. Imagine that you need to ask a neighbor to borrow twenty dollars. This *feels* different, doesn't it? And it should, because both social distance and the degree of imposition are now higher. In this situation, you would feel a need to provide a justification for the request and would probably want to reassure your neighbor that the loan is only temporary. No reason to stop there: What if relative power and social distance are high, and the degree of imposition is also very high? What if you had to ask your new boss for a thousand dollars? In this case, an elaborate song and dance would be required.

Of course, there's more to politeness than just relative power, social distance, and degree of imposition. Brown and Levinson also described specific linguistic strategies that speakers employ to be polite. These strategies revolve around Goffman's concept of face and what they refer to as *face-threatening acts*, which are challenges to the face of one of the conversational participants. People's face needs are under almost constant assault: we make mistakes, have accidents, or the gods simply decide to make us their plaything for a while. To mitigate the effects of these face-threatening acts, conversational participants in all languages use two strategies to prevent the loss of face.

The first of these strategies is called *positive politeness*. This refers to instances in which individuals seek to establish or maintain good rapport with others. We also make clear to others that their needs and wants are important to us. Brown and Levinson described many distinct strategies that speakers use; we will return to some of these throughout the book. However, an example would be uttering a statement that shows solidarity between a speaker and her conversational partner, such as "We're all in this together."

Brown and Levinson referred to the other category of linguistic politeness by using the term (surprise!) *negative* politeness. This term can be confusing, because negative politeness sounds like rudeness. But it is, in fact, a way of negating a face-threatening act. Individuals who use these interactional strategies are attempting to minimize the effects of face-threatening acts on their conversational partners. And here we see one of the interesting paradoxes of social interaction: even though we want to help others maintain their positive face, we are constantly engaging in activities that undermine our conversational partners' freedom of action. We want other people to give us things: their time, their attention, and even physical goods. Negative politeness helps lubricate these potentially awkward requests through displays of deference.

Brown and Levinson also described several negative politeness strategies that speakers employ, and we'll return to some of these later as well. But a good example for present purposes is the word "please." Think about the contexts in which we utter this "magic word." We often say it when we want others to help us, as in "Could you open the door for me, please?" A request for assistance is a face-threatening act: basically, one person is ordering another around. And by acceding to the request, the other person places himself in a subservient relationship to the requester. To paper over this potentially embarrassing state of affairs, we use "please" as a way of minimizing the imposition that we're making on someone else.

No one is born thinking this way, of course; young children need to learn about the importance of politeness through socialization. For example, before children leave the table after a meal, parents might request that they ask to be excused, and to use the magic word.[20] Many children find this display to be pointless—an empty ritual insisted on by their crazy parents. However, the parents are trying to instill a larger lesson about negative politeness. When a relative power differential exists, the individual with less power can't just come and go when he pleases. He may desperately want to leave the dinner table, but his parents have the authority to make him stay. To get his parents to grant his request—a potentially face-threatening act—the child is instructed to say "please" as an act of deference to them.

The concepts of face, face-threatening acts, and positive and negative politeness will take us a long way in making sense of the multifaceted world of social interaction. And these ideas will be particularly helpful when we turn to the complexities created by cross-cultural communication.

This Is Off the Record

Another useful way that language researchers describe intended meanings is as being either *on-record* or *off-record*. On-record utterances are those that mean what they appear to mean. Off-record utterances, on the other hand, are indirect. They can mean ... well, almost anything, as we will see.

Brown and Levinson used the term "bald on-record" to categorize statements in which no attempt is made to minimize the threat to the face of the hearer. And in many contexts, such direct statements are perfectly reasonable. If someone is kidnapping you, then your shout of "Let me go!" would be bald on-record. It would seem strange indeed to say, "I'd be ever so grateful if you could release me from these chafing restraints," to someone who has just taken you hostage. In this situation, your primary concern is not to avoid hurting the feelings of your kidnapper with a direct order. In a similar way, a surgeon requesting implements during an operation doesn't feel obligated to make her requests overly polite. It's fine for her to simply say, "Scalpel ... sponge ... retractor," in a context in which the focus should be on the job at hand.

Off-record statements have a literal meaning, as well, but they also have some other meaning (or perhaps multiple meanings) buried inside them. To make this clear, let's return to an earlier example. You and your spouse are trying to figure out who can be trusted to come by your house and attend to your dog a couple of times a day while you're on vacation. It turns out that none of your friends or relatives is available. You're running out of options and are starting to consider the cost of a kennel for Fido. Suddenly your better half suggests that John, an elderly neighbor, might be able to help you out. After thinking about this suggestion for a moment, you might reply:

Well ... John drinks.

The literal meaning is clear enough: John requires liquid to live. And as we have seen, another conventionalized interpretation would be that John is an alcoholic. But you might intend something even more specific in this instance. Your off-record meaning, for example, could be:

Since John is a recovering alcoholic, it may not be a good idea to tempt him with unfettered access to your extensive single-malt whiskey collection.

If your spouse understands your off-record intention, then he might reply with an on-record statement, perhaps something like "Right, I would need to be sure to lock up the liquor cabinet."

In this case, the off-record intention is a warning or perhaps a statement of concern. However, many other utterances can be delivered in this off-record way. We can threaten, entreat, flirt, display embarrassment, or tease by saying one thing but meaning another. And a great deal of the meaning of nonliteral language is, by definition, off-record. A metaphorical statement like

The lecture was a sleeping pill

has no real meaning in its literal sense, but it might allow several off-record interpretations. A conventional interpretation might be "The lecture was boring," but it could also mean "The lecture helped me get some much-needed rest," or even "I'm horrified that my lecture was so boring," and so on.

Going off-record affords several advantages. In many cases, it prevents people from having to state unpleasant truths directly. A listener should be able to infer an off-record, intended meaning if he shares common ground with the speaker.[21] Just to remind you, common ground refers to the knowledge, beliefs, and attitudes that people mutually possess. Someone might speak euphemistically so as to indirectly allude to an acquaintance's multiple arrests without having to do so on-record. An example might be "Billy has some issues with authority."

And sometimes a speaker wants to impart different messages to different members of his audience. This trick would be wellnigh impossible to accomplish on-record, but if you're clever, you can do so off-record. A good example of this occurs in the movie *Amadeus*.[22] The film, based on the play by Peter Shaffer, is a highly fictionalized account of the life of Antonio Salieri.

Salieri was the director of Italian opera for the Viennese court during the late eighteenth century. In the movie, he is secure in his privileged position, and life is good. Then, however, a young composer named Mozart arrives on the musical scene, and Salieri becomes insanely jealous of Mozart's tremendous musical gifts. Mozart, for his part, is dismissive of his colleague's modest abilities but realizes that maintaining good relations with Salieri will be helpful in the quest to secure royal patronage.

At one point during the film, we see Salieri conducting his own opera, *Axur, re d'Ormus*. When it concludes, Emperor Joseph II lavishly praises the composer. Salieri, however, only has eyes for the departing Mozart, who has attended the performance with some of his friends. Salieri is delighted when Mozart comes forward to congratulate him. Salieri asks, "Did my work please you?"

Salieri's question puts Mozart in a bind. It would be unwise, from a political perspective, for him to be anything but highly complimentary. At the same time, his friends have gathered around and are listening intently for his response. If he praises Salieri, Mozart will be seen as a hypocrite. So he pauses for a moment and then says:

I never knew that music like that was possible. One hears such sounds, and what can one say but—Salieri!

Salieri replies cordially, saying, "You flatter me," but it's clear he understands both the on- and off-record meanings of these ostensibly complimentary words. Mozart, however, has prevented a loss of face among his friends, who interpret his words as highly critical. And Mozart's response has given him plausible deniability; Salieri can't accuse him of being insulting,

since one interpretation of Mozart's words is, in fact, very complimentary.

Clearly, going off-record confers several advantages. But is there a downside to speaking in this way? Well, for one thing, you have to be fairly quick on your feet to craft such double-edged messages on the fly. And it can be a gamble, as well. A speaker has to make an educated guess about whether her conversational partner will actually comprehend the intended off-record meaning. In many cases, this isn't difficult. If you share a lot of common ground with someone (think of your spouse or parent or sibling), then you can be fairly certain that your hidden message will be received as intended. In cases like these, the *inferability* of the message can be thought of as relatively high.[23] But what about cases when inferability is low? You can't be certain that a new coworker will understand hidden criticism of your boss, for example.

There are also contexts in which off-record statements simply aren't helpful or desirable. As an extreme example, imagine that you're helping someone to defuse a bomb. If you are providing careful, step-by-step instructions, the last thing that's desirable would be vague or ambiguous speech. However, since off-record statements are so commonly used, it must be the case that their advantages usually outweigh their disadvantages.

In cross-cultural contexts, however, all of this becomes more complicated. Shared common ground will almost always be much lower than that shared by two members of the same linguistic community, and the inferability of off-record statements will be less certain. If you're speaking a language that you are not completely proficient in, you may not be able to engage in the verbal gymnastics of a Mozart to pull off the kinds of tricks we've been discussing. In such cases, where the communicative stakes are high, it is easiest and safest to be bald on-record—but it's not nearly as much fun.

To return to the dial metaphor we used earlier in the chapter, pragmatic dimensions could be thought of as being preset to certain cultural frequencies. We only discussed the range of settings for a few well-known dimensions, such as politeness and cultural type. However, there are potentially many more dials, some of which will be unique to a given culture. But it's important not to lock in these settings. Instead one needs to constantly monitor feedback from others to fine-tune them. In the chapters ahead, we continue to discuss the importance of adjusting one's responses to feedback, but perhaps one more example will be useful here.

Richard's colleague in Seoul had done a great deal of work organizing a conference. Richard's role was to give the welcoming remarks. Since he was kicking off the event, when he got up to speak, he thanked his colleague effusively for all he had done to make the conference a reality. Richard expected that after he had praised his colleague so warmly, the audience would clap in appreciation. Instead everyone sat stone-faced, and all Richard heard were crickets. Richard was surprised, but he kept going and finished his welcoming remarks as planned.

When it was over, Richard's colleague took him aside to thank him for his kind words. He said that he knew what Richard was trying to do, and he was grateful for the recognition; but in Korea, there is a strong sense of group membership. Since Richard and his colleague belonged to the same organization, Richard's remarks sounded to the Korean audience like he was bragging. This was the opposite of what he had intended, since he was trying to give credit to someone else, not to take it for himself. In that situation, Richard should have said nothing and allowed other conference participants to volunteer their appreciation. Richard was grateful to his colleague for helping him to adjust the setting of his individualistic–collectivistic dial. From that day on, he was careful to praise colleagues only at work, but not in public.

In the next chapter, we will see how different cultures set the dials differently as we consider the ways in which people can choose to accomplish their conversational goals. Some of these strategies include being indirect, insincere, or rhetorical.

3 How Speech Acts

What Shall We Talk About?

Given the vast range of things that people *can* talk about, is it possible to organize them according to some general scheme? Think about all the conversations that you had yesterday or during the past week. You may have been engaged in complex negotiations at work, or perhaps you had a fight with your spouse or significant other. Maybe you tried to persuade your son or daughter to do (or not do) something. You interacted with people in stores, in restaurants, on the phone, and in a host of other situations. At first blush, it seems unlikely that all these utterances could be classified into any sort of taxonomy. However, that hasn't kept scholars of language from trying.

One notable example comes from the work of John Searle, an American philosopher who attempted such a catalog in the 1970s.[1] Searle was working within a tradition called *speech act theory*, which attempts to explain how people use language. Let's return once again to the example of *John drinks*. This sentence could be uttered in many contexts for a variety of reasons: to remember to buy enough beer for a barbecue, or to revive a thirsty zoo specimen, and so on. There are many different reasons why someone might choose to say *John drinks*, and it would be impossible to catalog them all. But perhaps they could be grouped together according to the goals the speaker is trying to accomplish. These groupings are what are referred to as *speech acts*.

Searle proposed that speech acts fall into five general categories. He assigned the name *representatives* to one of these groupings. Representatives are speech acts that are statements about the world. They have an identifiable truth value: either they conform to reality (they're true), or they do not (they're false). "Humans drink water" would be a true assertion, while "The Earth has three moons" would not be. It's possible for people to be confused or mistaken, but that doesn't really matter here; if something is offered up as a statement of fact, then it's a representative.

In contrast, Searle's second category involves getting people to do things. These speech acts are called *directives*, and examples would be commands (Give me the remote) or requests (What time is it?). This is a special category for our purposes, because, as we will see, some languages and cultures require speakers to blunt the directness of such utterances by stating them indirectly.

A third category of speech acts is referred to *commissives*. With statements such as these, the speaker is committing herself to a particular course of action in the future. When someone makes a promise, such as "I swear I'll dry-clean your sweater if you let me borrow it," he or she is making such a commitment. It's important to note that Searle is silent on whether the person in question will, in fact, come through: you may never see your favorite sweater again, for example. All that matters is that a speaker is on record with a particular claim about future events.

Expressives are a fourth category and include speech acts in which a speaker expresses a psychological state, such as an attitude or an emotional reaction about something or someone. A great deal of the language usage that we explore in the rest of the book falls under this rubric: examples would include expressing thanks, providing opinions, offering congratulations, and making excuses, as well as greetings, complaints, preferences, and a host of others.

Searle's fifth category, *declaratives*, is perhaps the least common. Declaratives are statements that, by virtue of being spoken or written, change the state of the world. Examples would include a judge handing down a sentence, a religious official pronouncing that two people are married, a boss firing an employee, or a head of state declaring war on another nation. It should be noted that, for the declaration to succeed, you actually have to *be* a judge or a minister or so on. Anyone can *say* these formulaic words; you could, for example, pretend to marry two of your friends with the intent of teasing them, but that doesn't mean they need to start thinking about china patterns. In other cases, a group may give someone temporary world-changing powers, as in the case of asking someone to christen a ship. After that event, however, the power is gone: the individual couldn't simply show up at a marina with an armload of champagne bottles and rename all the boats riding at anchor.

Although Searle's taxonomy has been highly influential, other students of language have proposed other categorization schemes. At about the same time as Searle's proposal, John Dore, a psychologist, was trying to make sense of the intentions of young children who are at the one-word stage of language development. Dore put forward a system that differs from Searle's in important ways, which is hardly surprising, given that young children don't typically christen ships, for instance. Dore proposed that young children use language for labeling, repeating, answering, requesting actions, requesting answers, calling, greeting, protesting, and practicing.[2] This suggests that the world of young children, and therefore their pragmatic environment, differs fundamentally from the world of adults.

As a final example, let's consider a scheme proposed by two cognitive anthropologists, Roy D'Andrade and Myron Wish.[3] Whereas Searle's categorization scheme is essentially an armchair approach, these researchers tried to create a scheme inductively, by examining excerpts from the PBS documentary *An American Family*, which aired in twelve episodes in 1973. (This series is now regarded by many as the first reality television program and was groundbreaking in its day for presenting the unscripted and spontaneous interactions of the seven-member Loud family of Santa Barbara, California.) D'Andrade and Wish categorized the speech acts of the Loud family into ten categories. We don't need to list them here.

Our point is that there are a number of ways in which speech acts *can* be categorized. And none of these approaches is necessarily better or worse than the others. The different theories are like the paintings produced by different artists of the same tableau: a consensus about the major elements, but plenty of differences with regard to the details. From the perspective of speech act theory, we are interested not just in the meaning of words but also in the intentions behind the words themselves.

Although our description of speech act theory so far has focused on English speakers, as we will see, a speech act level of analysis turns out to be a fruitful one for explaining communicative success and failure in cross-cultural contexts, as well.

But Do You Really Mean It?

If you ran into a casual acquaintance at the post office, she might conclude a short conversation with you by saying something like:

Let's do lunch sometime.

Should you free up your calendar and ask friends for dining recommendations? If you are an American, probably not. But if you are from another culture, would you recognize this *ostensible* invitation for what it is—a politeness ritual? How is someone to know for sure?

When Richard was living in Germany, he was a student in a German language class with a Japanese student. During the class, the student remarked that she was always hungry and thirsty when she visited a German home. The reason was that when a German offered her something to eat or drink, she would always refuse the first offer (an *ostensible* refusal because she really wanted to accept), fully expecting a second and even third offer, as in Japan. But in Germany, she said, they offered once and never offered again.

On the surface, ostensible speech acts like these seem sincere, but they are not. Ostensible speech acts are meant to accomplish goals other than those in the literal statement. In our first example, the invitation to lunch substituted as a polite way to say good-bye. Refusing the offer of food and drink was a polite way to show deference and appreciation to one's host. Ostensible speech acts can be tricky even in one's own culture. You have probably found yourself suffering through a lunch that you really didn't want to happen. But these problems are magnified cross-culturally.

In many cultures, it's considered polite to pretend to refuse offers. This is true even when the proposed item, such as assistance, a gift, or a mouthwatering dessert, is greatly desired by the potential recipient. The statement of refusal might be accompanied by a gesture in which the refuser pushes both palms outward toward the giver, as if to ward off temptation. If the offer is repeated, the reluctant beneficiary will drop this token resistance and accept, perhaps with a self-conscious laugh and an expression of gratitude. Both parties understand that the initial refusal was ostensible, but the exchange serves the purpose of attending to the face needs of the giver, who is placing herself in a subservient position with respect to her conversational partner. The initial refusal by the recipient, therefore, is an example of negative politeness: "We are equals, so you don't have to offer me anything."

Depending on the culture, however, this refusal playacting is performed in different ways. For example, the complex and highly ritualized Persian custom of ta'arof dictates that a host offering food and drink must be forceful. In fact, the more forceful the offer, the more polite that offer is perceived to be. The guest, however, even if he wants to accept, must refuse at least once. Typically there will be several rounds of refusals and increasingly insistent offers before the two parties come to terms and decide whether or not the requests and refusals are genuine. For foreigners, this can create no end of confusion in the Iranian marketplace. In Iran, a storeowner will refuse to take money from a customer, expecting that her customer will persist in trying to buy something that she is ostensibly refusing to sell.[4]

The psychologists Ellen Isaacs and Herb Clark identified five characteristics that differentiate the ostensible from the genuine

in US culture.[5] The first of these is *pretense*: the speaker only pretends to make an invitation that is sincere. Crucially, a second property of such speech acts is *mutual recognition*: both parties involved must recognize the speaker's pretense. An invitation is only insincere if both parties recognize it as such. For this to work, there must be a third property: *collusion*. It's necessary for you to reply with something like "Yes, that would be lovely," knowing all the while it will never happen.

A fourth property of ostensible speech is *ambivalence*. What would happen if you actually accepted the invitation? You could, for example, whip out your phone to check your schedule and ask, "Does Thursday at noon work for you?" Now your invitee is trapped. To avoid being impolite, she must convert her fake offer into a genuine one. The only other option would be to revoke the invitation, which would result in a loss of face for both you and her. A final property of such invitations is that their purpose is off-record. And what is the off-record purpose here? The unspoken interpretation might be "I like you, but not enough to actually want to spend time with you." Ouch! Clearly, such a face-threatening act needs to occur off-record.

There are several clues to help you spot fake utterances. For example, if your would-be lunch date doesn't persist and follow up with something like "*Really*, we ought to take some time to catch up," her invitation is probably insincere. And if the speaker is vague or hedges, that's even more evidence that she doesn't really mean what she's saying. The use of "sometime" conveniently doesn't obligate her to a specific time frame. Finally, a host of nonverbal cues is also characteristic of such statements. If your conversational partner speaks hesitantly, avoids returning your gaze, or she speaks rapidly or mumbles, these may be further evidence of insincerity.

Isaacs and Clark's observations have been empirically supported by later research. Link and Kreuz found that people can reliably distinguish among ostensible, sincere, and ambiguous statements (i.e., those with multiple meanings).[6]

The psychologist Marsha Walton considered a different type of nongenuine speech act: ostensible lies. These could be invitations, but they can also be assertions, requests, or even compliments. Their purpose is to "impose a particular view of reality" onto one's conversational partner.[7]

People might tell ostensible lies for a variety of reasons. For example, instead of telling someone on record that he is *unwilling* to fulfill a request, the ostensible liar might claim that, for some reason, he is *unable* to fulfill a request (I have a parent-teacher conference). Both parties are aware that this isn't true.

But such assertions may go unchallenged if there is a difference in relative power between the speaker and listener. Although the powerful person does not need to observe social niceties, he may, in fact, use pretense as a mock show of politeness. As Walton points out, powerful others can lie to us because they know that we are not in a position to challenge their authority by calling them out on their lie.

Returning to the case of *ta'arof*, the ostensible features in Isaacs and Clark's description of English are insufficient for distinguishing invitations that are genuine from those that are ostensible. The consequences of these differences cause Iranians to sometimes perceive Americans' sincere invitations as ostensible. It's also the case that Americans may perceive ostensible invitations from Iranians as genuine and mistakenly attempt to accept them.

Ostensible invitations also appear to be more common in Farsi than in English. For example, they may be employed at the opening of telephone conversations, which would not be a typical behavior for American English speakers. Outsiders may perceive the flurry of insincere invitations and refusals to be somewhat hypocritical, but in fact these expressions are essential for enhancing the face of both speakers and listeners within this culture.[8]

The use of ostensible refusals in Iran is similar in many ways to ostensible invitations in China: in both cultures, a great deal of "ritual play" occurs. For example, someone may initially decline an invitation to another's home for dinner, even if she really wants to attend. This initial refusal, given without a specific reason and accompanied by certain formulaic expressions ("Don't bother" or "It's too much trouble for you"), is perceived by the inviter as ostensible. This sets the stage for a second ritualized round, in which the first party repeats the invitation several times. This eventually leads to a "pragmatic closure," in which the invitation is finally accepted.[9]

As is true in English, Farsi, Mandarin Chinese, and other languages, one clue that an invitation is ostensible comes from the number of times the invitation is repeated. The more it is repeated, the more sincere it is likely to be.

Once again, the facework involved here may seem needlessly elaborate to some. However, no matter how dilatory these rituals are perceived to be, they are essential for the smooth functioning of societies that place great value on harmonious relations.

Beating around the Bush

Speakers sometimes choose to be extremely indirect when making requests or demands of others. Within a given culture, this isn't typically a problem, since the inferability of conventional off-record requests should be high. It seems highly unlikely, for example, that an American adult would misconstrue what someone meant if asked "Can you pass the salt?" during a meal. Barring extremely unusual cases, like having two broken arms or being bound in a straitjacket, an American would instantly understand that this is a request for action and not a question about ability.

The issue of how, when, and where a person should be direct or indirect varies from culture to culture. Roger was reminded of the possibility for confusion when speaking with one of his German relatives. Roger's cousin, a retired engineer, is a native German speaker whose English is fairly good. He has visited the United States and Canada several times and is familiar with the

culture as well as the language. But he was extremely confused by an e-mail that he received from another relative, an American student who was studying in Paris at the time. She was unable to visit her family in the United States during her Christmas break, so she sent a request asking if she could visit him in Germany. Since she was a native English speaker, making the sizable imposition of intruding on someone she didn't know well during the holidays, her request was tentative and circumspect. She chose to employ an extremely indirect construction, something along the lines of "I wonder if I'd be able to visit you and your family during my Christmas break."

A native English-speaking American would not have been thrown by this "I wonder" construction. In fact, a study of American merchants, contacted by phone and asked, "I wonder what time you close," always interpreted the question as an indirect request for information.[10] Roger's cousin, however, was utterly flummoxed by the student's sentence. And, viewed literally as a statement about ability as opposed to an indirect request, it is highly ambiguous. What would prevent this woman from visiting? Does she not have enough money to afford the trip? Is she recovering from some sort of illness? The confusion was ultimately resolved, and the woman enjoyed her Christmas in Germany, but Roger's cousin was still pondering the miscommunication several months later when he asked Roger to make sense of it for him. Roger is always happy to discuss pragmatic issues, and the conversation turned into an impromptu mini-seminar on the American predilection for conversational indirectness. His cousin was astonished; it had never even occurred to him that the "I wonder" construction signaled a request and not some sort of philosophical speculation.

Do we find any differences among cultures that are deemed to express requests relatively indirectly? The psychologists Tom Holtgraves and Joong-nam Yang explored this issue by asking American and Korean participants to imagine themselves in situations in which they had to make a request of someone else. The researchers varied the size of the request, relative power, and social distance in these situations. You may recall that these are three dimensions that Brown and Levinson claim to be important in terms of politeness.

As expected, Holtgraves and Yang found that these three factors do have a significant effect on the way in which participants couched their requests. Although Koreans were not judged to be more polite overall, they were more influenced by the factors of relative power and social distance and were "more responsive to the interpersonal features of situations."[11]

In later research, Holtgraves created a conversational indirectness scale to measure this construct. He found that, in comparison to Americans, Koreans are in fact more likely to use indirect speech and to look for potential indirect meanings in the things that people say.[12]

It is important to remember that being indirect does not automatically equate to being polite. Richard was teaching psychology one evening on a US Marine Corps base in Okinawa, Japan. Each night he always gave his students a fifteen-minute break around 6:00 p.m. One evening, during the break, his students were talking and laughing in the hallway. They seemed loud to Richard, so he went into the hallway to ask the students to be quiet. When he did, the Japanese teacher in the room next door glared at him and then slammed his own classroom door. A few days later, Richard was in the administrative offices of the university, talking with the director of the program. The same Japanese teacher came into the office and apologized for interrupting but said he needed to ask the director a question, which was "What time should teachers give their students a break during the evening session?" The director replied that it was up to the teacher and added, "Why do you ask?" The Japanese teacher replied, "I just want to make sure when my students take their break they don't disturb the other classes." Clearly the entire exchange was not a genuine request for information but an indirect criticism of Richard.

Oblique exchanges like this one show that indirectness and politeness are different concepts. Likewise, being direct does not equate to being rude. Obviously, Germans don't consider themselves rude by speaking German to each other. And the Japanese do not seem especially polite to each other when speaking Japanese. Even in Korea, it's perfectly acceptable to say directly, "Please bring me some water." In fact, in Korea, whenever Richard tried to turn a direct request into a more

indirect request along the lines of "Can you please bring me
some water?" people always looked thoroughly confused. Perhaps a final anecdote can illustrate both the pleasures and the
perils of being indirect.

Richard was in Korea, having brunch in a nice restaurant on a
US military base with his American friends George and Sylbeth.
The server, who was Korean, came over and wanted to know
if she could bring them something to drink—and announced
that "today is a champagne brunch, so you can have free champagne." George said to her, "Champagne is my middle name!"
They all laughed, and then Richard ordered coffee, and Sylbeth
ordered tea.

The server brought the coffee and tea. When she came by the
table about fifteen minutes later, Richard asked about the champagne for George. She seemed surprised and replied, "Oh—do
you want some champagne?" They all had a good chuckle, but
Richard wondered why the server, as accustomed as she was to
working with Americans, did not recognize the indirectness of
the request. Although it is possible in Korean to say, for example,
that someone's family name is "beer" (meaning that they like to
drink beer), it wouldn't commonly be used between a server and
a patron. Moreover, there's really no way the server could have
known that Americans don't usually have a middle name like
"champagne."

But why be indirect in the first place? The potential for ambiguity or confusion should make it *less* likely for people to speak
in this way. However, there is also much to be gained. In the
United States, if I tell you to pass the salt and you comply, then
I have demonstrated that I have power over you. I can order
you around if I feel like it. This is a face-threatening act, and
complying would cause you to lose face. However, if I ask you

a question about whether you *can* do something, then you can *choose* to interpret it as a request. No one is ordering anyone to do anything; therefore no one's face is threatened. In Brown and Levinson's terminology, indirect speech acts can be viewed as an off-record politeness strategy and yet another example of negative politeness.

You Call That a Question?

Ain't I a woman?
—Attributed to Sojourner Truth, address to the 1851 Women's Convention in Akron, Ohio

If you prick us, do we not bleed? If you tickle us, do we not laugh?
—Shylock, *The Merchant of Venice*, act 3, scene 1

As we have seen, not all questions are genuine information-seeking ventures. In fact, people frequently ask questions for which they expect no answer at all. In English, queries like "Who do you think you are?" or "What are you, a three-year-old?" are meant to admonish, and actually answering the question— perhaps by stating one's real age—would run the risk of antagonizing the questioner even further. However, in many other cases, it may not be clear if an answer is expected or desired. And in many languages, there seems to be no hard-and-fast dividing line between so-called *rhetorical* questions, on the one hand, and sincere questions, on the other.

In English, rhetorical questions can be employed in a variety of ways. Using Brown and Levinson's analysis of politeness, we can think of rhetorical questions as an off-record strategy to fulfill a variety of discourse goals, such as to make excuses (How could I have known that?), as well as criticisms (How many times must I tell you?). Rhetorical questions can be used to clarify (Can't you see that it's raining?), as well as to show negative emotion. Similarly, Leggitt and Gibbs found that rhetorical questions were perceived as being relatively hostile and negative ways of achieving one's communicative ends. Rhetorical questions are also employed to make claims and assertions (Aren't those your glasses?). Finally they can be used for supposed humorous effect (Is rain wet?).[13]

Throughout history, rhetorical questions have often been employed in persuasive contexts, as in the Sojourner Truth speech quoted at the beginning of the section. Most research on this topic related to American English suggests that such questions do increase the persuasiveness of messages, although they can also be distracting and may reduce the processing of such messages.[14]

In some languages, speakers explicitly mark utterances as rhetorical. Tzeltal, the language spoken in Mayan Mexico, allows speakers to indicate that a statement is rhetorical via the language's grammar or by using certain prefixes. Similarly, the southern Indian language of Tamil has grammatical forms that are associated with rhetorical questions. Korean allows certain discourse markers to signal questions for which an answer is not expected. And rhetorical questions in Jordanian Arabic are often formulaic and proverbial in nature, which makes clear that they are not information seeking.[15]

In a range of languages, including English, rhetorical questions are sometimes marked by adding interrogative tags to declarative questions, as in "It's beautiful, isn't it?" However, such tags are used in a variety of other ways, such as to signal sarcasm (You're really something, aren't you?) and even in sincere questions (You see the dentist next week, don't you?).[16] So it really is up to the hearer to determine if such a statement requires a response or not.

Tag questions in English are more complex than they are in some other languages. Modern Polish, for example, has only five words that can function as tags, whereas speakers of English can exploit a large number of auxiliary verbs, along with a variety of tenses and moods. This allows tag questions in English to display subtle gradations of certainty, hope, or expectation.[17] For example, a statement like "It's beautiful," followed by a tag like "Don't you think?" may be a clearer signal of a genuine question, and the expectation of a response, than a more neutral tag like "isn't it?" It may be difficult, however, for a nonnative speaker of English to pick up on such subtleties. To do so, all the usual pragmatic suspects need to be called in for the lineup: the relationship between the speaker and hearer, the situation, and the culture must all be considered.

In general, academic writers are encouraged to avoid rhetorical questions in English, since they are perceived as appealing to emotion and sentiment, rather than letting the facts speak for themselves.[18] We find a different view of rhetorical questions in many Asian cultures, however. Eli Hinkel, who has conducted extensive research on teaching English as a second language, suggests that stylistic traditions influenced by Confucianism, Taoism, and Buddhism have resulted in greater comfort with the use of rhetorical questions. She tested this idea by asking native speakers of English, as well as Chinese, Korean, Japanese, and Indonesian speakers of English as a second language, to write essays in English. Although the nonnative English speakers had an average of thirteen years of English language study, she hypothesized that they would still make greater use of rhetorical questions when writing essays in English. And this turned out to be the case for all four nonnative English groups.[19]

Other studies support the notion of a cultural divide with regard to the role of rhetorical questions in written language. Keiko Hirose asserts that in Japanese, rhetorical questions are seen as a good strategy because they allow writers to state their opinions in a polite way. In addition, rhetorical questions are also seen as an effective way to conclude one's arguments in that language. And a study of native Turkish and English speakers writing argumentative essays showed higher rates of rhetorical question use in Turkish compared to English.[20]

In contrast, some languages show less-frequent use of rhetorical questions than English. For example, a comparison of Arabic and English newspaper editorials found relatively low rates of rhetorical question use overall, but they were used more by the editorialists writing in English.[21]

Before we move on to examine some cross-cultural issues related to topics such as humor, profanity, and small talk, we'd like to end with an out-of-this-world example that shows how the avoidance of indirectness, ostensible speech acts, and off-record statements played a role in accomplishing a cross-cultural mission. Interesting, yes?

Pragmatics and the Final Frontier

On July 17, 1975, Thomas Stafford, a brigadier general in the US Air Force, wriggled through a narrow passageway and into history. Waiting on the other side to shake his hand was Alexei Leonov, Hero of the Soviet Union and the first person to walk in space. Stafford's *Apollo* command module had docked with Leonov's *Soyuz 19* spacecraft three hours earlier, 130 miles above the coast of Portugal. The *Apollo-Soyuz* Test Project (ASTP), as the mission was known, was the first time that representatives from the world's two spacefaring nations had collaborated in orbit.[22] The mission was part science, but also part theater: it was a tangible expression of détente, the warming of relations between the two superpowers during the mid-1970s.

The mission planners had to overcome many engineering and logistical hurdles. In addition, they faced the more prosaic issue of communication: what language (or languages) should the three astronauts and two cosmonauts use to speak to one another? The most straightforward solution might have been to have both crews use just one language. But which language? The American planners were undoubtedly concerned that an all-Russian mission might play poorly on US television: everything would need to be translated, and the whole enterprise would take on a decidedly foreign cast. The Russians probably had similar misgivings: détente notwithstanding, cosmonauts speaking the language of the capitalists could be seen as a propaganda coup for the West.

Alternatively, the crews could speak their respective native languages and learn, as best they could, to understand the language of the other crew. And in fact, this is what the original ASTP agreement called for. The astronauts and cosmonauts dutifully began intensive programs of study with teams of instructors.[23] Even with this training, however, Stafford was concerned that it might be insufficient to carry out the procedures required on the flight. In his memoir *We Have Capture*, he describes the solution he arrived at for this problem:

One night at a party, I found myself talking with Anatoly Filipchenko, commander of the second [backup] ASTP craft. It was almost as if we had ESP—the first thing we did was try to speak each other's language.

When you do that, you naturally speak more slowly and distinctly. The next day, we presented this arrangement to the other crew members and flight planners. Since nobody thought what we had was working especially well, we all agreed to give this a try. It became our standard method.[24]

So the Russian cosmonauts learned to speak English, and the Americans learned to speak Russian. Such an approach might seem like the worst of both worlds, since the two crews would still need to sacrifice valuable training time to achieve some measure of oral proficiency.

And communication problems did occur. Stafford spoke Russian with a pronounced Oklahoma drawl, later dubbed "Oklahomski" by his Russian counterparts. At one point during the mission, he repeatedly asked the cosmonauts to turn off their ship's beacons but kept using the word мягкий (*myagky*, or "soft") instead of маяки (*mayaki*, or "beacons"). The Russian crew members were puzzled by his persistent requests to "turn off your soft," but they eventually figured out what Stafford meant and complied with his request.[25] However, such misunderstandings could have had more serious consequences. Was this cross-linguistic system really the best solution?

Although Stafford doesn't consider the issue in his memoir, the approach adopted by the crews neatly bypassed a number of thorny pragmatic issues. The Americans' imperfect understanding of Russian would not have allowed them to easily grasp the connotations of the Russian language—and vice versa. Stafford points out that Americans speaking Russian will speak more slowly and more distinctly, but in addition, they are continually reminding their Russian counterparts that they are grappling, imperfectly, with a foreign language.[26] Therefore, instead of unconsciously assuming proficiency on the part of the Americans, the cosmonauts interpreted the Americans' productions as simple and literal: no indirectness, no ostensible speech acts, and nothing off-record.[27] Because each crewmember was communicating with a (linguistic) hand tied behind his back, the two crews were, in fact, less likely to misinterpret each other.

4   The Elements of Pragmatic Style

That's a Good One

Not being funny doesn't make you a bad person. Not having a sense of
humor does.

—David Rakoff, *Fraud* (2001)

In the fall of 2001, the British psychologist Richard Wiseman
set out to identify the world's funniest joke. People from around
the world were invited to submit their favorite jokes to him via
a website. The data were collected over a twelve-month period,
and ultimately more than 40,000 different jokes were submitted.
In addition, nearly 2 million ratings were made.[1]

So what's the world's funniest joke? After crunching the
numbers, Wiseman reported that the best thigh-slapper was the
following:

Two hunters are out in the woods when one of them collapses. He
doesn't seem to be breathing and his eyes are glazed. The other guy
whips out his phone and calls the emergency services. He gasps, "My
friend is dead! What can I do?" The operator says, "Calm down. I can
help. First, let's make sure he's dead." There is a silence, then a shot is
heard. Back on the phone, the guy says, "OK, now what?"

Chances are, you found this joke to be fairly humorous—even if you've heard it before. Wiseman reported that it has universal appeal, for men and women of all ages.[2] However, he also asked his participants to indicate the country they lived in, and found some striking national differences. Here, for example, is the top-rated joke from the German participants:

A general noticed one of his soldiers behaving oddly. The soldier would pick up any piece of paper he found, frown and say: "That's not it" and put it down again. This went on for some time, until the general arranged to have the soldier psychologically tested. The psychologist concluded that the soldier was deranged, and wrote out his discharge from the army. The soldier picked it up, smiled and said: "That's it."

Unless you're German, the soldier joke is probably amusing, but less funny than the hunter joke. And consider the top vote getter from the Belgian participants:

Why do ducks have webbed feet?
To stamp out fires.
Why do elephants have flat feet?
To stamp out burning ducks.

Perhaps you're reading this in Antwerp or Ghent and are now wiping tears from your eyes. If not, there's a good chance that your reaction was somewhat less than mirthful. And this underscores the culture-bound nature of humor.

In societies characterized as high context, individuals share a great deal of cultural knowledge, and most people have had similar experiences. The import of a story doesn't have to be spelled out explicitly, because it is assumed that everyone will know and understand what it means. In contrast, low-context cultures are often much more heterogeneous, and shared cultural frames aren't taken for granted. Not surprisingly, this affects how humor is perceived. The American linguist Audrey

Adams has pointed out that inside jokes exemplify high-context humor. These sorts of witticisms make perfect sense to a particular group's initiates but will be understood imperfectly, or not at all, by those on the outside. In a low-context culture like the United States, it's not unusual to hear a member of a particular subgroup say, "It's a [name of group] thing; you wouldn't understand." And when a comedian laments to an unresponsive crowd, "You're not my audience," he means exactly what he says. And, of course, once an inside joke has been explained by using explicit, literal language, the joke loses much of its power to amuse.[3]

Given the myriad ways in which cultures differ, it's not surprising that what is considered humorous varies greatly, as well. Although only a handful of cross-cultural studies have explored this phenomenon, the results suggest that there are reliable differences between countries. One project asked college students in Singapore and the United States to fill out self-report humor questionnaires and to supply their favorite joke. The results suggested that the Americans rely more on humor as a coping mechanism than the Singaporean subjects. The content was also different: The Singaporeans provided jokes with a higher proportion of aggressive content than the Americans. In turn, the US participants provided more jokes with sexual content than the students in Singapore. The authors interpreted the findings as reflective of the two culture's mores, as Singapore is more conservative. It's against the law, for example, to sell or possess pornography, and the Ministry of Education blocks access to pornographic websites.[4]

Several other cross-cultural differences have been documented. For example, compared to Germans, Italians have a greater appreciation for sexual humor and are less amused by nonsense humor (like the elephant joke recounted earlier). Egyptians, Lebanese, and Americans use aggressive and affiliative humor (telling jokes and funny stories to each other) to a similar degree, but Americans are more likely to employ humor to be self-deprecating or self-enhancing. Speakers of French tend to make humorous remarks about third parties, whereas Australian English speakers are more likely to direct their humor at their conversational partners. In Japan, jokes that involve puns and wordplay and amusing personal anecdotes are extremely popular.[5]

Jokes and wordplay can be thought of as the set pieces of humor, but a great deal of what is considered amusing is spontaneous and unfolds over several conversational turns. A good example of this is playful mockery, which has been studied by the linguists Michael Haugh and Derek Bousfield. Although such teasing could be construed as face threatening, it functions in a way that is very similar to small talk: this sort of banter encourages social bonding and creates connectedness between pairs or small groups of conversational participants.[6]

A nonnative speaker of a language is doubly disadvantaged in appreciating the humor of native speakers and in producing her own witticisms. She may lack the cultural frame for *why* something is considered funny by others, and her grasp of the language may not allow the verbal proficiency necessary to engage in wordplay or other types of culturally appropriate humor. The American linguist Catherine Davies has studied how this process unfolded in an intensive English program, in which small groups of nonnative speakers interacted casually with each other and a native speaker. She observed that humor was often a joint project: the conversational participants would collaborate in their banter, with the native speaker providing scaffolding that the nonnative speakers could use as a springboard for their own contributions. In this way, the nonnative speakers developed competence in informal English that should help them create social networks in their new environment.[7]

What the &#?@!!?

You see what happens when you find a stranger in the Alps?

—John Goodman as Walter Sobchak, in the bowdlerized version of *The Big Lebowski* (1998)

On August 15, 1998, twenty-five-year-old Timothy Boomer, a native of Detroit, fell into frigid waters while canoeing with some friends on the Rifle River. Somewhat vexed by his tumble, and in reaction to being laughed at by his buddies, he expressed his anger by uttering profanity. According to his own account, he said the "f-word" a couple of times. However, others who witnessed the event said that he used that term, quite loudly, between twenty-five and seventy times. A woman in a canoe bore witness to the harangue and reported that she felt compelled to cover her toddler's ears. And because Mr. Boomer unleashed his tirade within earshot of the other canoeists, he was in violation of an 1897 Michigan law that bans swearing in the presence of women and children. A sheriff's deputy who was patrolling the river also heard the verbal volley and issued Mr. Boomer a ticket. In court, Mr. Boomer's invocation of free speech did not carry the day: he was found guilty and fined. He was, however, successful on appeal because his attorney characterized the law as being unconstitutionally vague.[8]

A similar appeal to vagueness kept the Fox television network out of hot water with the Federal Communications Commission (FCC). In this case, the offender was Bono, lead vocalist of

the Irish rock band U2, who uttered the same expression as Mr. Boomer, albeit in a very different and much more public context. During a live telecast of the 2003 Golden Globe Awards, Bono excitedly said, "This is really, really, f*ing brilliant!" when his band received the award for best original song.[9] In general, appellate courts have not supported the FCC's indecency policy concerning the use of so-called fleeting expletives. Despite this, certain four-letter words are still forbidden or are bleeped over when uttered on American television, even during late-night programming when minors are assumed not to be watching. Images that might be offensive to some viewers are pixelated. And since 1985, recordings with explicit musical lyrics sold in the United States have been accompanied by a parental advisory warning.[10]

There is, in fact, a long history of censoring potentially objectionable language in both the UK and the United States. Nearly two centuries after the publication of Shakespeare's plays, for example, the English physician Thomas Bowdler published *The Family Shakspeare* (*sic*), in which he omitted from the Bard's works events and characters that he thought might cause offense to women and children. Changing Lady Macbeth's exclamation of "Out, damned spot!" to "Out, crimson spot!" may not have elevated the Scottish Play's language, but Bowdler's actions did have lasting impact. His name is now applied to the changing of text or dialogue that might otherwise be considered offensive.[11] Such changes, like those in the quotation at the beginning of this section, are frequently undertaken to allow adult-oriented movies to be broadcast on commercial television—no matter how strange or illogical the end result.

Most English speakers use the words "swearing" and "cursing" interchangeably, although lexicographers do make a distinction, since the words have different histories. Broadly speaking, swearing involves appeals to a supreme being or a sacred object, and the term is historically linked to promises and oaths. Cursing involves the profane as opposed to the sacred and includes a broad set of referents, such as bodily elimination, genitalia, and sexuality.[12] In other words, swearing is blasphemous, whereas cursing may be vulgar or offensive. As a result, when a need arises to refer to such functions, body parts, and acts, many speakers will fall back on euphemisms (such as "visit the little boys' room" or "make love") to avoid offending others.[13]

Whereas swearing and cursing are broad subjective categories, "obscenity" has been codified into legal statutes, although which terms and images fall under this category has varied over time, and from place to place. Even within a particular culture at a given time, what is considered obscene can be noto-riously subjective. US Supreme Court Justice Potter Stewart's pronouncement of "I know it when I see it," uttered in the con-text of determining criteria for obscenity, is well known. These examples illustrate how perceptions of profanity are driven by a variety of factors within the same culture, such as genera-tional and regional differences, ideological orientation, religious adherence, and whether minors are being exposed to such language.

Swearing and cursing can, of course, fulfill a variety of impor-tant discourse goals. In English, profanity is strongly linked with the expression of emotion (as with Timothy Boomer), being funny, or emphasizing something (as with Bono). Swearing can also create social bonding and can be used in constructing and displaying one's identity.[14] A good example of this can be found in the language used by a New Zealand soap factory work team. The use of expletives on the factory floor was interpreted as an example of positive politeness by the researchers who observed the workers, because it seemed to function as a marker of solidarity.[15]

Researchers have described a wide range of communicative functions for profanity in other languages, as well. A study of Turkish cursing found that women curse much more than men. The researcher who made the observation suggests that it says a great deal about the place of women in Turkish society. For women who lack power and influence, there are relatively few ways to protest treatment they feel is unfair.[16] Viewed from this perspective, cursing provides relatively powerless people with a voice—albeit a profane voice.

Some have argued that the relative acceptability of cursing and swearing reflects whether a culture is *tight* (with strong norms and low tolerance for nonconformity) or *loose* (weak norms and a high tolerance for nonconformity). A study of thirty-three countries found that inhabitants of Pakistan, Malaysia, India, and Singapore exhibited the most tightness, whereas residents of Ukraine, Estonia, Hungary, and the Netherlands were the most loose. The United States was ranked as relatively loose, although English-speaking Australia was looser and the United Kingdom a bit tighter.[17]

Cliff Goddard, an Australian linguist, has explored the looseness of Australian English in comparison to American English. While many aspects of swearing and cursing are similar in the two countries, Goddard suggests that Australians have a greater tolerance of, and even an appreciation for, irreverence in public life. By contrast, American culture has a tradition of civility in public life.[18] It remains to be seen whether the embracing of incivility by some in the American political realm has permanently dented this tradition.

An awareness of taboo words within a given culture is yet another example of how native speakers of a language are socialized. Children gradually learn what they can and can't say, and to whom, either by observing others or by receiving explicit instruction (You can *never* say that to your grandmother!). And while nonnative speakers understand the concept of taboo language, they may not possess the pragmatic competence needed to always succeed in not giving offense to others. The American psychologists Timothy Jay and Kristen Janschewitz tested this idea by giving hypothetical scenarios involving taboo language to both native and nonnative English-speaking college students. They found that the native speakers had a more nuanced view of the appropriate use of swearing. For example, it is less appropriate for a dean to swear than a college student, but more appropriate for a dean to swear in her office than somewhere else on campus.[19] Since students learning a second language rarely receive instruction in the proper use of profane language, they may know the meanings of such expressions but not know how to employ them as a native speaker would. Perhaps not surprisingly, therefore, people who are multilingual are more likely to swear in their dominant language.[20]

it's a Shame

It took me about a second before I realized I'd done it again. My mouth seriously needed a chaperone.
—Cara, in the novel *Populazzi*, by Elise Allen (2011)

O shame, where is thy blush?
—Hamlet to Gertrude, *Hamlet*, act 3, scene 4

The universally experienced states of embarrassment and shame are keenly felt by virtually everyone. The sudden shift from our normal sense of ease and competence to self-consciousness and awkwardness can happen quickly, leaving us feeling sheepish or even humiliated. And for people who are extremely shy, such experiences can be debilitating. Not surprisingly, therefore, cultures have developed codes of behavior to minimize the embarrassment and shame that we experience. Ranging from simple and almost unconscious rituals to elaborate facework, these acts can serve to protect our own egos, as well as the self-esteem of others. A great deal of what is referred to as etiquette can, in fact, be characterized as helping people to avoid embarrassment in situations in which expectations may not be clear. However, since different cultures have different ways of accomplishing these ends, befuddlement and confusion can occur when these strategies clash.

The universality of emotions and attendant facial expressions has been a topic of debate in the social sciences since the time of Darwin.[21] And in the case of embarrassment, the situation is complex. Blushing, for example, is associated not only with embarrassment but also with anxiety, romantic attraction, and anger. A study of participants from Quebec and Gabon found no reliable facial indictors for posed examples of embarrassment (that is, asking people to "look embarrassed"), although the same study found such indicators for many other emotions, such as happiness and sadness.[22] And unlike many other emotional displays, people spontaneously try to conceal their embarrassment by using a hand to cover their face, especially the mouth or eyes, or even try to hide their face behind large sunglasses.[23]

Another way to express embarrassment is through a combination of tongue biting and shoulder shrugging. Although this gesture is common in much of some parts of Asia, its meaning was lost on college students in Wisconsin, who found it baffling. In fact, they tended to interpret it as amusement or happiness.[24] In contrast, both American students and participants from India interpreted a hand covering the face as reflecting shame or embarrassment.[25]

Even within one's own culture, certain desires and requests can be difficult to convey via language alone. Making clear to someone that you are attracted to him or her might fall into this category. Most of us dread the acute embarrassment that results when our feelings are not reciprocated, so we resort to a variety of off-record behavioral displays, such as laughter and eye contact, to signal our interest. However, there are situations in which individuals must ask questions or make requests that, in any other context, would be extremely face threatening.

A classic study of language used by pediatric allergists in Sweden found that the physicians were often extremely indirect in their face-threatening recommendations and directives. For example, when one allergist found that a child with a severe cat allergy was petting cats, he said, "Well, that's really not so smart," leaving it to the child's mother to ratify the statement by saying, quite directly, "You SHOULD NOT do that." The researchers also documented many instances of the physicians employing positive politeness strategies, such as accompanying requests with overly respectful forms of address. For example, one doctor softened a recommendation that a child should get more exercise by referring to her as "your ladyship." In general, the physicians frequently used jokes and playful behavior when interacting with their young charges, clearly aware that their face-threatening and potentially embarrassing requests needed to be leavened with humor.[26]

In looking across the world's languages, we can observe some differences with regard to these concepts. It is claimed, for example, that Chinese has more than one hundred terms for shame, guilt, and embarrassment, in comparison to no more than a few dozen in English. This is consistent with the notion that shame, and the avoidance of losing face, plays an important role in contemporary societies rooted in Confucian traditions.[27]

The idioms used to describe embarrassment and shame show a great deal of similarity across the world's languages. Many of these terms map onto the physical and experiential aspects of such states, such as being "red-faced" (a reference to blushing, mentioned earlier) or being tongue-tied. In Japanese, one might say, 穴があったら入りたい (ana ga attara hairitai), or "If there was a hole, I'd want to get into it," which is perfectly interpretable in English. On the other hand, describing an unanticipated and embarrassing situation as "a banana skin" is a term used in British but not American English.

Rebecca Merkin, a communications researcher, asked participants from six countries to imagine an embarrassing situation in which, while visiting another country as a tourist, they knocked a glass of red wine onto the floor of a restaurant, shattering the glass and sending the wine flying. The participants then rated the degree to which other people from their culture would employ a variety of face-saving strategies. Merkin used this scenario to assess the participants' uncertainty avoidance (UA), which refers to the way people avoid unpredictable situations by adhering to strict codes of behavior. She found that participants from strong-UA cultures (such as China and Japan) endorsed more ritualistic strategies for uncertainty avoidance than participants from weak-UA cultures (such as the United States and Canada). Furthermore, participants from the high-UA cultures imagined that such situations would lead to more anxiety and hence more-aggressive and less-harmonious behaviors, such as walking out of a meeting. In contrast, participants from weak-UA cultures were more likely to respond by cultivating an air of calmness and collectedness.[28] These results support the Dutch psychologist Geert Hofstede's view that people from strong-UA cultures, with established formal codes for UA avoidance, can become more confrontational when these norms are violated. People from weak-UA cultures, which do not have strong scripts for UA avoidance, are less likely to respond confrontationally.[29]

A study with similar results involved American and Korean college students, who were asked to imagine themselves in a situation in which a classmate fails to keep a social engagement, and another in which a younger person addresses an older person informally, failing to use the appropriate form of address. The researchers asked the participants to characterize the interactions in terms of politeness, avoidance, and confrontation. The Korean participants viewed the outcome in both scenarios more unfavorably than the American subjects and showed a greater tendency to resort to confrontation as a result. These findings are consistent with yet another cross-cultural study, which found that American college students were more likely to use humor as a coping response to embarrassing situations in comparison to Japanese participants.[30]

The results of such studies should be interpreted with some caution, however, since they employed a limited number of scenarios for the participants to consider. However, these studies do suggest that cross-cultural behavior in embarrassing and face-threatening situations may be affected by how people are socialized to deal with ambiguity and uncertainty.

Shooting the Breeze

Small talk is the biggest talk we do.
—Susan RoAne, *What Do I Say Next?* (1997)

Praten over koetjes en kalfjes (To talk about little cows and little calves)
—Dutch expression for small talk

Chew the fat. Chitchat. Palaver. Schmooze. How you react to seeing or hearing such expressions probably says a lot about the language you speak and where you were socialized. Many people in the West equate these terms with idleness and gossip. Consider, for example, encountering a coworker who is taking a break away from her desk. This may lead to what is referred to in the United States as a "water cooler" conversation. The term is used to describe perfunctory exchanges about current events, or perhaps sharing opinions about a recently released movie. Anything more than that would probably be perceived as wasting time.

This negative view of small talk is typical in cultures that are *monochromic*. Such a label is applied to societies in which people typically do one thing at a time, and one is either "on the clock" or not working.[31] As a result, working and socializing are perceived as being two separate activities that cannot be done at the same time. (This explains the briefness of water cooler conversations.) In contrast, cultures in many parts of the world can be characterized as *polychromic*. In such cultures, multitasking is the norm, interruptions are common, and plans change frequently. There is also a less rigid separation of work and play, and casual conversation is seen as a significant part of one's daily interactions. The British anthropologist Bronisław Malinowski used the term *phatic communion* (or what is now referred to as *phatic communication*) to describe these sorts of exchanges, in which the goal is not to share information but rather to be sociable and to build rapport.[32]

Brown and Levinson characterize both gossip and small talk as positive politeness strategies, achieved by invoking the common ground shared between two conversational participants. The commiseration of two acquaintances about a loss by the home team may serve the goal of catharsis, but it also reinforces the social bonds that exist between people who live in the same community. In a similar way, gossip, despite its bad reputation, plays an important role in the dissemination of news and information within groups.[33]

In many societies, a question like "How are you?" which appears to be a legitimate inquiry, is in fact ostensible and not intended as a genuine concern about one's health. A recitation of one's medical conditions or state of mind is not called for and would almost certainly not be welcome. However, recognizing an expression like "Did you have a good weekend?" as an invitation for small talk or as a sincere question varies even among Western cultures. A study of a French corporation in Australia found that queries about one's weekend led to cross-cultural confusion. The English-speaking Australians regarded the question as ostensible and provided brief replies, whereas the French employees regarded it as sincere and provided long, detailed responses. The employees interpreted this as reflecting personal, rather than linguistic, differences. The French viewed the Aussies' terse responses as reflecting indifference, while the Australians characterized the native French speakers' long-winded replies as emblematic of insensitivity and self-centeredness.[34]

In many contexts, phatic communication can provide an important mechanism for promoting social interaction, especially between groups that do not always get along. A study of transactions between Korean shopkeepers and their African American customers in the American Midwest, for example, found that phatic communication occurred frequently in this context. The storeowners and their patrons often discussed the weather or their children at length, though these topics had little to do with the transactions being conducted. In this situation, small talk played a big role in building rapport between the merchants and their clientele.[35]

Not surprisingly, expectations about small talk can loom large in consequential interactions, like cross-cultural negotiations. Among the many books that are intended for international businesspeople, the following is typical (the topic under discussion is behavior at cocktail parties):

Germans simply do not believe in it [small talk], Finns and Japanese are frightened to death by it and Swedes usually dry up after about 10 minutes. Russians and Germans—more than willing to have long, soul-searching conversations with close friends—see no point in trotting out trivialities and platitudes for two hours to a complete stranger. ... Finns, unused to chatter, actually buy booklets on small talk.[36]

It turns out that these observations contain some elements of truth. Researchers have, in fact, documented an aversion to phatic communication in many parts of Europe and Asia. The linguist Juliane House, for example, has pointed out that the German language does not even have a term for "small talk." And the Finns really do seem to have an aversion to small talk.[37]

However, Europe is not monolithic in this regard. A comparison of telephone calls found that phatic communication occurred less than one-third of the time in German phone calls, but over two-thirds of the time in Greek calls. Not only that, but the phatic statements seemed to serve different purposes for the two groups. Whereas the Greeks used small talk to enhance their relationships with each other, the Germans often used phatic utterances to reduce any face threats that were associated with the reason for the call.[38] And these differences can vary within a particular language. A comparison of Spanish spoken in stores in Quito, Ecuador, and Madrid, Spain, found differences in phatic communication, with the Ecuadorians interacting in a ritualistic, almost ceremonial way, using extended greetings and openings. The Spaniards, by contrast, were more informal and got down to the business at hand more quickly.[39]

Finally, when we turn to non-Western countries, we see that small talk plays an important role in many cultures. When Richard lived in Niger, he had to learn how to slowly wade into the conversation and not just dive in feet first. Similarly, in Arabic-speaking countries, conversational participants avoid jumping quickly to the topic at hand and instead begin with pleasantries, then loop back and forth between business and more general issues.[40] And contrary to the earlier quotation, speakers of Japanese do engage in small talk, although it differs in important ways from the Western conception. Americans engage in more self-disclosure and are more informal and spontaneous, whereas residents of Japan are more reserved and guarded about personal matters.[41]

Me and *Vous* and Everyone We Know

In Korea, Richard once referred to one of his younger brothers by using an honorific term that basically means "gentleman." He was corrected and told that it wasn't appropriate to use this word to refer to a younger brother—even though his brother is a university professor. But it's not reciprocal. If Richard's younger brother ever wanted to refer to Richard in Korean, he would be obliged to use that respectful term. Age differences, therefore, even among siblings, are coded into the honorifics of the Korean language.

And it's not just foreigners who have trouble with honorifics. Tensions arise even among Koreans about the proper term someone should or should not use. One of Richard's colleagues once correctly referred to someone with a PhD as "doctor." This individual became upset, however, because he expected the even more elevated term "professor."

As these examples show, a fundamental aspect of language use involves making reference to other people. In theory, this should be simple, but in practice, it is governed by all sorts of cultural, social, and situational factors. And just to keep you on your toes, the rules that govern reference to one's self and others in a given language may change over time.

If you are a native English speaker, then you are probably only dimly aware of all of this. Nowadays, honorifics in English are most commonly used in titles, such as "Your Honor" or "Reverend" or "sir." But it wasn't always this way. For example, throughout its complex history, English shed one of the honorific distinctions still observed in many of the world's languages: different forms of "you." For example, French and German (from which English is descended) still retain the distinction among three types of "you":

1. The familiar singular *you*

2. The formal singular *you*

3. The plural *you*

In Modern English, these three forms are all the same. It doesn't matter whether you're addressing your brother (form 1), a head of state (form 2), or a mob of thousands (form 3); it's all *you* to you—and to them, as well.

But as recently as the seventeenth century, speakers of English distinguished among *thou* (form 1) and *you* (form 2) and *ye* (form 3). The archaic *thou* can still be found today in the King James version of the Bible (published in 1611) and in the plays of Shakespeare (written between the 1590s and the 1610s).

Many people mistakenly assume that *thou* is the formal form, since it's the one that biblical figures use to refer to God, as in "Thy kingdom come, thy will be done" in Matthew 6:10 (*thy* is the possessive form of *thou*). And if God doesn't rate the formal form, then who does? But, in fact, *thou* was used by earlier speakers of English to indicate intimacy as well as familiarity.

As in some modern European languages, the archaic second-person distinction in English was reflected in its grammar. Verbs that followed the two forms of *you* were modified (declined) differently. For example, in *As You Like It* (ca. 1599), Rosalind tells Celia, "Nay, thou goest from Fortune's office to Nature's" (act 1, scene 2). The change of "go" to "goest" is exactly how things still work in modern German: the verb *gehen* becomes *gehst* when the familiar form of *you* is used (as in *Wohin gehst du*? or "Where are you going?").

So how about the third form, the plural *you*? Shakespeare and his contemporaries used the word *ye* to refer to more than one person. And once again, vestiges of this live on in institutions that are slow to change, such as in liturgical and judicial contexts. When bailiffs announce that court is now in session, they say *Hear ye! Hear ye!* which is basically a call for silence and attention, directed at everyone (hence the plural form of *you*).

Should we assume, then, that the plural form of *you* also ended up on the ash heap of English's history? Interestingly, it's still alive and kicking—but only in nonstandard forms of the language. For example, the term *y'all* (as a contraction of *you all*) is widely used in the American South to address multiple people. And there's even a variation of this variant—*all y'all*, which some people use to refer to even larger groups or for emphasis.

In a similar way, plural forms of *you* can be found all over the English-speaking world—*yous* in the British Isles and Australia, *you guys* in large parts of North America (even when addressing mixed groups of men and women), and *you lot* in England. And back in the United States, *yous guys* is used in the Northeast, and even *yinz* can be heard in Pittsburgh, Pennsylvania. Clearly, speakers of English still find it convenient to distinguish between the singular and plural forms of *you*, even if there isn't universal agreement about which term to use.

So that's the complicated state of affairs in a language that (in theory) has only one form of *you*. Things should be simpler, therefore, in languages that make explicit distinctions between the second-person familiar, formal, and plural forms, right? Well, as you've probably figured out by now, the answer is no. In fact, things can be a good deal more confusing.

German would be a fairly typical example of how things work in many European languages. The formal form is *Sie*, and the same word is used for both singular and plural others. *Sie* is used by children to address adults, and by adults to address strangers and people who would otherwise be referred to using honorifics (Mister, Miss) or by title (Doctor, Professor). *Sie* is also used with one's coworkers. The familiar form is *du*, and the plural is *ihr*. Adults use *du* and *ihr* to address family members, close friends, children, animals, inanimate objects, and God. The use of *du* also implies the use of first names. If a switch from *Sie* to *du* is made, it is maintained consistently by both parties. There is even a specific verb to refer to this change: *duzen*.

It all seems fairly straightforward and rather tidy, doesn't it? But in practice, the distinction is anything but. It can be a linguistic minefield for the unwary—and not just for nonnative speakers. If it's *du* for kids and *Sie* for adults, then when does one cross over? One online guide breezily suggests "about age fifteen" as the dividing line.[42] Is someone who celebrates her sixteenth birthday addressed as *du* one day and *Sie* the next? Does a third cousin whom you don't know well get included on the familiar or the formal side of things?

There are some general guidelines, of course. In the workplace, a superior may explicitly choose to address a subordinate with the familiar *du*, at which point the subordinate can also make the switch. At one time, it was customary for the two individuals to mark the occasion with a little ceremony, often over a glass of beer or wine. Interestingly, the police in Germany are required to use the formal form at all times. Even if they catch a criminal in the act, they must use *Sie*, and if they don't, they can be fined.[43] It also works the other way. Not addressing a police officer with *Sie* in Germany can also result in a fine.

Michael Agar, an American anthropologist, relates a number of stories about his experiences in Austria in his book *Language Shock*. In one case, a female acquaintance changed from using *Sie* to *du* with him, which he found pleasant but otherwise unremarkable. An exasperated colleague had to explain later that the woman had been flirting with him.[44]

And German is not the only language where "you" is a loaded term. The Swedes are also struggling with formal and informal distinctions in terms of address. The informal *du* is too familiar for business and professional settings, but the formal *ni* is seen as maintaining class distinctions in egalitarian Sweden. One proposed solution is to do away with *you* altogether.[45] But such a change would require some linguistic gymnastics to accomplish. What do *you*—er, *those individuals reading this now*—think?

On the other side of the globe, languages such as Japanese and Korean not only formalize distinctions in how a person is addressed but also use specific verbs to show respect. Richard has found that Japanese and Korean speakers tend to have relatively low expectations regarding the linguistic abilities of foreigners learning the language. For example, native speakers generally aren't offended when nonnative speakers mistakenly use more familiar constructions.[46] However, this tolerance does not seem to hold for emigrants and their descendants. In these cases, there is an expectation that ancestry should compel them to achieve a high level of proficiency in the language.

It doesn't take much imagination to see how a pragmatic distinction that trips up even native speakers could wreak havoc on the psyche of a foreigner who is trying to learn the language. One of the ironies of language learning is that the better you speak a given tongue, the more that native speakers will assume you understand the underlying culture. If you've just begun to learn the language, then most native speakers would shrug off a *du* versus *Sie* type of error as a beginner's mistake. If, on the other hand, your accent is good and your mastery of the syntax is high, such an error would be more likely to lead to confusion or annoyance.

It appears that "all speech communities have linguistic means of distinguishing different social relationships."[47] But, of course, they don't all do it the same way. In Korea, one's age, relative to another's, is an extremely important variable that must be taken into consideration with every conversational partner, as the next example shows.

It's Only a Number

Indeed, no woman should ever be quite accurate about her age. It looks so calculating.

—Oscar Wilde, *The Importance of Being Earnest* (1895)

It was a cold day in January, and Richard and Roger were enjoying a meal at a restaurant in Seoul. It was Roger's first visit to Korea, and he was struggling to manipulate the chopsticks that he had never quite mastered during his forays to Chinese restaurants in the United States. To help him, Richard modeled the proper technique, and Roger did his best to emulate his example.

The restaurant was fairly empty, but there were a few other patrons, including a table of older Korean men. And as Roger was to learn later, he and Richard were being observed with some interest. Although Seoul is a cosmopolitan city, the presence of foreigners is still something that might be remarked on. And most Koreans would assume that visitors to their country would not understand the language, or at least not very well. This assumption would be warranted: the US State Department classifies Korean as a "super hard" language to learn, and some diplomats who are attached to the embassy in Seoul receive nearly two years of full-time language instruction before assuming their posts. Richard, with the benefit of this language training, was able to follow the conversation of the men who were watching them.

After Richard had paid for the meal, he returned to the table for a few moments, and then he and Roger left the restaurant. Richard then told him that the table of older men had been discussing them—in particular, their relative ages, for it turns out that their behavior didn't make any sense to the Korean men.

At first the men in the restaurant probably assumed that Richard and Roger were social peers of about the same age (and they are, in fact, just two years apart). However, by setting out the chopsticks and the napkins and by getting the water, Richard was taking on the role of a *younger*, subservient person by attending to the dining needs of his elder. The men at the nearby table noticed this and mentally tagged Roger (the bleary-eyed, jet-lagged one) as the older member of the pair of foreigners. But then Richard violated this implicit understanding by paying for the meal. In Korean culture, it's customary for an older person to pay for his younger guest. So who was, in fact, the older foreigner, and who was the younger? This conundrum was remarkable enough to become the topic of the men's conversation, which Richard overheard and understood.

This anecdote may seem rather curious unless you're aware that one's age plays a major role in Korean social interaction.[48] And by age, we mean one's age relative to others, as opposed to one's absolute age. The proper roles for older and younger people are clear, so it is common to be asked one's age shortly after meeting someone new in Korea. This peremptory query would seem odd at best to Americans and could even be considered quite rude.

In Korea, however, ignorance of one's age would make it impossible to employ the proper etiquette that the culture demands. Korean society is more hierarchical than most Western

societies, and age is an important component of this social organization. In addition, both the Confucian tenet of social harmony and the acknowledgment of the feelings of others are
essential. So what seems to be a nosy question about one's age
allows the requester to place his or her conversational partner
into the appropriate social stratum.[49] As a result, this seemingly
impolite request is actually required to follow the appropriate
rules of etiquette and decorum within Korean culture.

But why would someone need to know your age? Korean, like
Japanese, Vietnamese, and other Asian languages, uses a complex set of honorifics. Relative age is an important part of this
system. Age is tied up with showing appropriate deference and
respect, and this affects the level of speech that is employed in
social encounters. Age is calculated by one's birth year, and in

fact, the word for "friend" (친구, or *chingu*) means people who are the same age—specifically, those who were born in the same calendar year. In such cases, people can get away with using the lowest level of politeness in speaking with one another. However, under this system, even if you were born just a few weeks after your conversational partner, but in the following year, then you must use the appropriate honorifics in addressing your "elder." If two people have a close relationship, then the older may be referred to as "big brother" or "big sister," but not as "friend." In fact, in the music video "Gangnam Style," Psy calls himself "Oppa," a word girls use to refer to their big brothers, in a way that suggests "call me Big Daddy."[50]

And just to keep you on your toes, Koreans calculate age in a highly specific way.[51] To begin with, you're at least one year older than you would be in a Western country (sorry about that). That's because when a baby is born, he or she is already considered to be a year old. And everyone becomes one year older on the following first of January, as opposed to on their respective birthdays. This means that everyone born during the same calendar year is the same age, and everyone's age changes at the same time, as they ring in the new year. Consequently, one's "Korean age" could be, at least for some people, two years more than their biological age. A baby born in late December might be only a few days old chronologically but will be two "years" old on January 1.[52] Obviously, this can be confusing, so the term "full age" is used to refer to one's chronological age when it is required, as in legal or medical contexts.

So in comparison to biological age, one's "Korean age" is an abstraction—but an exceedingly useful one. If everyone's age did not change on the same date, then the fixed honorific conventions that people observe would be changeable. Under a strict full age system, people born a few months apart in the same year would have different ages until the second party caught up with the first by celebrating his or her own annual birthday. And for a few months, they would technically have different ages, with all the attendant linguistic consequences for their interactions. The Korean system for calculating age is a stark reminder of the power of language and culture to override something as basic and as consequential as one's true chronological age.

Up to this point, we have looked at broad pragmatic principles, and some specific stylistic variations, that are central to creating the content of utterances. In the next chapter, we examine the mechanics involved in the production of these utterances.

5 The Mechanics of Cross-Cultural Communication

Really! Go On ...

Drawing on my fine command of the English language, I said nothing.
—Robert Benchley, quoted in *With Truth as Our Sword* (2005)

During face-to-face conversations, listeners periodically provide confirmation to speakers that they are attending to what is being said. They do this in a variety of ways, such as by nodding their heads or through exclamations like "Uh-huh," "Wow!" "No kidding!" and "Oh dear!" Other verbal and nonverbal cues, such as smiles and laughter, can also serve this function.[1] This is called *backchanneling*, and it could be considered a form of positive politeness, since the listener is making clear that she is attending closely to a speaker. It can also implicitly signal that the listener is not trying to take the floor away from the speaker and is, in fact, encouraging him to continue. This behavior was first given a label by the American linguist Victor Yngve and has become an important topic of research in conversational analysis and cross-cultural communication.[2]

Although backchannels have primarily been characterized as empathetic responses, they can serve a variety of other functions. In addition to displaying understanding, agreement, and support of the speaker, they can also signal strong emotional responses (Wonderful!) or provide the speaker with information (inserting "August" when the speaker says "Later this year"). Backchannels can also be requests for clarification (Really?) or a way of signaling a lack of understanding (What?). Finally, linguists have argued that backchanneling can, in fact, signal disagreement ("Uh-uh," accompanied by a headshake). Research has suggested that these diverse discourse goals undermine the idea that backchannels constitute a specific type of speech act.[3] What all these functions have in common, however, is that they are not attempts to take the floor away from the speaker but rather helpful signals that she should continue. A backchannel is not a new conversational turn but a brief parenthetical interlude before the speaker's turn continues.

It can be unnerving when one's conversational partner backchannels only rarely (is he really listening?) or does so too frequently or at the wrong times (his interest doesn't seem genuine). And a person's keenly developed sense about proper backchanneling can be thrown off when she interacts with someone who is from another culture or speaks a different language. This is because there are significant cross-cultural and cross-linguistic differences in how backchanneling functions.

Several studies have explored differences between English and Japanese backchanneling, for example. Senko Maynard, a Japanese linguist, videotaped college students engaged in one-on-one casual conversations in Tokyo and New Jersey and analyzed the backchanneling behaviors of these pairs. Many aspects of the backchanneling were similar. For both groups, the most common form of backchanneling was what she calls a "brief utterable," such as "uh-huh," "yeah," and "right" for the Americans, and *un* (Uh-huh), *honto* (Really), and *soo* (I see) for the

Japanese students. Maynard also found that backchannels for both groups were most likely to occur at or near speaker pauses and at the junctures of clauses and sentences. By backchanneling at these times, the listener avoids interrupting or overlapping with her conversational partner and provides feedback only when the speaker has completed a thought, rather than while he is speaking.

However, some significant differences in backchanneling were found in the conversations that Maynard observed. With regard to frequency, she found that backchanneling occurred far more frequently—about twice as often, in fact—in conversations between Japanese speakers than in conversations of the same duration between the Americans. (Other studies have found even larger differences.) With regard to nonverbal cues, the American students used head movements about twice as often as Japanese speakers and used laughter as a backchanneling cue more often.[4]

It's easy to imagine how cross-cultural communication might be affected by such backchannel differences. An American, encountering brief utterables about twice as often as she is used to, might conclude that her hearer is being overly solicitous or even obsequious. A Japanese speaker, on the other hand, might perceive an American's relative dearth of spoken backchannels as indicating a lack of interest in what she is talking about.[5]

As we saw in the discussion of linguistic alignment, people are flexible and can adapt their linguistic behaviors on the fly to accommodate their partner. Sheida White, an American literacy scholar, explored this issue by recording Japanese and American participants as they spoke with partners from the same country and with partners from the other country. White found that the American subjects backchanneled more frequently when speaking with the Japanese participants; the Japanese subjects, however, showed no significant change in their backchanneling behavior when conversing with the Americans. Since both groups of participants provided evaluations of their conversational satisfaction and perceptions of their partner, it's possible to speculate on why this was so. White notes that the Japanese participants, on average, spoke less than a third as much as the Americans, possibly because they lacked confidence in their English ability. It's likely, then, that the Americans were backchanneling as a way to encourage their nonnative English-speaking partners to talk more.[6]

At the other end of the backchanneling continuum, Bettina Heinz has shown that speakers of German typically backchannel less than Americans do. However, as German speakers increase their proficiency in English, they produce more backchannels than their monolingual German counterparts. Heinz points out that backchanneling is a largely unconscious act and one that is not taught explicitly to native speakers or to second-language learners. She suggests that becoming consciously aware of backchanneling differences in a target language can help the learner achieve greater proficiency in the new language.[7]

The topic of a conversation can also affect the process of providing feedback. For sales negotiations, parties have competing agendas (buying at the lowest possible price versus selling at the highest possible price). Ron White explored this dynamic by creating sales simulations between American and Japanese businesspeople who were familiar with the give-and-take of negotiation. In this discourse context, backchanneling can be ambiguous. Is the listener saying "yes" because she likes what the speaker is offering, or is she encouraging him to continue and to perhaps offer a better deal? As expected, White observed examples of miscommunication based on the interpretation of such feedback. He also found that the Japanese comfort with long pauses created a problem for the American negotiators, who found lengthy silences unnerving, motivating them to fill such pauses with a counteroffer, which worked against their own interests.[8]

Studies of other languages have revealed additional cross-cultural differences. Lars Fant, a Swedish researcher, has documented the ways in which Nordic and Hispanic cultures differ with regard to backchanneling. Specifically, he notes that such feedback is common in Swedish, but far less common in Spanish. Not surprisingly, this difference can lead to cross-cultural difficulties. For example, Fant suggests that a Hispanic speaker might mistakenly interpret a Swedish listener's backchanneling as a genuine expression of agreement and not simply as a way of saying "go on."[9]

No Doubt!

Doubt is an uncomfortable condition, but certainty is a ridiculous one.
—François-Marie Arouet (Voltaire)

Positive, adj.: Mistaken at the top of one's voice.
—Ambrose Bierce, *The Devil's Dictionary* (1911)

In his classic science fiction novel *Stranger in a Strange Land* (1961), Robert Heinlein introduced readers to the concept of the Fair Witness. Individuals belonging to this profession were rigorously trained to observe and report what they saw and heard as accurately as possible, and not to make inferences of any kind. For example, when asked about the color of a nearby house, a

Fair Witness in Heinlein's novel reported it to be "white, on this side."[10] Most of us would be comfortable with the assumption that houses are usually painted the same color on all sides, and wouldn't feel a need to qualify such a statement with a phrase like "on this side." Ironically, the very act of restricting a statement, presumably to ensure its accuracy, can have the opposite effect on the hearer. If someone believes what they are saying, why should they feel compelled to qualify it?

Students of language refer to such equivocations as *hedges*. The term was introduced by the American cognitive scientist George Lakoff in the context of modifying the truth value of an utterance but has since grown to include the pragmatic aspects of such phrases, as well.[11] In English, hedges can run the gamut from a minor tweaking of meaning (kind of, a little) to more elaborate constructions, such as "would you mind" or "I was wondering if" in the context of making requests.[12] The act of issuing such a qualification is called *hedging*.

In terms of politeness theory, hedges can be thought of as a type of negative politeness, since the qualification by the speaker minimizes the imposition of her views on the hearer. Brown and Levinson suggest that, by acting in a way that isn't presumptuous, the speaker makes it easier for the hearer to assert his own beliefs on the topic at hand. Hedges can also be used to deflect criticism about potentially controversial positions, as when a politician makes a statement about a technical subject by prefacing it with an acknowledgment of a lack of expertise (I'm not a scientist, but …). The opposite of hedging is referred to as *boosting*. Boosters are words and phrases that suggest a great deal of confidence in what is being said (We firmly believe …, Without a doubt …, Obviously …).[13]

The linguist Robin Lakoff argued that women use hedges like "I think" or "If I'm not mistaken" to implicitly apologize for expressing opinions or making assertions, even when they are quite certain about the accuracy of such statements. Lakoff saw women's uncertainty and lack of authority in speaking as the result of pervasive gender socialization in the West that views assertive, more powerful speech as the province of men, and men only.[14] These ideas were popularized by the American linguist Deborah Tannen, whose best-known work, *You Just Don't Understand*, expands on the notion that men and women use language in very different ways. We should note, however, that research has not always supported such claims; for example, the linguist Janet Holmes did not find gender differences in the use of hedges by men and women. She also found that men used hedges to express uncertainty more often than did women.[15]

The expression of uncertainty is a perennial issue in scientific and academic writing.[16] Researchers are well aware that the results of their experiments are only probabilistically conclusive. Probability theory dictates that the result of any study could have occurred by chance, even if such an outcome is highly unlikely. It's also the case that generalizing from one group of research participants to the population at large entails some risk. For these reasons, responsible scientists are trained to make liberal use of words like "may," "might," "probably," and "perhaps" when discussing their findings.

Importantly, there are also cross-linguistic differences in how academicians use such hedging statements. For example, a study of English and German academic publications found that scholars writing in English use hedges to make the subject matter more approachable (for example, by using phrases like

"I think" or "I suspect"). In contrast, German writers tend to employ hedges to cultivate an air of objectivity and detachment (for example, by using terms like "arguably" and "admittedly").[17] Unfortunately, when academic research is reported on by the media, these qualifiers may be lost, leading to public perceptions about certainty in scientific results that are frequently unwarranted.

The ability to express just the right level of doubt or uncertainty is a skill we acquire along with all the other aspects of our native tongue. When we learn another language, however, these subtle gradations may be learned only imperfectly. This phenomenon was the subject of a large-scale analysis that compared the output of native Cantonese students writing in English for examinations with a similar group of British students. The second-language learners relied on a smaller range of hedging expressions and, in general, showed more difficulties in expressing various shades of certainty. For example, the researchers found that the use of the verb "think" (in the sense of expressing uncertainty, as in "I think") was nearly three times more frequent in the writing of the native English speakers. And the lexical verb "appear" was used *thirty-three* times more often by the British students. The authors of the study suggest that second-language learners may require explicit instruction to achieve the proper degree of tentativeness expected in academic discourse written in English.[18]

Similar results have been reported in several studies of research articles written by native and nonnative English speakers.[19] However, a study of indirectness and hedging in conference proposals written by native and nonnative English researchers found a more complex pattern of results. Native English speakers and nonnative English-speaking Indian scholars used relatively low rates of indirectness and hedging, while Turkish and Japanese nonnative English-speaking researchers used relatively high rates.[20]

Cross-linguistic studies of hedges and boosters have revealed other differences, as well. Ken Hyland, a linguist working in Hong Kong, asked Cantonese-speaking college students to read and answer questions about academic texts written in English. He found that the participants showed a sensitivity to the presence of boosters in the passages, but the hedges seemed to largely escape their notice. Specifically, third-year students of English mentioned boosters in their answers about twice as often as they referred to the hedges, even though both types of qualifiers were critical to understanding the meaning of the passages that they had read. Hyland concluded that these two forms differed in their "visibility" to the nonnative speakers and that the hedges were largely invisible to them.[21]

As with other pragmatically complex forms, cross-linguistic differences in the use of hedges and boosters may be embedded in the culture of the languages' speakers. This can create difficulties in cross-linguistic communication, because the use of hedges in particular seems to be tied to ways of expressing deference. And since English has become the lingua franca for scientific communication, nonnative scientists writing in English may need to pay close attention to how they discuss their results.

Changing Gears

As Roger and a colleague were driving to a meeting, the colleague's wife called him, and he chose to route the call through the car's speakers. Roger's colleague and his wife are bilingual, and when talking to each other, they typically employ her native language, which is German. It was a routine conversation about mundane matters, and Roger was torn between trying not to eavesdrop and taking advantage of the opportunity to brush up his German. Suddenly, his colleague switched from German to English: he used the term "storm windows" and then went back to German for the rest of the conversation. This is an example of a phenomenon referred to as *code switching*, and it may occur for a wide variety of reasons.

To begin, it's important to note that code switching isn't the same as the blending of two languages. An example of the latter would be what is referred to as *Spanglish*. This term is used in North America to refer to the speech of some Spanish-English bilinguals, and it involves using hybrid words or employing the grammar of one language while speaking the other.[22] Code switching can occur in Spanglish, of course, but these blended elements go beyond a simple switch between the standard forms of two languages.

If both parties in a conversation have nativelike proficiency in two languages, these so-called *balanced* bilinguals may switch from one language to another for practical reasons. For example, it may be a conscious attempt to prevent a conversation from being overheard and understood by others. However, code switching may also be the result of uneven linguistic ability. An *unbalanced* bilingual may have greater facility in one of her languages than the other, and so her partner may switch to the other's stronger language to facilitate the conversational flow. A change of this sort could be characterized as a positive politeness strategy, since it reflects an attentiveness to the partner's wants and needs. It can also be a way of showing solidarity, perhaps by emphasizing a shared community membership.

In other cases, the parties may switch back and forth several times between two languages during the same conversation. Or, as with Roger's colleague, it may occur just once. What governs code switching in cases like these?

In the case of a single switch, the issue may simply reflect a difficulty in retrieving a particular word. All of us experience "tip of the tongue" states, in which we know we know a word but are temporarily unable to recall it.[23] The bilingual, however, has at her disposal a second conceptual system, and a desired word may be accessible in one language while being inaccessible in the other. So rather than hesitate or struggle to produce the term in one language, she may simply elect to code switch—as long as she believes that her listener will understand.

Some support for this notion can be found in the research of the American anthropologist Leigh Swigart. When she asked Wolof- and French-speaking bilinguals in Dakar, Senegal, about their code switching, they responded that intermingling words from the two languages was simply "easier," "faster," or "more convenient." In fact, in many cases her informants told her they weren't even aware that they *were* code switching.[24] Other studies have supported this finding of a lack of awareness; while most bilinguals will admit to occasionally engaging in code switching, they express surprise when confronted with evidence of their own frequent switching.[25]

Different linguistic communities seem to have evolved different approaches with regard to this behavior. The linguist Shana Poplack has studied code switching among Spanish-English bilingual Puerto Ricans in New York, and French-English bilingual Canadians in Ottawa and Hull. She found, for example, that the New Yorkers minimized the impact of their linguistic switches on the ongoing discourse, while the Canadians conspicuously called attention to their code switching. For example, they would repeat or emphasize words and phrases in the second language. Poplack speculates that a variety of historical, social, and political issues may govern the differences in code switching she observed, such as issues of identity and attitudes toward the dominant (English) language.[26]

Another reason for code switching has to do with the topic of conversation. To study this aspect, Carol Scotton and William Ury recorded conversations of the Luyia of western Kenya as they switched back and forth between local dialects of Luyia, Swahili, and English. The researchers then played these recordings for other Luyia speakers and asked them to describe what was happening in these interactions. Most of the participants spontaneously mentioned the occurrence of code switching in their responses. A switch into English, for example, was associated with attempts to assert authority, whereas a switch into Swahili was seen as being appropriate for discussions of business or commerce.[27]

In other cases, a speaker may code switch if a concept doesn't really exist in either the currently used language or within the speaker's culture. For example, a study of Bulgarian speakers residing in Canada documented a switch from Bulgarian to English so that a speaker could employ the term "glass ceiling" (as in a barrier to advancement because of one's gender). The authors of the study assert that there is little gender discrimination for employment in modern Bulgaria, so the concept doesn't have an equivalent term in that language. And it would have made no sense to translate the English idiom into Bulgarian. As a result, the speaker resorted to English to communicate the idea.[28] And in case you were wondering, this was true for Roger's colleague, as well. Most windows in the United States aren't constructed like their German counterparts, so there is no exact equivalent for the American term "storm windows" in German.

Code switching may also occur to encourage informality. A study of code switching in Norway examined the differential use of highly prestigious local dialects of Norwegian and the so-called standard version of the language, which is used for official purposes and by the media. The standard language is also used by teachers to deliver lectures, but when the instructor wants to encourage free and open discussion among his students, he will shift to using the local dialect. Learning which language is most appropriate in which context seems to start at a very young age. The Norwegian linguist Elizabeth Lanza has claimed that children as young as two years of age engage in code switching.[29]

Code switching can serve a variety of other complex pragmatic functions, as well. In an analysis of an interaction between Chinese-English bilinguals who are mother and daughter, a switch back to Chinese by the daughter was seen as representing an attempt to soften a refusal.[30] It may also be the case that switching to a second language allows people greater emotional distance from memories and thoughts that are disturbing to them. An individual's first language may tap into deeper and more elaborated affective states, and if someone is trying to talk about something that is unpleasant, it may be easier to do so in a second language than in one's first.[31] This is supported by a study of Cantonese-English bilinguals, which demonstrated that participants found it easier to talk about embarrassing topics in their second language and were able to speak about them at greater length.[32] Likewise, nonbalanced bilinguals are likely to make less-emotional, more-practical decisions when faced with a moral dilemma in their nonnative language. As language proficiency improves, they tend to resolve moral dilemmas similarly in their native and nonnative tongues.[33]

Finally, code switching may reflect many other social and societal forces. A study of Turkish-Danish elementary school students, for example, highlighted the importance of the perceived prestige of a given language. Among these students, French, German, and English were viewed as high in prestige, whereas the heavily accented Danish of a Turkish immigrant was perceived as low in prestige. In the same way that a speaker may choose to affect a haughty, upper-class tone to mock the values of the wealthy, these children used different languages to achieve similar ends.[34]

Getting a Word In

I'mma let you finish, but …
—Kanye West to Taylor Swift, 2009 MTV Music Awards

The graduate student was horrified: her thesis advisor was on fire. Cora Friedline watched with concern and then growing alarm as Edward Titchener's beard, ignited by his cigar, began to burn. Lost in thought, perhaps, Titchener failed to notice the curling tendrils of smoke rising from his own body and continued to drone on about her research project. Friedline finally spoke up, exclaiming, "I beg your pardon, Dr. Titchener, but your whiskers are on fire!" By the time the flames had been smothered, they had burned through Titchener's shirt and undershirt. Why hadn't Friedline alerted him to the danger more quickly? As she later recalled, "His imposing manner made [me] reluctant to interrupt."[35]

What might seem unimaginable today can be better understood with a little context. Titchener's inadvertent self-immolation occurred at Cornell University, in upstate New York, during World War I. Friedline was in her mid-twenties, and Titchener, who was then America's most prominent experimental psychologist, was twice her age. Titchener had been born in England and trained in Germany, where academicians were accorded great respect and deference. All of this seems to have conspired to prevent Friedline from promptly breaking into Titchener's monologue with some important news.[36] Considerations about who can interrupt whom, and under what conditions, are ultimately driven by the relationship between conversational partners. But as might be expected, cultural factors play a role, as well.

To begin at the beginning, let's consider the concept of *the floor*. In a well-ordered exchange, conversational participants take turns, and the floor is amicably passed back and forth between them. However, that doesn't necessarily mean that only one person is speaking at a time. As we saw when we considered backchanneling, the listener may make exclamations or provide clarifications, but these aren't attempts to take the floor—in fact, they are explicit encouragements for the speaker to continue. Not all conversations, however, are well-ordered. Sometimes the speech of both parties will overlap, and this simultaneous speech will continue until one or the other ends up with the floor. And if the listener is anxious to take the floor, he may choose to interrupt, but typically only at certain junctures within the speaker's turn.[37]

It should also be kept in mind that not all interruptions are unwelcome. It seems likely that Dr. Titchener would have appreciated knowing that he had set himself ablaze, for example. Researchers differentiate between interruptions that are *intrusive* and those that are *cooperative*.[38] Imagine a couple telling a funny story to a third party. If the couple has related the anecdote many times, they may interrupt each other with additional details or provide parenthetical commentary as the story unfolds. In this case, the interruptions are serving the larger discourse goal of recounting the story in a lively and interesting way. At the other extreme, we have Kanye West interrupting Taylor Swift's acceptance of the Best Female Video award before a televised audience of millions.

Interruptions may be aligned with general cultural orientations and norms. Lars Fant, for example, suggests that misunderstandings might arise because there is a greater level of comfort with interruptions in Hispanic culture than in Scandinavia.[39]

The psychologist Han Li has proposed that members of collectivistic cultures, such as Chinese speakers, may tend to use cooperative interruptions more frequently than intrusive interruptions, as demonstrations of loyalty and group solidarity. On the other hand, members of individualistic cultures, like Americans or Canadians, would be more likely to employ intrusive than cooperative interruptions, since self-assertion is valued in such cultures. Li conducted a study of preferred interruption styles by having Canadian and Chinese participants simulate interacting as doctors and patients both intraculturally (for example, two Chinese conversational partners) or interculturally (a native Chinese speaker interacting with a native Canadian English speaker).

As expected, the Chinese-Chinese dyads showed significantly more cooperative interruptions, and the individualistic Canadians were more likely to engage in intrusive interruptions. However, in the intercultural conditions, there were more intrusive than cooperative interruptions. A likely reason for this is that the Chinese participants were changing from their normal cooperative style to match the more intrusive style of the Canadians. This is an example of linguistic alignment. In addition, the roles played by the conversational partners also influenced their behavior. Since doctors have more power than patients, we might expect that the "doctors" would be more likely to intrusively interrupt their "patients"—which is indeed what Li found.[40]

The Chinese propensity for cooperative interruption has been documented in other research. Speakers of Chinese were recorded as they interacted with other Chinese speakers, as well as with Finnish and Dutch speakers—via English—in both real and simulated business negotiations. The Chinese speakers interrupted their conversational partners more often than the Europeans. And interestingly, the Finnish and Dutch speakers increased their number of interruptions when interacting with speakers of Chinese (another example of linguistic alignment). The researchers concluded that although they found differences in interrupting behavior, the interruptions were not necessarily impolite, since they may have been the result of an eagerness to conduct business or simply efforts to assist the speaker.[41] A more accommodating view of interruption is also a part of Japanese culture. Studies have shown that Japanese speakers are more likely than Americans to engage in cooperative interruptions.[42] Japanese even has a word for such interruptions, *kyowa*, which means to coproduce or to cooperate.[43]

We've now explored some verbal behaviors that can vary cross-culturally. We've seen how they can influence how a message is interpreted. Now let's look at some nonverbal behaviors that also play a role in communication. These visual signals are even less likely to be considered when making attributions about someone's intentions.

Don't Stand So Close to Me

It happens so naturally that most people never even think about it, but the amount of space that they maintain between each other is not random. It depends in large measure on where you're from and who you're talking to. Furthermore, these distances vary from culture to culture. If you run into an acquaintance on the street and stop to ask her how her new job is going, you'll unconsciously choose to stand a culturally specific distance from her. For Americans, it would be considered quite disconcerting to hold this sidewalk conversation with only an inch or two separating your bodies. At the other extreme, it would be strange to stand several yards away, raising your voice so that the other person can hear you. In the first case, your friend might back up a bit, and in the second, she might make a point of moving closer to you.

It turns out that this whole "how far apart do we stand" business has a name, *proxemics*, and it can be defined as how personal space is maintained as a function of one's culture. The term was coined by Edward Hall in 1966 and is just one aspect of nonverbal communication.[44]

Hall interviewed large numbers of people from all over the world to see whether there was any regularity to personal distance. It might be the case, for example, that this is simply a personal idiosyncrasy, an individual difference that varies from person to person. Devotees of the American TV program *Seinfeld* may remember an episode in which Elaine's new boyfriend, played by Judge Reinhold, is shown to be a "close talker." Part of the episode's humor revolved around how disconcerting this was to the other characters, culminating with Kramer falling over backward as he moved away from the close talker's verbal assault. What Hall found, however, was a great deal of consistency about personal space. In fact, he even derived exact measurements for the size of the zones that surround an individual's body. We will dispense with the exact numbers, but we think it's important to summarize Hall's four main zones of personal space.

The closest of these zones is referred to as *intimate distance*, which includes the space from bodily contact, such as a hug, to the distance it would take to whisper to a confidant. Very few of our public interactions occur within intimate distance. Even handshakes, which involve physical contact, tend not to take

place within intimate distance: instead the two greeting parties stand apart while extending their arms outward from their bodies to clasp hands.

A second zone, extending out beyond intimate distance, is *personal distance*. This is the zone within which people interact with family members or good friends. Of course, there are times when personal space or even intimate space is violated by strangers. This might occur, for example, in a crowded elevator. However, the discomfort that people feel is likely to be transitory, since most elevator rides last only a moment or two. A packed subway car is another matter. In this case, the unwanted closeness may go on for considerable lengths of time, accompanied by physical jostling as the train moves and when people enter and exit the car. People often deal with the violation of their space by psychologically removing themselves from the situation, for example, by closing their eyes or by listening to music through earphones. In Tokyo, Seoul, Rio de Janeiro, and other cities, subways have special cars that are to be used only by women to avoid violations of their personal or intimate space by men.

When it comes to interacting with acquaintances, we've now entered a third zone, moving outward from personal distance, called *social distance*. If you're chatting with a colleague at work, it's likely that you're maintaining a social distance. In fact, if two of your colleagues at work are carrying on a secret affair, they may unconsciously adjust their personal space from a social distance to a more intimate one. What they may not realize is that they are broadcasting a signal to others, as well.

Finally, there is *public distance*, which is the distance used in public speaking. Individuals make a number of unconscious changes to their behavior when presenting at a public distance. For example, they typically speak more loudly and may change their bodily posture to project their voice so that it carries farther. And as is often the case, we're really only aware of these changes when they create a problem. When Roger gives a lecture to a roomful of undergraduates, he makes a point of speaking loudly and clearly. After class, however, a student may approach him to make a comment or ask a question. When Roger first began teaching, he was frequently surprised when these students would draw back from him when he began to answer. At some point, he realized that he was continuing to use his public-distance voice in a one-to-one setting. This caused the students to spontaneously back away from the unexpectedly loud voice that was answering them.

You probably won't be surprised to learn that personal space varies from culture to culture. In Saudi Arabia, for example, if a stranger moves close to you to converse, you might find yourself unconsciously backing away (as in the case of Kramer and the close talker). In the Middle East, social distance is closer than it is in the United States, so as you back up, your conversational partner may attempt to close the gap once again. It's easy to imagine an awkward dance down a sidewalk, with one party retreating and the other advancing as the conversation progresses.

The point here is that where you stand when you talk to someone is reflexive. Although you certainly don't measure the distance physically, you are calculating it mentally. When a mismatch occurs between what you think the distance should be and what the distance is, you then must make an attribution. Why is this person standing so close? Hall's theory about personal space can help answer this question. Sometimes a person is standing too close because it is typical of their culture. Sometimes a person is standing too close because they really are pushy or aggressive. Cross-cultural miscommunication arises when you make the wrong attribution. For example, you might decide someone is pushy (personal attribution) instead of realizing that their idea of social distance may be different (situational attribution).

In Mongolia, when two people inadvertently bump each other (such as kicking someone's leg under a table), they must immediately shake hands, which in a sense reestablishes the correct personal distance. But when someone bumps into you on a crowded sidewalk in Ulaanbaatar, should you shake his hand or tighten your grip on your purse? Unfortunately Hall's theory won't help you there.

As we've mentioned before, it's important neither to underestimate nor to overestimate the influence of cultural factors. With luck, an awareness of proxemics and differing cultural attitudes about personal space might prevent you from executing a backward two-step when someone is, quite literally, getting too close for comfort.

Posture, Gaze, and Gesture

There's language in her eye, her cheek, her lip,
Nay, her foot speaks; her wanton spirits look out
At every joint and motive of her body.
—Ulysses, in *Troilus and Cressida*, act 4, scene 5

I speak two languages, Body and English.
—Mae West

On April 1, 2009, President Barack Obama stooped to greet King Abdullah of Saudi Arabia at a Group of Twenty summit meeting in London. Conservative pundits saw the gesture as a major faux pas committed by the newly elected US president. One newspaper referred to it as "a shocking display of fealty to a foreign potentate" and "an extraordinary protocol violation."[45] Obama's intentions in greeting the king in this way quickly became a matter of dispute. Was it a bow or something else? A White House aide explained: "It wasn't a bow. He grasped his [the king's] hand with two hands, and he's taller than King Abdullah."[46] However, the following November, when the president greeted Emperor Akihito of Japan, he executed a deep bow while shaking his hand. Once again, a difference in height may have been a factor: Emperor Akihito is eight inches shorter than

President Obama. And if it was a bow, the act was viewed positively by many: a British newspaper, for example, characterized it as "a well-intentioned show of respect to a head of state [at] his home." In addition, Obama's act was viewed quite favorably by the Japanese people.[47]

As should be clear from these examples, the pragmatics of nonverbal communication can be just as problematic as they are for spoken language. And the ambiguity inherent in bodily posture and gesture undoubtedly plays a role, as well. A diverse collection of such behaviors is integral to the greetings and farewells in many cultures, and they vary according to pragmatic factors such as relative power, formality, and shared common ground.[48] Greetings are so tricky that a best-selling six-hundred-page handbook for businesspeople provides advice on whether one should "kiss, bow, or shake hands" in dozens of countries around the world.[49]

Within a given culture, the rules about such things are often well specified. The British royal family, for example, has a strict protocol about who bows or curtseys to whom. Kate Middleton is a member of the British royal family, complete with a fancy title (Duchess of Cambridge). However, she was not born a royal but became one by marriage. Therefore, when unaccompanied by her husband, Prince William, she must curtsey to the "blood princesses" of the royal family (Anne, Alexandra, Beatrice, and Eugenie). However, when accompanied by him, she need only curtsey to Queen Elizabeth, Prince Philip, the Prince of Wales, and the Duchess of Cornwall. The rules that the royals follow are updated regularly as their family's membership changes.[50]

As we have already seen, the real problem arises when individuals from different cultures greet each other. The US president's greetings abroad are not the only ones that have attracted attention. Some in the UK were aghast when Michelle Obama partially embraced Queen Elizabeth in April 2009, for example.[51] So do the rules that apply to the queen's British subjects extend to those from other countries? And does a visitor's use of the host country's protocols imply submission or respect? The answers seem to be a function of the inferences that the observer chooses to draw, and these can be colored by one's ideological orientation.

A great deal of our communication occurs through nonverbal means, although estimates of how much vary widely and go as high as 90 percent.[52] But some commonly held assumptions about the cultural universality of such acts have not survived close scrutiny. For example, romantic kissing, long thought to be culturally ubiquitous, has been documented in fewer than half of 168 cultures surveyed around the world.[53]

Even a behavior as universal as a handshake shows regional variation. Job seekers in the United States, for example, are taught to disguise their nervousness by shaking hands briefly but firmly with a potential employer. On the other hand, a light grip is customary throughout much of Asia. Gender, age, and social status can also play a role. In addition, these customs change with the times. In the United States, for example, it was once customary for a woman to initiate a handshake with a man, but this is no longer the case and has become more egalitarian.[54]

According to some interpretations of the Koran, it is forbidden for a man to touch a woman not related to him. This has become an issue in Switzerland, a country in which shaking hands with one's teacher is a long-standing tradition. It is seen as a sign of respect and often occurs at the beginning and end of a school day. The issue came to the fore in the spring of 2016, when two teenage Syrian brothers were granted a temporary exemption from shaking hands with their female teachers in a town near Basel. However, it was later ruled that if the boys refused again, they would be fined the equivalent of $5,000.[55]

As another example, studies have shown that the mutual eye contact that occurs during communication differs by culture. Whereas many Americans tend to expect direct eye contact with their conversational partners, it is more common in Japan for people to look down or away from the person they're talking to.[56] Americans may interpret this gaze behavior as signaling a lack of interest or even deviousness, which can greatly impair perceptions of trust. And even in the United States, gaze patterns may differ along racial lines. Some black parents instruct their children not to look their teachers in the eye, telling them that doing so can signal disrespect. This seems to be the opposite of what many white teachers believe, and these differing attitudes can create issues in the classroom.[57]

Finally, hand gestures also create potential for cultural misunderstandings. The "A-OK" sign in the United States, for example, involves touching the tip of one's thumb and index fingers together while splaying the other three fingers outward. The circle this creates, however, is considered obscene in large parts of Europe and also in Brazil.[58]

In closing, we believe it is important to remember that when communicating with people from other cultural backgrounds, it's not just what they say that matters. It's also how

they say it. Behaviors like where people stand, how they signal that they are paying attention, and whether and how they interrupt are not merely background noise. These are the kinds of cultural differences that are likely to go unrecognized and unacknowledged.

6 Pragmatics in Action

Hello and Good-bye

Parting is such sweet sorrow that I shall say goodnight till it be morrow.
—Romeo, in *Romeo and Juliet*, act 2, scene 2

Greetings and farewells are fundamental rituals that everyone performs on a daily basis. And as with many such rituals, their formulaic nature serves to harmonize interpersonal interactions and promote solidarity. These social exchanges typically have a verbal component, but they can also involve behaviors like kissing, bowing, or shaking hands, which we described in the previous chapter. In this section, we'll limit the discussion to the structure and linguistic content of such interactions, which are generically referred to by researchers as *openings* and *closings*.

These interactions can be formulaic and can also differ greatly from culture to culture. In Japan, it is so important to welcome customers with いらっしゃいませ! (*Irasshaimase*, or "Come in!") that some establishments use a recording to greet people as they enter, just in case someone comes in without being seen by a clerk. Compare this to Germany, where Wal-Mart shoppers complained about having been "harassed by strangers" as they entered the store.[1] Wal-Mart exited the German market in 2006 and incurred a loss of a billion dollars on the venture. Although there were many other reasons for their failure in Germany, the negative reaction to store greeters certainly didn't help.

Greetings frequently refer to the time of day (Good morning!) or ask an often ostensible question about the other person's health or their family's well-being (How are you?) or simply offer an informal query along the lines of "How's it goin'?" or just "Hey!"

If two people haven't seen each other for a long time, a more extensive interaction is typical and expected. On the other hand, a coworker with whom you've just spoken may not merit any more acknowledgment than a smile if you pass her in a hallway a few minutes later. And sometimes the person to be greeted may look away or avoid the eye contact necessary to initiate a greeting. Sociolinguists have, in fact, described several social and cognitive prerequisites for such encounters.[2]

In most languages, openings and closings also provide some leeway with regard to formality. In German, for example, an opening like *Guten Tag* (Good day!) is relatively formal, whereas *Hallo* or *Wie geht es dir?* (How's it going with you?) are less so. *Wie geht's?* and *Alles klar?* (What's up?) would be perhaps the least formal. Unlike in English, however, an inquiry like *Wie geht's?* is not perfunctory; in fact, it may elicit a detailed response from the person being greeted. Closings in German show both formal and regional variation. *Auf Wiedersehen* is about as formal as "Farewell" would be in English, whereas *Tschüss* (Bye!) and *Bis bald* (See you soon!) are informal. In southern Germany and the Alpine countries, *Grüss Gott* ("Good day," but literally "God greets you"), *Grüezi* (a shortening of this), and *Grüss Sie*

(Greetings to you!) are also common. And *Servus* (At your service) can function both as a southern German greeting and as a closing.[3]

Who greets whom? It's common for people entering a house or room to be greeted by those who live there, or by those who arrived earlier. In practice, however, the person entering may have to initiate an opening to get the attention of someone already present. Individuals of higher status will often initiate the greeting of someone of lower status, but once again, there are many exceptions to this practice. In Islamic countries, for example, a younger person is expected to greet an older person, and smaller groups expect to be greeted by larger ones.[4]

Native speakers of a language develop great proficiency in composing greetings that are sensitive to the other person's status, time, and location. For example, if it's obvious that the person being greeted is in a hurry or preoccupied, the greeter may craft a less-intrusive hello on the fly. A study of nonnative speakers in the United States found that since they often lack high verbal proficiency in English, they tend to stick to ritualized openings that are overly formal for more casual interactions.[5] In addition, some choose greetings that are appropriate in their native culture but are perceived by Americans as odd ("Have you eaten?" or "Where are you going?"). The former could be misinterpreted as an invitation; the latter seems nosy to many Americans, although it is commonly employed in languages like Samoan.[6] On the other hand, nonnative speakers may be greatly surprised when Americans greet them with indirect complaints (Can you believe how hot it is today?). Not surprisingly, therefore, even relatively scripted interactions like openings can be a source of anxiety and frustration for people coping with a new language and culture.

If greetings are hard, farewells are even more difficult. For example, when is a closing required? Americans don't always feel the need to say good-bye to cashiers or roommates, but there are many contexts in which a farewell is expected, and ending a conversation without one may seem quite rude. One clue about closings in English can be found in a study of US telephone switchboard operators. The researchers reported that callers were more likely to say good-bye to operators when they were grateful for the assistance they received or when there had been some exchange of personal information. In other words, as an interaction becomes more like a conversation and less like an impersonal exchange of information, people feel a greater need to provide an explicit closing.[7]

By their very nature, closings are rarely simple or cleanly executed. The person doing the closing is, in essence, committing a face-threatening act—essentially announcing he wants to stop talking to someone and go do something else instead. As would be expected, therefore, closers use positive politeness strategies, like positive comments (So nice to talk with you!) or excuses (I have to study for a test tomorrow).[8] However, the off-record strategies of indirectness and hinting are often employed, as well (I'm really tired; I think the dog needs to go out). And there is no guarantee that the other party will take the hint. There may be several, sometimes awkward, conversational turns before the interaction winds down and both parties feel free to go their separate ways.

The American sociologists Emanuel Schegloff and Harvey Sacks first wrote about closing sequences in the early 1970s.[9] They argued, for example, that before a closing can begin, there is usually a "preclosing," in which one party initiates the closing sequence, perhaps by saying, "Okay ...," "So ...," or "Well ..."

with falling intonation. But this is only a *potential* preclosing; it must be accepted by the other party, who now has the conversational floor and may choose to steer the conversation off into another direction entirely. In short, a successful closing is a joint project, one that must be agreed to, and then engineered by, both parties.[10]

Given the problems that speakers of the same language encounter, it's not surprising that negotiating smooth closings between native and nonnative speakers can be even more problematic. The linguists Beverly Hartford and Kathleen Bardovi-Harling explored this possibility by recording academic planning sessions between graduate students and their advisors to decide on coursework for the next semester. Although such interactions have a well-defined end point (the advisor signs the student's course ticket), many of the nonnative English students experienced difficulties in bringing the meetings to a smooth conclusion. On the one hand, the students were aware that the faculty members were extremely busy and that time was at a premium. On the other hand, many had questions about terminology and procedures that were unfamiliar to them. To their credit, the faculty members dealt with the students' queries with great forbearance. But afterward, several told the researchers they felt frustrated when their charges returned to previously discussed issues, even after they had initiated a closing sequence.[11]

Finally, in a study of telephone closings in Ecuadorian Spanish, Placencia found that repetitions and restatements, which can prolong closings in ways that English speakers might find tedious or irritating, were quite common. Similar extended closings have been described in the phone calls of Persian speakers.[12] It should be noted, however, that these can certainly occur in

English and are stereotypically associated with the closings of love-struck teenagers, as in *"You* hang up!" "No, *you* hang up!" "No, *you* hang up!!"

No, No, I Couldn't Possibly

Regrets … I've had a few …
—Frank Sinatra, *My Way* (lyrics by Paul Anka, 1967)

Suppose you are out to dinner and your host orders some expensive caviar. You aren't allergic to caviar, but you don't really like it. When your host kindly offers you some, would it be polite to say, "No, thank you?" If your host insists, believing your refusal to be ostensible and saying that he ordered it especially for you, should you be honest and say you don't like caviar? Should you lie and say you are allergic to it? Would it matter if your host were your boss or your future father-in-law? In this section, we explore the issue of refusals and how the components of refusals vary cross-culturally.

The production of a refusal in a language like English can be compared to the list of ingredients required for a recipe. Polite refusals typically consist of three parts: a *regret*, an *excuse*, and a face-saving *closing* or an *offer*. If any of the three components is missing, then the result will not be pragmatically well formed (or appetizing, to complete the culinary analogy).

Hongyin Chen, for example, found that when making refusals, native Chinese speakers typically did not produce the regret component that would be expected by English speakers. As a result, their refusals were less likely to be perceived as sincere.[13]

Issuing refusals requires a delicate balance between making one's preferences known (I don't want any more buffalo milk) and not threatening the face of one's host (Hey, what's wrong with my buffalo milk?) One way to do this, in English, is to offer specific excuses for the refusal, for example, in refusing assistance (I have to do the work myself as a condition of my parole) or a gift (This rhinestone-studded cowboy hat is far too valuable for me to accept) or dessert (I'm on a diet). But even if the reason for the excuse is perceived as legitimate, refusals may also be tempered by closings like "Thanks for offering!" or "I really wish I could accept!" as an additional face-saving gesture.

The importance of concrete refusals in English was demonstrated in a study of native Persian speakers learning English. The researchers found that, when declining an offer, the Iranian participants' reasons were more clear and their excuses were less specific than those of native English speakers. Whereas the second-language learners might say, "Sorry, I'm busy," the English participants in the study, who were Boston University students, were more likely to be specific, saying things like "I'll be attending a wedding that day." As mentioned earlier, refusals that include concrete reasons are perceived as more genuine by Americans than are generic refusals. Therefore the Iranian participants' excuses were seen as less sincere. In addition, the native Persian speakers were typically more polite in issuing their refusals than their native English-speaking counterparts. For example, the Persians were more likely to issue an apology as part of their refusal, especially when the other person was higher in status. Although this may sound like a good thing, it created a perception that the Iranian speakers were being overly formal.[14]

Sharyl Tanck compared refusals given by native English-speaking graduate students with those generated by students of various nationalities (Chinese, Korean, Polish, Spanish, and Thai native speakers) enrolled at the same university. The native English speakers typically produced refusals that contained all three components: regrets (I'm afraid I can't), excuses (I have a test tomorrow), and offers (How about next weekend?). Although both groups were as likely to craft a refusal that contained a regret, the nonnative speakers were less likely to follow up with an excuse or to offer an alternative.[15] Once again, without the additional components that are characteristic of the American refusal frame, the nonnative speakers could easily be perceived as brusque or rude.

The refusal behavior of Americans and Mexicans was studied by asking participants to role-play situations in which offers are refused. In general, the US participants would suggest alternatives or ask for more information, while the Mexican participants more commonly mitigated their refusals (perhaps by saying "I believe") or gave replies that were indefinite (such as "Well ... let me see, all right?").[16]

Speakers of Thai are sometimes perceived as rude when speaking English because they are less likely to express some form of gratitude when refusing an offer or an invitation from someone of equal or lower status. Over time, they learn to include gratitude in more of their refusals in English but typically still do so less frequently than native English speakers.[17]

As in Thai, status plays a greater role in refusals in Korean than in English. Speakers of Korean are more likely to mitigate their refusals, perhaps by apologizing or offering an alternative, when replying to someone of higher status. American English speakers, by contrast, are more egalitarian: their refusals aren't particularly influenced by the status of the person making the offer. Speakers of Korean are also more likely to hesitate, and they generally issue direct refusals far less often than speakers of English. As a result, their refusals can seem "less transparent and more tentative" to speakers of languages in which more direct refusals are the norm.[18]

In Japanese, a genuine refusal can be signaled by failing to complete the refusing sentence, thereby allowing the recipient to infer the face-threatening conclusion. Another strategy is to provide a formulaic, nonspecific reason for the refusal, such as *Yakusoku ga aru node ...* (I have an engagement ...).[19] An American might be offended by an English-speaking Japanese individual who refuses an offer in such a way, concluding that "he didn't give me a good reason for saying no."

Going to the opposite extreme has its dangers as well. Thi Minh Nguyen compared the refusals of requests by Australians who were native speakers of English and Vietnamese speakers who were learning English. The native Vietnamese speakers expressed their refusals in English more elaborately than did the native English-speaking Australians, who were rather direct in their refusals.[20] It would be easy to imagine the misperception of an overly elaborate refusal as a falsehood or as sarcasm.

As with other face-threatening actions that we have reviewed, efforts have been made to incorporate more effective refusal strategies into second-language instruction. Research has demonstrated, for example, that explicit instruction in English refusals, in which teachers explain the use and function of refusal strategies, was more effective than methods that were less direct and more passive. Teaching methods that consist of several components, such as translation and role-playing activities, have also been proposed.[21] By making the complete "script" of refusal expectations in the target language clear to students, they can learn, as in the English idiom, to "let someone down easy" (or at least somewhat more easy).

The Honor of Your Presence Is Requested

Nothing annoys people so much as not receiving invitations.
—Oscar Wilde, *The Importance of Being Earnest* (1895)

Invitations can be thought of as a special type of offer. However, they are frequently more formal, and a refusal can be seen as more face-threatening to the one who makes the invitation. The stakes are high for the would-be host, but also for the recipient, who might have to carry out some elaborate facework to prevent a refusal from damaging the relationship with her inviter. And when we consider the different expectations held by members of different cultures, it becomes clear that invitations, and responses to them, can be laden with pragmatic difficulties.

Part of the problem with invitations is that it is not always clear they are genuine. We have already seen, in the discussion of ostensible speech acts, that what appears to be an invitation may actually be just a social nicety. An invitation to "do lunch sometime" could be a heartfelt offer, but most English speakers would recognize it for what it is and not follow up by proposing a date or an offer to make reservations.

Such ambiguity can create difficulties for second-language learners when their native cultures favor more direct communication. An example of this can be seen in the dissertation of Agnieszka Rakowicz, who studied native Polish speakers learning English. Polish culture equates directness with sincerity, and the Poles in her study tended to view ostensible invitations issued by English speakers as being sincere offers. In addition, the Polish participants tended to make direct refusals of invitations. This violates the US pragmatic norm of offering some sort of excuse.[22]

In other cases, although an invitation might be sincere, it may be delivered in a highly ambiguous or indirect way. A good example can be found in the dissertation research of Elinor Ochs, as reported by Brown and Levinson. Ochs found that in Madagascar, a request can be constructed by issuing a string of hints, as in the following invitation to have the listener visit the speaker. One can easily imagine such a vague and indirect offer going over the head of a visitor from a culture that favors more direct invitations: "My house isn't very far away ... [intervening material]. ... There's the path that leads to my house."[23]

Some linguists have argued that simply announcing one's presence at a certain location can be construed as an invitation. Christian Licoppe has examined the use of location checks by Parisians via the social media app Foursquare. Users of the app "check in," which broadcasts that they have arrived at a specific place, like a bar or restaurant. These check-ins then become visible to one's friends and acquaintances who also use the app. As in the case of the solicitous homeowner in Madagascar, no actual invitation is issued, but the preconditions for a meeting have been put in place. Furthermore, the face-threatening aspects of invitations and potential refusals are eliminated. Users of Foursquare are only indicating their receptivity for social interaction, and their friends are spared the awkwardness of having to explicitly reject a social overture. Such arrangements seem to work well for large groups in which the members are only weakly linked to each other.[24]

In our earlier discussion of offers, we mentioned that the Persian custom of *ta'arof* requires offers to be made repeatedly. This is true in other cultures as well. In Spanish-speaking countries in Central and South America, this insistence is seen as polite, and it functions to strengthen the bond between the conversational participants. In fact, *not* insisting is seen as rude and can create the impression that the offer was not sincere. In contrast, insistence is not a typical part of the US invitation-refusal sequence; it is face threatening and may be perceived as impolite and ill-mannered. Americans who spent time studying in Latin America learned this new cultural norm but still found multiple instances of insisting to be "rude, bothersome, or confusing" and reported that the practice left them uncertain about how to "negotiate a refusal across several turns" in a socially acceptable way.[25] Multiple acts of insistence in the face of refusal are also viewed positively in Palestinian society, where it is seen as a way of expressing sincerity and hospitality.[26]

There are also cultural differences in the zeal with which it is appropriate to accept an invitation or gift. In Chinese society, the acceptance of an invitation is only gradual; being overly eager is considered impolite. This apparent lack of enthusiasm is often construed by foreigners as a lack of interest in their offers. In Chinese society, it is also expected that a recipient will pretend to refuse a gift. As we have seen, ostensible refusals are common in other cultures, as well, but it is considered perfectly acceptable to offer up only token resistance. In the United States, a brief exclamation along the lines of "Oh, you shouldn't have!" or "It's wrapped so beautifully, I hate to open it!" is sufficient, at which point an eager unwrapping can follow.

In China, Japan, Korea, and other countries, however, a present is not usually unwrapped in front of the giver; instead it is put aside to be opened later. Doing so spares both the giver and the receiver any face threats in case the gift disappoints in some way. However, not opening the gift in front of the giver could be construed as indifference or unhappiness with the gift in many Western cultures.[27]

Wedding invitations have become a fruitful genre for students of culture and language, since they display many of the unspoken (and often unacknowledged) norms within a society. Studies have noted, for example, that societies as diverse as the United States and Iran have many commonalities, but also some notable differences. In Iran, wedding invitations commonly come from the couple's fathers. In the United States, invitations traditionally come from the bride's parents, although nowadays they frequently come from the couple themselves. However, in both countries, invitations tend to mention the bride's parents first. Researchers can use these features to assess the importance of factors like paternal authority and masculine power within a culture.[28]

Given that such differences exist, it's easy to see how complications can arise in the case of intercultural marriages. Some of the difficulties faced by such couples were documented in a study of online wedding message boards. The modification of ritual elements from both cultures into one ceremony was a common topic of discussion, often leading to the creation of a hybrid to satisfy the expectations of the couples' families and friends. These concerns included issues related to the invitations themselves, such as whether they should be printed in one or two languages.[29]

As we will see in the next section, love means sometimes having to say you're sorry.

I'm Sorry ... So Sorry

Experience is what you get when you didn't get what you wanted.
—Randy Pausch, *The Last Lecture* (2007)

For of all sad words of tongue or pen, the saddest are these: "It might have been!"
—John Greenleaf Whittier, *Maud Muller* (1856)

An important function of linguistic politeness is to express contrition when things don't go as planned. Expressions of regret, as well as full-blown apologies, function as an essential lubricant for social interaction. We experience many episodes of rejection and disappointment throughout our lives, over events both major and minor. Since some of these experiences may be deeply felt, we become especially attuned to whether expressions of regret from others are appropriate and sincere. Regardless of whether such statements are perfunctory and formulaic or deeply heartfelt, there are cultural expectations regarding the appropriate display of such feelings.

Given the earlier discussion of positive and negative politeness, it should come as no surprise that both strategies can be employed to modify apologies. Such statements can be intensified, which displays deference to the hearer, as in "I'm so terribly, terribly sorry." They can also be used to minimize an imposition, as in "I'm sorry, but could you move just a little to the right?"[30]

Like all languages, English has a variety of expressions to convey regret. In terms of responsibility and magnitude, they run the gamut from interjections or phrases that are informal and casual ("Oops," "Whoops," or "My bad!"), to the extremely formal, typically reserved for more consequential outcomes (We regret to inform you ...). As would be expected, when given hypothetical situations to consider, US college students varied their apologies to match their perceived level of responsibility, as well as the degree of consequence for the wronged party. Expressions of remorse and offers of help increased as the consequences became more serious (accidentally knocking someone to the ground, for example, as opposed to merely bumping into them). And requests for forgiveness and statements of self-castigation (I feel foolish) were primarily affected by perceived degree of responsibility.[31]

Expectations about *when* it is necessary to apologize also show cultural differences. In one telling anecdote, a Japanese researcher who had recently moved to Australia returned to a store soon after purchasing a product that was defective. The store's employee simply asked if she wanted to exchange the item. The transplanted Japanese speaker was very surprised by this reaction, since she expected the clerk to express great embarrassment and to proffer an extravagant apology. And learning *how* to apologize can be tricky, as well: American students learning Russian without exposure to the target culture tend to formulate overly polite apologies.[32]

Because an apology can be construed as accepting responsibility for an undesirable outcome, there are legal ramifications for using such language. Physicians, for example, run the risk of being sued for malpractice, and therefore must choose their words carefully when expressing condolences to a family grieving over the death of a loved one. Some have argued that a simple statement of regret, such as "I'm sorry," can lower the likelihood that survivors will seek legal redress. A recent survey of physicians, however, suggests that apologies can actually make things worse, because the apology can later be used against the physician in a lawsuit.[33]

An expression of regret is not the same as a full-blown apology. And an apology that is perceived as perfunctory or insincere can inflame the passions of the disappointed party. Since apologies entail responsibility, statements made by politicians, sometimes about events that occurred decades or even centuries earlier, are carefully parsed to measure the exact degree of culpability that is being admitted to.

Given that apologizing or expressing regret can be a delicate undertaking even within a culture, it should come as no surprise that cross-cultural communication adds a layer of complexity. Naomi Sugimoto studied American and Japanese college students' differential use of apology strategies in response to hypothetical situations that varied in severity. These included canceling a meeting or accidentally deleting a friend's paper on a computer. The participants were asked to write out exactly what the offender would say or do for the wronged party. In all the situations, the Japanese participants included statements of remorse more often than did the US subjects. The responses of the Japanese students were also more likely to include direct offers of remediation ("I'll buy you a new one" in the context of breaking a friend's Walkman). When the US students did offer remediation, it was more likely in the form of an inquiry (Would you like me to buy you a new one?).[34]

Sugimoto interpreted this finding as reflecting cultural differences, with Americans' presuppositions about autonomy leading to less-direct offers of compensation. In general, the Japanese participants generated more involved and wordy apologies than their US counterparts. This reveals a significant issue for cross-cultural communication, because an apology that is perceived as more elaborate than is required can have unintended consequences in the United States. An outsized display of contrition, for example, might be misconstrued as sarcasm. But in Japan, an *un*elaborated apology might be misconstrued as insincere.

Second-language learners have an understandable tendency to map expressions like "I'm sorry" and "excuse me" onto seemingly analogous expressions in their target language. This can create difficulties when the pragmatic factors concerning apology in one's native language don't map perfectly onto expressions in the second language. The result can be nonnative speakers of English who decline invitations by saying things like "Excuse me. I'd like to go, but I don't have time."[35]

Perhaps because expressing apology and regret can be so difficult, there are entire websites, such as sorrywatch.com, devoted to analyzing such statements. Sorrywatch.com has over sixty categories (automotive, culinary, religious, and sports, to name just a few), testifying to the broad scope of apologies that are perceived as problematic in some way.

How Typical!

Do nothing, say nothing, and be nothing, and you'll never be criticized.
—Elbert Hubbard, *John North Willys* (1922)

If you can't say something good about someone sit right here by me.
—saying embroidered on a pillow owned by Alice Roosevelt Longworth

In many respects, complaints and criticism are the ultimate face-threatening activities. Instead of expressing disapproval indirectly or humorously, such statements are bald on-record and clearly run the risk of antagonizing the hearer.[36] When the source of the problem is a third party, the complainer may be turning to others for commiseration or support. And even if we aren't able to make lemonade from the lemons that life hands us, complaining about the lemons can make us feel better.

When speakers of English complain, they typically do so indirectly. In one study of this phenomenon, the American linguist Laura Hartley provided US university students with four situations, ranging in severity from the minor (a friend makes a mess in your kitchen) to the major (you have to take a summer course to graduate on time because of bad advising). The most common responses were indirect statements, for example, "It looks like you've made yourself right at home." Even in the more serious advising situation, the students resorted to directly criticizing the advisor only a quarter of the time.[37]

As we saw with refusals, there seems to be a recipe for expressing disapproval. In one study, a group of American graduate students was given the hypothetical task of asking a professor why they received a low grade on a paper. These participants invariably crafted a four-part argument, consisting of (1) an *explanation* of purpose that stated why they were contacting the professor; (2) a *complaint* that they thought their grade was too low; (3) a *justification* that pointed out that they had spent a lot of time and effort on the paper; and (4) a potential *solution* phrased as a request, for example, asking the professor to reconsider the grade.

A second group, this one of Korean graduate students studying in the United States, engaged in the same task, but their recipe for disapproval differed from that of the Americans. The Korean subjects also provided an explanation of purpose (1), a justification (3), and a potential solution (4). However, rather than complain (2), they *criticized* the professor (You didn't recognize my point of view). And while 80 percent of the Koreans' candidate solutions were requests, 20 percent were demands (The grade is not fair and must be changed).

The Koreans' productions were also judged as more aggressive, and as less respectful and appropriate, than the Americans' responses. Apparently the judges perceived the criticisms as denials of responsibility and as personalizing the situation; that is, the fault lies with the professor. In contrast, the complaints were perceived as a partial acceptance of responsibility, and as a way of depersonalizing the problem.[38] We should point out that the judges were all American undergraduates. Had Korean undergraduates judged the responses, the results could have been different.

Another study compared Canadian English speakers, native speakers of Persian in Iran, and Iranian students studying English in Iran. These participants were given short dialogues that contained complaint situations and were asked what they would say in such circumstances. Of the three groups, the native speakers of English were most likely to ease into the conversation with phrases like "Good morning" or "Do you have a minute?" perhaps to soften the impact of an upcoming complaint. The speakers of Persian were more direct, beginning the interactions with expressions like *Mishe bedonam* (May I know ...) or *Mixastam bedonam* (I wanted to know ...). The students of English in Iran fell in between, using phrases like "Hi, I have something to discuss with you." It appears that they were aware that native speakers of English may perceive such abrupt openings as rude or disrespectful, and they modified their opening statements accordingly.[39]

As mentioned earlier, sometimes the purpose of a complaint is not to seek redress from an offending party but to solicit comfort and support from others. Such speech acts are referred to as *indirect complaints*, and they have different pragmatic functions from their direct counterparts. Far from being mere griping, indirect complaints can play an important role in social bonding. Two coworkers, for example, venting about an insensitive boss, are aware that they can't change their employer's behavior, but they can commiserate with each other, which makes them feel better. Indirect complaints are therefore another example of positive politeness: such statements build solidarity between people by emphasizing the common issues and problems that they face. In the United States, complaints like "I can't believe I have to work on Saturday!" are also functioning implicitly as invitations to greater intimacy, creating a shared perception that "we're all in this together."

The American linguist Diana Boxer found that about 75 percent of indirect complaints between English speakers functioned to build rapport. This commiseration function can clearly be seen in an interaction between a graduate student (GS) and a library assistant who is also a graduate student (LA):

GS   They never have what you need in here! You'd think they'd at least have the important books and articles.

LA   They didn't have what you were looking for?

GS   No.

LA   That's typical!

The assistant is employed by the library, but she isn't responsible for the library's collection. And as a student, she is also aware of the library's limitations, so her response ("That's typical!") can be characterized as a sympathetic, commiserative reply.[40]

In later research, Boxer examined responses to indirect complaints in the conversations of Japanese and American speakers of English. Commiseration was by far the most frequent response to indirect complaints in conversations between the American speakers. And commiseration was also the most common response by the Americans speakers to indirect complaints made by the Japanese participants (who were speaking English to them).

However, Boxer found that commiseration response rates dropped significantly when the Japanese speakers replied to the complaining Americans. Instead of commiserating, the Japanese participants gave *nonsubstantive* replies more than half the time. Nonsubstantive replies are essentially nonresponses, such as verbal or nonverbal backchannels like "hmm" or gestures like head nods. In contrast, Boxer found that only about 2 percent of the indirect complaint responses between the Americans themselves were nonsubstantive.

By failing to commiserate or engage with the speaker in a substantive way, the Japanese speakers of English were missing out on a chance to bond with their conversational partners. And as a consequence, the native English speakers frequently abandoned the topic under discussion and switched to a new one.

We should note that these pragmatic choices were not due to limited English proficiency of the Japanese speakers. Boxer describes them as "intermediate and upper level learners" of English. She provides the following example between two of her participants:

Native speaker   I found it very hard in France, when I was there to take a regular French university course because it was structured differently.

Nonnative speaker Yeah.

Native speaker And I found it really hard to understand the structure and to be able to understand what he wanted us to read and what kind of things to do. Sometimes I didn't study the right thing.

Nonnative speaker [no response]

The nonnative speaker could have shown some degree of empathy or offered up a similar experience. By not doing so, the nonnative speaker has left the native speaker no recourse but to move on to a different subject. And these pragmatic difficulties were clearly apparent to the native English participants. In a different conversation, after getting several empty responses from her conversational partner, a native English speaker remarked: "It's so funny, I sit here going on and on and you just say, 'uh huh,' it's like I'm in an interview or something," after which both parties laughed.[41]

Boxer's research illustrates once again that knowing the vocabulary and grammar of a second language is not enough. It's also important to be aware of the social strategies that native speakers of a language employ. Without knowledge of pragmatic expectations, a bonding experience like a griping session can degenerate into a self-conscious monologue.

This Old Thing?

I have been complimented many times and they always embarrass me; I always feel that they have not said enough.

—Mark Twain, speech (1907)

She kept up her compliments, and I kept up my determination to deserve them or die.

—Mark Twain, *The Innocents Abroad* (1869)

When Richard was living in Niger, a friend went to a bakery and noticed that the woman behind the counter was wearing a striking pair of earrings. Without thinking, she complimented her on them. As is traditional in West Africa, the woman reached up and removed her earrings and handed them to Richard's friend. As would be expected in that culture, she reached up to take her own earrings out to exchange them. Only then did she realize that she was wearing a pair of expensive gold earrings that had been a gift from her mother. But it was too late, and her heart sank as she handed her earrings over to the woman. Because Richard's friend had started the exchange with her unthinking but well-meaning compliment, she felt that she had no choice but to follow through.

It may appear that compliments are an unalloyed pragmatic good: they exemplify Brown and Levinson's notion of positive

politeness. However, just as with fertilizer and chocolate, there really can be too much of a good thing. And as the previous example shows, there can be unintended consequences.[42] If someone compliments someone else excessively, the praise can curdle into suspicions about ulterior motives. Flattery is, in fact, easy to spot when it is being lavished on a third party, but many studies suggest that our own positive self-image prevents us from suspecting ingratiation as a motive when those beautiful words are directed at us instead.[43]

Everyone, it seems, likes to be praised—right up until they have to say something in return. At that point, many people become embarrassed and tongue-tied as they struggle to respond to the kind words they've received. Compliments are typically followed by what researchers refer to as *compliment responses*, which is some sort of acknowledgment of the flattering words. And as with many other behaviors that we describe in this book, there are linguistic, pragmatic, and cultural differences with regard to compliments and how people are expected to respond to them.

In many cultures, people's discomfort with praise and compliments may reflect modesty: one should minimize self-praise. For most people, though, a compliment creates a conflict between modesty on the one hand, and an implicit desire to agree with the speaker on the other.[44]

Who compliments whom? Janet Holmes recorded and analyzed several hundred compliments in New Zealand and found a strong pattern with regard to gender. The most common pairing was females complimenting other females, followed by males praising females. Females complimenting males was less common, and rarest of all were cases of men praising other men. This would seem to reflect stereotypic cultural norms in which it is unseemly for women to show explicit interest in men (but not the reverse), as well as a general aversion by men to expressing any sort of positive affect toward other men.[45]

Researchers have documented a variety of methods by which people negotiate the treacherous territory of praise. For example, one could choose to simply *accept* a compliment, such as "I just love your dress!" with a formulaic "Thank you." However, there are also other, less-direct forms of acceptance. The speaker could choose to qualify the compliment in some way (Yes, I think it looks okay) or offer a compliment in return (And I think yours is fantastic!).

A recipient could also choose to reject the compliment, perhaps by disagreeing (I'm not so crazy about it) or by questioning the sincerity of the speaker (You're being far too kind). Finally, the recipient could attempt to deflect or evade the praise, perhaps by giving credit to someone else (My mother picked it out) or by simply ignoring the compliment (I'm starving—where did you find those appetizers?).[46] All these strategies have their pros and cons, and their use is heavily influenced by factors like the relationship that exists between the parties involved and their cultural background.

Many differences in compliment responses can be seen throughout the world. For example, Hawaiian Pidgin English speakers frequently deny compliments in their responses, such as "Nah," "Stop it," and even "Shut up, hah?" Researcher Candis Lee suggests that there are important Asian influences in this culture, since it has been heavily influenced by immigration from China and other Asian countries. As a result, extreme modesty, to the point of self-denigration, is normative.[47] However, it is easy to imagine an outsider's surprise at a seemingly rude dismissal of a proffered compliment by a Hawaiian Pidgin speaker.

A study of compliment responses by Mandarin Chinese and Australian English speakers showed a similar pattern. Compared to the Australians, Mandarin speakers employed fewer acceptance strategies (Thank you) and more evasion (That's what friends are for) and rejection strategies (Don't say that).[48]

In societies undergoing rapid cultural change, one might expect to see pragmatic shifts occurring, as well. This seems to be happening in the case of China, where earlier studies of compliment responses showed an overwhelming preference for rejection strategies. However, it now appears that speakers of Chinese show a preference for acceptance in their compliment responses.[49] This suggests that as a culture shifts away from being more traditional, Confucian, and collectivistic, there is a corresponding shift in comfort with accepting compliments. Over time, then, the gap between Asian and Western compliment response strategies may decrease.

Studies have also documented differences between American English and German compliment responses. Although Americans may accept compliments in their responses, they are more likely to reject or qualify the statement in some way. For example, a remark about how nice one looks in a dress might trigger a response like "You really think so? It's just a hand-me-down from my sister." In contrast, German speakers were far more likely to accept the compliments in their responses. However, they didn't use phrases like "Thank you," which is the go-to expression in English. Instead the Germans often provided assessments, such as *schön* (That's nice) or simply *ja* (yes). This may reflect a preferred conversational style that places greater weight on the information content of discourse rather than its social functions.[50]

A comparison of British English and Spanish compliment responses reveals other cultural differences. In one study, university students in Cardiff and Valencia were given a number of hypothetical scenarios that involved receiving a compliment, and they were asked what they would be likely to say in response. The study found that the British participants were more likely to question the truth of the assertion (Do you really think so?) than were the Spanish subjects. Although both groups used humor and irony in their responses, the male Spanish subjects were especially likely to employ humor and irony in so-called *upgrades*, in which the complimenting assertion is agreed with and then made even more extreme, as in "I'm a great chef!" in response to "I didn't know you were such a talented cook."[51]

Of course, not all compliments compliment. Consider the "backhanded compliment," which is a statement that sounds positive at first but, on further examination, is really an insult. The sting of the insult comes precisely from the fact that the venom is delivered in the form of a compliment. "You speak Chinese well for an American" could be such an example. A backhanded compliment, therefore, blends the negative with the positive.[52]

The combination of both positive and negative aspects in a compliment is also part of the feedback mechanism called the *compliment sandwich*. In a compliment sandwich, a person delivers negative news between more positive information. The following is an example: "You show a lot of enthusiasm for your work, but you are rather sloppy in your delivery. However, I really like how much you care." But this technique has its detractors. Research has shown, for example, that confident individuals benefit from this type of feedback, whereas those with low self-esteem find it disturbing.[53]

In this chapter, we've explored some specific speech acts and how they are accomplished in English and other languages. It should be clear by now that this kind of information is crucial to building pragmatic competence. Our goal has been to facilitate a heightened awareness to the range of pragmatic options available around the world. In the final chapter, we look at how the social use of language must adapt to a changing world.

7 Pragmatics in a Changing World

Return to Sender: Improper Address

All the topics we've discussed so far become even more problematic when communication doesn't occur face-to-face. When we speak with someone, we rely on reading her facial expressions to determine if she has gotten a joke, or if our words have made her angry, or simply to gauge whether she is pausing to think or has been rendered speechless. Even on the telephone, we can still take advantage of many nonverbal cues, such as laughter, intonation, volume, and speech rate. But what happens when even these indicators are absent?

The unfortunate result is that communication becomes much more difficult when the medium for transmission is electronic, as it is via e-mail, social media, or text messages. Virtually everyone has had personal experience with the misunderstandings that can arise as a result of these impoverished modes of communication. Add in the cross-cultural issues we've explored in previous chapters, and we have the ingredients for a perfect storm of misunderstanding.

Let's consider some of the specific issues that arise from the use of an electronic medium like e-mail. One important characteristic is that it is *asynchronous*. In other words, the exchange doesn't play out in real time, with both parties immediately responding to each other. Instead there may be a delay of minutes, hours, or even days between conversational turns. And it's only natural to make attributions about the recipient when his response is delayed. We tend to perceive a slow response as emblematic of a lack of commitment to the relationship, when in fact it may be due to how busy the recipient is, or even external factors like the recipient's time zone. In Korea, the verb "to chew" was previously used as a vulgarism for ignoring someone. Now it is used colloquially to nudge someone whose texts and e-mail responses are not seen as rapid-fire enough.

Electronic communication is also different from face-to-face communication in that it is relatively *permanent*. Whereas the words we speak are ephemeral, the sounds dying away within fractions of a second, electronic messages can be read and reread in search of alternate meanings, passed along to others, and otherwise obsessed over. So an offhand remark that might not have been given a second thought in face-to-face conversation can take on a life of its own when seen as disembodied words on a screen.

As one of the oldest forms of computer-mediated communication, e-mail has been studied extensively by researchers. Several studies have shown that e-mail exchanges make it even more difficult to manage the face needs of the recipient. And misunderstandings can accumulate and fester, ultimately causing permanent damage to relationships. One study, for example, documented a five-month exchange between a male American college professor and a female staff member at a Chinese university. The professor was on a one-year contract to teach in China, and through a cascade of misunderstandings and unrecognized cultural differences, the exchange degenerated into a series of personal attacks and ultimately a rupture in the relationship. The first part of the article's title can give you a sense of exactly what happened: "You think I am stupid?"[1] It seems unlikely that either individual was ill-intentioned or malicious. Rather, the cause of the breakdown seems to have been the impoverished mode of communication, which was simply not up to the task for which it was used.

Researchers have also demonstrated that people believe they can communicate more effectively via e-mail than is actually the case. When asked to communicate sarcasm, seriousness, anger, or sadness over e-mail, study participants were quite confident that their intentions would be understood clearly and unambiguously. In fact, across a series of experiments, the actual accuracy (as measured by other participants classifying these statements correctly) was much lower and sometimes approached chance levels.[2]

This is simply one manifestation of a larger phenomenon referred to by social psychologists as *egocentrism*. We tend to view the world from our own perspective, and it takes time and effort to appraise things more objectively. As a result, we rarely bother to do this. And most of the time, it may not matter—we spend our days with family, friends, and coworkers whose outlooks, values, and cultural expectations are shared by us or at least known to us. All bets are off, however, when we are communicating with others outside our social circle, and especially with individuals from other cultures. After all, as we have seen, even something as innocuous as a hand gesture can mean different things in different cultures.

It can take time to craft a polite request, and in this regard, written communication should be superior to more synchronous forms of communication. For example, when we compose an e-mail message, we can take as much time as we want to choose our words, editing and reediting as necessary. We don't have this luxury when, for example, we leave a voice mail message. Normally we are hoping to reach our recipient directly, but instead we are forced to craft a short monologue on the fly. One might predict, therefore, that voice mail messages are perceived as less polite than e-mail, and the evidence supports this prediction.[3]

As we've already seen, making requests of others can be a pragmatic minefield. We might therefore expect the difficulties in crafting polite requests to be magnified in situations where feedback is not available in real time and when cultural differences are in play. This seems to be the case. One study examined e-mail sent by nonnative English-speaking university students (Greek Cypriots) to their English-speaking teachers. These students simply failed to take into account the power differential and degree of imposition involved. As we have seen previously, there are many ways to signal deference in English. Instead of using these, the students omitted salutations or closings, did not use proper forms of address, and made very direct requests, often expecting immediate answers. Needless to say, the English-speaking faculty were not impressed.[4] Roger can testify that this failing is not limited to Greek students; his own undergraduates frequently begin their e-mail messages to him with very informal openers like "Hi" or "Hey." (He's gotten used to it, but he still doesn't like it.) However, this isn't just a question of the youth or inexperience of students. Even professionals can fail to show proper deference by e-mail. Korean academics also felt that e-mails from overseas colleagues were less formal and therefore less polite.[5]

It's clear, therefore, that the decontextualized nature of e-mail only exacerbates the chances for miscommunication and misunderstanding, both within and between cultures. But communication is simply a conventionalized set of behaviors, and like any other behavior, it is malleable: it can adapt and change. Perhaps it is possible to augment e-mail and other forms of computer-mediated communication to make intended meanings clearer. As we will see in the next section, this is exactly what has occurred, although the efficacy of these augmentations is open for debate.

A New Type of Facework

An impoverished text-based form of communication like e-mail is particularly bad at communicating things like emotion or the seriousness of one's intent. For example, the meaning of a message like

Better get to work soon—the boss will be looking for you.

depends crucially on context. Is it a playful reminder, a taunt, a dire warning, or simply a joke? Punctuation can help—a series of exclamation points after the final word might suggest that the message is both serious and urgent—but even this interpretation is problematic, since it could still be intended humorously. On the other hand, consider the following:

Better get to work soon—the boss will be looking for you. :-)

Here the potentially serious statement is followed by a smiling face (albeit on its side), suggesting that the intent is indeed playful.

The so-called smiley face or smiley (with or without a nose) has been a fixture of computer-mediated communication for many years. Its first explicit use as a "joke marker" seems to have been in an e-mail written by Scott Fahlman of Carnegie Mellon University on September 19, 1982. In the same e-mail, Fahlman also proposed using :-(to mark things that are not jokes, and this is now universally referred to as the "frowny face."[6] Collectively, these markers are called *emoticons*, and when e-mail was only a text-based medium, they were the principal way in which emotional nuance could be communicated.

Pre–digital age examples of emoticons have been found as early as March 1881, in an issue of *Puck*, an American humor magazine.[7] It's also been claimed that a smiley was used as early as 1648, in the poem "To Fortune," by Robert Herrick.[8] It seems likely that such affective symbols were spontaneously invented several times by different individuals. And it's important to note that in the digital age, their use spread rapidly, not because they were imposed in a top-down manner by linguistic fiat or government edict. People simply began using them because they were so useful in clarifying what they intended. Not content with using only a few of these symbols, people delighted in creating thousands of new emoticons, even when they were of limited utility. For example, <+]:¬) can be used to represent the pope (with the symbols over the eyes representing the pontiff's miter).

As emoticons based on the limited set of ASCII characters were becoming popular in the Western world, a different form was arising in Japan. Called *kaomoji* (顔文字, or face marks), they fulfill the same functions but depict a face horizontally instead of vertically, such as (^^), in which parentheses define the sides of the head, and carets denote the eyes. The hands and arms may also be depicted, as in └(^∀^)┘. The double-byte character codes used for representing the Japanese *kana*, Western characters, and other symbols allow for a far larger number of signs; and groups of them, called "dongers," can be strung together to create a wide range of *kaomoji*, such as the "shruggie": ¯_(ツ)_/¯.

The purely character-based emoticons and *kaomoji* have now been joined by graphic icons, called *emoji*. These first appeared on Japanese cell phones in the early years of the new millennium and only became popular in the West in 2011, when they debuted on the Apple iPhone. The Unicode-based system allows for a vast number of such icons, and they have been put to all sorts of creative uses. *Emoji* have been used, for example, to translate the entirety of Melville's *Moby Dick. Emoji Dick*, as it is known, was a crowd-sourced effort, conceived of and edited by Frank Benenson.[9] And an *emoji* (a face spouting tears of joy) was chosen as Oxford Dictionaries' "word" of the year in 2015, though the company has no plans to add these icons to its reference works.[10]

Although still popular in the West, emoticons have lost ground to *emoji*; many software programs now automatically change emoticons to *emoji*. Microsoft Word, for example, will convert the text string of punctuation that makes up the smiley face to ☺. And as cell phone text messaging replaces e-mail as a primary form of electronic communication, the popularity of *emoji* has exploded. The *emoji* in instant messaging apps, such as LINE and KakaoTalk, have been augmented by stamps and stickers, and still more complex forms of *kaomoji* are being created.[11]

As early as 2001, a study of American college students showed that they were familiar with, and agreed about, the meaning of the smiley and frowny emoticons. A third form, ;-) (or the "smiling wink"), was seen as having several possible meanings: it elicited labels of "happy," "sarcastic," and "joking" from the participants.[12] This suggests that the meaning of an emoticon might not be as straightforward as it appears. Although emoticons may reduce the ambiguity of an electronic message, they do not eliminate it altogether.

Not surprisingly, emoticons are also often used as politeness markers in text-based systems like Twitter. An analysis of English and Czech tweets found that they were commonly employed in both languages to welcome, say farewell, and give thanks.[13]

But are there cultural differences in how these symbols are used? As previously mentioned, Western emoticons are read vertically, while Japanese *kaomoji* are read horizontally. And some researchers have claimed that whereas emoticons emphasize the mouth, *kaomoji* emphasize the eyes; the mouth is often only a straight line or is omitted altogether, as in (^o^).[14] Some researchers have argued that this reflects the difference between East and West in representing emotion via facial expression: Americans are more likely to smile broadly than Koreans or Japanese, who tend to communicate emotions with the eyes.[15]

In fact, evidence suggests that emoticons are largely culturally bound, with cross-cultural adoption being extremely rare. Jaram Park and his colleagues analyzed millions of postings on Twitter between 2006 and 2009 and determined, for example, that "sweat drop" emoticons, such as ^^; or ^_^; are much more common in Japan and Korea than in other countries. This marker of embarrassment, shyness, or confusion is frequently seen in the graphic novels and animated cartoons of Asia, in which characters are shown with large beads of sweat on the sides of their heads. The researchers also found almost no examples of tweets with emoticons written in the vertical style in English-speaking countries. The majority of emoticons in Twitter postings by

Koreans, on the other hand, were of the vertical type.[16] It will be interesting to see if this symbolic insularity holds in the future, given the increasing popularity of various entertainment forms from Asia in the West, such as anime and K-pop.

Flaming, Shaming, and Trolling

Without a doubt, the Internet and other forms of online communication have enriched our lives in a myriad of ways. The ability to keep in touch with friends and loved ones, whether across town or across the world, is a luxury that would have seemed like science fiction to previous generations. This seemingly miraculous mode of communication, however, has a darker side: it also facilitates the expression of negative emotions in the form of insults, gossip, censure, and bullying. And once again, this form of communication is intertwined with issues of culture.

Face-to-face criticism differs in important ways from online disparagement. For example, virtual communication allows people to express negative impulses without having to directly see the impact of their words on another person. And if the criticism is anonymous, it deprives the recipient of the ability to respond. Bad behavior, of course, has existed for as long as there have been people, and scholars have argued that these new forms of online incivility simply reflect contemporary culture.[17]

The Internet and its decentralized structure have facilitated the emergence of thousands upon thousands of *microcultures*, and this process had begun even before the emergence of the World Wide Web in the mid-1990s. The Usenet and bulletin board systems of the 1980s and 1990s led to the creation of discussion groups devoted to extremely specific topics, such as favorite bands, specific cuisine, software programs, and types of pets. It became possible, for example, for fans of Pomeranians to visit alt.pets.dogs.pomeranians on the Usenet to discuss their favorite breed without having to bother with postings about American pit bull terriers, German shepherds, or Labrador retrievers. If someone were a rabid Pomeranian devotee (pun intended), the existence of such a microculture provided all sorts of benefits: the chance to learn from, and to ask questions of, other devotees and to feel connected to a larger group with the same specific interests. One drawback of microcultures, however, is that they can become narrow, insular, and self-referential.

Some of these early newsgroups were moderated, which meant that a designated person vetted all posts before they were made public, deleting any that were hostile or off topic. Not surprisingly, given concerns about censorship and the amount of effort that moderation entailed, most newsgroups were unmoderated; all postings were immediately visible to all users of that group. Unfortunately, this could allow Pomeranian partisans to log on to newsgroups devoted to, say, Alaskan malamutes, and to leave disparaging comments about that breed so as to upset the regular readership. Such a posting, or "flamebait," would inevitably be responded to by someone who found the comment offensive, and a "flame war" between the two parties might ensue.

In other cases, the disruptive behavior might be far subtler. For example, a poster with malicious intent might initially pretend to be a sincere but possibly inexperienced and uninformed enthusiast, who over time becomes accepted by the other posters. However, the miscreant might then attempt to sow confusion and discord by "luring others into useless, circular discussion, without necessarily involving argument."[18] Challenges to the poster's intentions could be countered with protestations of innocence, leading to even more upheaval. Collectively, such behaviors have become known as "trolling," and their practitioners as Internet trolls. A common piece of online wisdom is not to engage with such disruptors (don't feed the trolls), but this may be easier said than done, since new group members might also ask naive questions and thus be mistaken for trolls themselves.[19]

As the Internet has morphed into the present-day World Wide Web, these types of undesirable behaviors have insinuated themselves into all forms of online commentary. From news stories to blog postings to YouTube videos, no place on the Web has been safe from the influence of the trolls.[20] One unfortunate consequence of this has been the abandonment of comment sites by the online versions of many newspapers.[21] Commercial enterprises, as might be expected, have to be careful not to offend any customers and accordingly judged the risks of flaming and trolling on their sites as too great to allow unfettered posting to continue.

Of course, criticizing a preference for a dog breed or a product on Amazon is not the same as a direct personal attack on a specific individual. And once again, this form of behavior is nothing new. Acts of public shaming can be found throughout history, as well as in the arts (think of Hawthorne's *The Scarlet Letter*). What has changed, however, is the speed and the scope of such attacks. A good example would be the so-called Gamergate controversy of 2014, which began as a debate about journalistic ethics in the video game industry but then devolved into targeted harassment and misogyny, including "doxing" (the releasing of personal information onto the Web), criminal hacking, and threats of violence.[22]

One of the root causes for such bad behavior is the existence of so many microcultures online. It is all too easy for a *micro*culture (We all love Pomeranians!) to transform, over time, into a *mono*culture (Pomeranians are better than all other kinds of dogs!), and for this to lead to a clash with different monocultural adherents (Shelties are the best!). A factor that undoubtedly contributes to online flaming, shaming, and trolling is a lack of empathy displayed by members of one monoculture toward members of other monocultures.[23] In such cases, the monoculture can become a self-perpetuating echo chamber in which hostility to alternative points of view can build.

It is indeed ironic that the same tools that allow for instantaneous worldwide communication also enable behaviors like trolling and cyberbullying. Moreover, the same issues that can lead to cross-cultural misunderstandings in face-to-face communication are also in play in computer-mediated communication.[24]

If the online world simply mirrors offline existence, it would be unrealistic to expect some sort of cyber-nirvana, in which online interactions are devoid of aggression and hostility. Not surprisingly, therefore, the establishment of micro- and monocultures online has led to a host of unintended pernicious consequences.

But if misunderstandings can arise based on computer-mediated miscommunication, then understanding can arise through computer-mediated communication, as well. In the wake of tragedies such as terrorist acts or natural disasters, Twitter hashtags like #BringBackOurGirls or Facebook banners such as "We Are Orlando" can serve to remind us that the glass is also half full.

Sign Up!

On December 10, 2013, US President Barack Obama spoke in Johannesburg, South Africa, at the memorial service for former South African President Nelson Mandela. Standing next to him was Thamsanqa Jantjie, who was there to translate Obama's remarks into South African Sign Language (SASL). However, during the president's remarks, and those of other world leaders,

Mr. Jantjie merely gestured with his hands. He did not translate what was said into any recognizable form of Sign language.

Cara Loening, Director of Sign Language Education and Development in Cape Town, said of Mr. Jantjie's performance, "He's a complete fraud. He wasn't even doing anything. There was not one sign there. Nothing. He was literally flapping his arms around." Mr. Jantjie subsequently apologized, saying that he was experiencing a schizophrenic episode during the service. He asked to be forgiven if he had offended anyone.[25]

It is true that the security lapse that resulted in this astonishing event is troublesome. But perhaps there is an even more disturbing aspect to the story. Despite pleas from viewers who could tell he was gesticulating nonsensically, Mr. Jantjie remained on the stage. Moreover, it appears that this was not an isolated incident. In describing the agency contracted to provide the interpretation, South Africa's Deputy Minister for Women, Children, and People with Disabilities said, "They have been providing substandard sign language interpreting to many of their clients, and nobody has picked up."[26]

But how could such a thing happen? Imagine how quickly an interpreter would have been whisked away if he had been asked to translate from English to French but merely babbled with a pseudo-French accent. As one blogger wrote, "On a day when the world saluted a man who fought oppression, a guy stood on stage and effectively oppressed another minority—Deaf people, by making a mockery of our language."[27] Incidents like this one are all the more harmful because they serve to perpetuate misconceptions about Sign languages and the Deaf communities that use them.[28]

It is important to realize that there is not one universal sign language. In fact, it has been estimated that there are "271 identified sign languages, dialects and other sign systems." Some of these are true Sign languages used by Deaf communities, whereas others are more limited sign systems used only in extremely specific circumstances, such as the underwater sign language used by scuba divers or the signing systems used in monasteries to avoid speaking.[29]

Furthermore, although Sign languages can share similarities with each other, they are not necessarily mutually intelligible. For example, the most widely used Sign language in the United States and Canada is American Sign Language (ASL). ASL is also used as the primary language for Deaf communities in many countries in Africa and other parts of the world. Although it has become something of a lingua franca, ASL is a specific language that will not automatically be understood by those who use a different Sign language.[30]

Like spoken languages, Sign languages can also be grouped into linguistic families based on their similarities with other Sign languages. Because of its history, ASL is closely related to French Sign Language (LSF, or Langue des Signes Française), but not to British Sign Language (BSL). In fact, LSF and ASL signers find that they have many signs in common. ASL and BSL signers do not. Even the fingerspellings of the letters of the English alphabet (called a manual alphabet) are different in ASL and BSL. Likewise, Mexican Sign Language (LSM, or Lengua de Señas Mexicana) is different from both the Spanish spoken in Mexico and Spanish Sign Language (LSE, or Lengua de Signos Española) used in Spain.[31]

Sign languages are as rich and complex as spoken languages. And like spoken languages, they are inextricably linked to the community in which they are used. Each Sign language, therefore, has its own pragmatic system that will differ from both other sign languages and from the spoken languages used in that geographic area.

Every aspect of pragmatics that we discuss in this book has an equivalent in Sign language. For example, people who sign can show a "slip of the hand" as opposed to a "slip of the tongue." Sign languages also use puns as a way of creating humor. And there are bilingual signers—which can refer to those who code switch between Sign languages or those who switch between spoken languages and Sign languages. Basically, if it happens in spoken language, there is a Sign language counterpart.

Because Sign languages are the equal of spoken languages in every way, they also interact with culture in complex ways. Although we have concentrated our discussion on cross-cultural differences among spoken languages, these issues apply to Sign languages, as well.

For example, ASL is not English. Nor is it a watered-down version of English. In fact, it even includes grammatical structures that English lacks. As a result, Americans who speak English and Americans who use ASL will both share in some cultural aspects and differ in others.

In the United States, the opportunity to compare and contrast ASL with English keeps getting easier. As of June 2016, there were 185 US colleges and universities that allowed students to take ASL to fulfill their school's foreign language requirement. Of course, there is an inherent irony in the fact that *American* Sign Language can count at US schools as a *foreign* language.[32] But Sherman Wilcox at the University of New Mexico sees only good in this trend:

Students who know a foreign language commonly find that their perceptions of themselves and the world are richer than their monolingual peers. The study of a language, culture, and literature different than their own propels students beyond the limits of their own world. In all respects ASL affords students the same challenges and rewards as more traditional foreign languages.[33]

We still have much to learn about Sign languages, Deaf cultures, and their associated cross-cultural components around the world.[34] But perhaps the best advice in moving forward comes from the motto of Gallaudet University, *Ephphatha*, which is Aramaic for "Be opened."

Cant Help It

Argot is the language of misery.
—Victor Hugo, *Les Misérables* (1862)

As we mentioned earlier, the Internet is a place where micro-cultures flourish. For the first time, people in widely different places with similar interests can find each other online. Imagine how *Great Expectations* would have turned out had Miss Havisham been able to get on Tinder and meet someone else after her fiancé left her at the altar.

Offline as well, groups of people with shared interests or similar pressures, or who are simply not part of a mainstream society, will bend language to suit their needs. For example, in Japanese there are many different ways to refer to oneself. The most straightforward pronoun is *watashi*, which means "I" or "me." *Watashi* is a multipurpose pronoun that can be used by both men and women and is polite enough to function in most situations.

There are, however, many other ways to refer to oneself in Japanese, and these vary by gender, age, and intention. An additional choice for women is *atashi*. Two additional choices for men are *boku* and *ore*. *Boku* is a term used by boys and young men and has a rather youthful feel. *Ore* is rougher and much more informal, which means it also has the potential to be seen as rude. Richard once tried to use *ore* to refer to himself when he was talking to a friend. She burst out laughing (apparently Richard is not much of a tough guy).

Because pronouns in Japanese can be gender specific, Japanese gay men will sometimes refer to themselves in the feminine rather than the masculine. This pronoun reversal is part of a gay-specific speech pattern called *onee kotoba* (big sister speech). But *onee kotoba* involves much more than just switching pronouns. The pragmatics of *onee kotoba* include a mixture of the masculine and the feminine. For example, users may speak in an exaggeratedly feminine style in terms of pronunciation and grammar but use crude words to discuss topics like sex or bodily functions.[35]

Onee kotoba is just one example of the ways in which LGBTQ individuals around the world have created their own way of speaking to each other. Known as *argots*, *cants*, or *antilanguages*, these secret languages serve to build a sense of community, challenge stereotypes, protect group members and separate insiders from outsiders.[36]

LGBTQ argots can be found in all parts of the world. South Africa alone has at least two: isiNgqumo, which is used by gay men who speak isiZulu,[37] and Gayle,[38] an English- and Afrikaans-based argot, which derives in part from a more ancient cant language spoken in Britain, known as Polari.[39] In Indonesia, the gay argot is called Bahasa gay;[40] in the Philippines it is Swardspeak.[41] Hijra Farsi (a mixture of Urdu, Hindi, and Persian) is spoken in the hijara community of South Asia.[42] The study of so-called lavender linguistics is a growing field, and these are just a few examples.[43]

Of course, argots, cants, and antilanguages are not created only by LGBTQ communities; they are created anytime a group feels the need for secrecy or a way to communicate separately from those around them. Polari, for example, has roots that stretch back centuries to Elizabethan thieves' cant.[44] In Japan today, young people are using a special texting code meant to be indecipherable by adults. And in China, bloggers and others are reconfiguring Chinese characters, using them creatively, and blending them with non-Chinese symbols into what is called "Martian" so as to get past both parents and government censors.[45]

Because argots are secret languages, those who use one must become adept at code switching back and forth between it and the wider vernacular. But unlike code switching between English and Icelandic, for example, in an argot, many words and phrases are also words in the standard language, used in nonstandard ways. By using the same words in unexpected ways, argots convey on-record and off-record meanings simultaneously. Such utterances will be clearly understood by group members, and although they are intelligible to a wider audience, an outsider who is eavesdropping would be unlikely to figure out what's really going on. For example, if you know that bears, cubs, otters, and pandas aren't only found in zoos, then you may have some familiarity with the LGBTQ community in the United States.[46] In this way, argots have a unique duality of purpose: their goal is both to communicate and to conceal at the same time.

It has been argued that antilanguages lose their importance as groups become more fully accepted by a society. Paul Baker, for example, has described Polari as "'endangered' if not 'dead.'"[47] Likewise, as LGBTQ individuals make strides in their quest for full freedom and equality, gay argot is becoming more mainstream. For example, the word *outed*, which was once reserved for the practice of revealing someone's sexual orientation against his or her will, is now used regularly to mean divulging anything without the consent of the person or organization being referenced.

It's unlikely, however, that argot will disappear anytime soon, since there will always be groups of individuals who will need to create and maintain a common language to discuss matters of importance to themselves in contrast to others. But in using argot cross-culturally, there are a couple of points to keep in mind. First, it's important not to confuse the way people are speaking the argot with the way in which the language is spoken more widely. Richard has an American friend who was working in Okinawa and inadvertently outed himself by using a gay slang term for the word "muscular." Because he was learning Japanese from gay friends, he didn't know what was *onee kotoba* and what wasn't. It follows, therefore, that people who use an argot don't use it all the time in all situations. Moreover, many members of a community specifically reject argot because they feel it perpetuates stereotypes. Therefore using argot will not always be accepted by all members of the group, and an attempt to seem like an insider could make one an outsider.

As we discuss in the next section, the goal of pragmatic competence is to find a place for oneself in a particular linguistic community. To do this, one must develop skills that allow for appropriate language based on membership in that community. And it's likely there will be more than one (for example, a lesbian doctor from France living in Vietnam). Argots can help, but it is important to learn how to use them. There's a thin line between trying to identify with a culture and cultural misappropriation. In other words, there are many ways to say "I" in a language, but it's important to find the I that works for you.

We Wouldn't Say It That Way

The gentle reader will never, never know what a consummate ass he can become, until he goes abroad.

—Mark Twain, *The Innocents Abroad* (1869)

When people learn a second language later in life, they may speak it with an accent. This is because, consciously or not, they transfer the pronunciation of sounds from their native language to their new one. The reason, of course, is that there are subtle articulatory differences between languages. The English *r*, for example, is not pronounced the same way in Spanish or in French.

In a similar way, people carry over pragmatic knowledge from one language and cultural context to another.[48] Of course, some degree of *pragmatic transfer* is desirable, and even necessary. When learning a new language, it's crucial to learn how politeness is signaled in various communicative contexts— even though the *concept* of politeness doesn't need to be relearned. There will always be some overlap between the pragmatics of any two languages, but the match is rarely, if ever, perfect.

It makes sense that language learners would have a natural tendency to rely on their understanding of politeness, indirectness, and other pragmatic strategies in their native language. When this happens, it could be said that someone is speaking with a *pragmatic accent*.[49] With a verbal accent, as long as the person is intelligible, the accent could be considered charming or possibly even distinguished. Similarly, as long as a pragmatic accent doesn't interfere with the inferability of a speaker's true intentions, it could also be viewed positively, or at least not negatively. For example, you may not apologize to someone from another culture in precisely their way, but if your apology is understood to be sincere, the person receiving the apology is unlikely to be offended. Likewise, funeral and wedding rituals differ greatly around the world. But you don't need an interpreter to condole or celebrate with others whose language and culture you don't share.

Pragmatic accents become problematic, however, when there is an overreliance on one's native language, or if the speaker has an insufficient understanding of how the new language differs from the native one. As we have already seen, native speakers of German tend to be relatively direct in expressing themselves. This can create problems when they learn English, since that language requires more indirectness with regard to face-threatening acts, such as complaints.[50]

Building pragmatic competence, therefore, is crucial because pragmatic errors can have serious consequences. Inexact pronunciation or a mangled grammatical construction are mistakes a nonnative speaker could be expected to make, whereas pragmatic missteps risk being perceived as intentional rudeness or thoughtlessness. In fact, the better you speak a language, the less likely it is that a pragmatic mistake will be recognized as such.[51] So how can someone develop pragmatic competence?

It may be helpful to distinguish between learning a *second* language and learning a *foreign* language. In the case of learning English as a second language (ESL), the nonnative English speaker is learning the language while living in a country where English is commonly spoken. In contrast, studying English as a foreign language (EFL) refers to acquiring the language in a place where English is not commonly employed. In theory, this shouldn't make any difference; both ESL and EFL students can and do learn new languages to high degrees of proficiency throughout the world. A motivated student working with a competent teacher should be able learn English in Ulaanbaatar just as easily as in Ulster. In practice, however, the outcome may be very different.

Whereas learning the vocabulary and grammar of a new language does not crucially depend on experiencing the language's culture, developing pragmatic competence is much easier in ESL than in EFL contexts. The linguist Gila Schauer demonstrated that German EFL students studying in Germany weren't as aware of their pragmatic errors as were German ESL students who were learning English at a British university. Additionally, she reported that the pragmatic awareness of the ESL students in Great Britain significantly improved during their stay.[52]

There is another reason why it's important to get as much pragmatic context as possible when learning a foreign language. In the classroom, a second-language learner may be taught about only one pragmatic strategy. But native speakers usually employ a range of strategies. For example, English speakers learning Japanese are taught that it's polite to deny compliments, often by simply saying no. And although Japanese speakers frequently invoke this negative politeness strategy, responses to compliments in Japan are also affected by psychological distance. Specifically, a response that would be appropriate between friends differs from one that would be proper when interacting with a teacher. In English, it doesn't really matter who is doing the complimenting—whether your officemate admires your tie or the president recognizes your humanitarian works, saying "thank you" is appropriate in both situations. As a result, American students of Japanese typically don't take psychological distance into account and may respond inappropriately to those paying them compliments.[53]

Obviously, living in an environment where a language is spoken has many advantages. For example, doing so allows for increased recognition and reinforcement of the cultural expectations and routines that native speakers take for granted. But not everyone can do this. Fortunately, there are ways to develop pragmatic competence that don't involve moving to another country. What is needed is an ability to read social cues and then to make adjustments based on these observations.

The psychological concept of *self-monitoring* describes the extent to which people observe their social environment to control how they appear to others.[54] At opposite ends of this continuum are high self-monitors and low self-monitors. High self-monitors are individuals who pay particular attention to what is happening around them and then modify their behavior accordingly. That is, the more someone is self-monitoring, the more his behavior is based on what he thinks is expected of him. Low self-monitors, however, are less likely to vary in their responses to social situations. They will act more consistently across different situational landscapes.

Neither personality type is better than the other. Each has its strengths and weaknesses. High self-monitors are likely to make friends easily, get along well with most people, and be considered socially adept. However, they also run the risk of appearing false and chameleon-like. Low self-monitors, while steady and predictable, can come across as inflexible and unwilling to make necessary adjustments for the sake of sociability. Of course, most of us fall somewhere between these two extremes, and our discussion is meant to illustrate the range of possibilities, and not to stereotype anyone.[55]

It should stand to reason, therefore, that high self-monitors would be more skilled at modifying their language use in a cross-cultural setting. And that seems to happen. Among German students who were studying Dutch in the Netherlands, high self-monitors showed better adaptation to Dutch and had fewer social and academic problems than did low self-monitors.[56]

The take-home message is this: pay close attention to what's going on around you, and be willing to modify your language use as needed. In cases where a conversational participant's response is unexpected, stop right away and consider what just happened (John seems angry, but I didn't mean to make him angry; I need to figure out why). It's also a good idea to align your usage with others whose pragmatic competence you trust.

Of course, being aware of situational cues is not always easy. For example, if you tell an off-color joke to a colleague, he may smile out of embarrassment rather than delight. The fact that he is offended could escape your notice. Such a state of affairs could lead you to tell more risqué jokes to this person, which could spiral downward to the point that one person feels harassed and the other is incredulous when a complaint is filed against him.

That is why it is extremely important to be perceived as approachable about such issues. By showing an openness to correction, you signal to others that they will not upset you if they point out where you've blundered.

A person who, by words or deeds, discourages others from expressing themselves, cultivates an environment where tensions can build. This may seem elementary, but especially in cultures that highly value saving face, inappropriate language use may go unacknowledged unless someone has shown, by everything she does, a willingness to adapt her own behavior.

Here is an example. When Richard was studying Korean, he learned the word for driver (as in chauffeur). Later he began using this word to refer to the drivers at work. One evening, when he and one of the drivers were alone in the car, the driver asked if he could be so bold as to offer a suggestion. The driver said he didn't think Richard was trying to be insulting, but his use of "driver," while technically correct, made it sound like Richard was talking down to him and the other drivers. He then told Richard the preferred term. It was the Korean word for "teacher," but when used in the work environment, it can also have the connotation of "colleague."

Richard was mortified. He was very grateful the driver had pointed out his mistake. This colleague told Richard that he wouldn't have said anything if he'd thought Richard would not have accepted the criticism in the spirit with which it was intended. Showing a willingness to be corrected allowed Richard to speak more sensitively and salvaged his relationship with these colleagues.

Sometime later, Richard used the word "teacher" with a taxi driver. But this time, he was corrected again. The taxi driver told Richard to use the word for "driver" he had learned in class. The point here isn't that Richard's Korean needed repair. Rather, it's that pragmatic competence is a process of continual adjustment, which cannot occur without feedback from others. If someone is unwilling to receive such feedback, then his ability to become pragmatically competent is impaired.

It is clear that pragmatic competence comes about by paying close attention to the responses of others and through a willingness to receive their feedback. What may be less apparent is that understanding the pragmatics of another language should allow you to fine-tune pragmatic awareness in your native tongue. As Goethe said, "He who knows no foreign languages knows nothing of his own."

Epilogue: Smooth Sailing

Mark Twain was the pen name of Samuel Clemens. In his twenties, he was a steamboat pilot on the Mississippi River. "By the mark twain" was a river term that signified a depth of two fathoms (twelve feet), which was the minimum safe depth for the navigation of a steamboat. In places where the river was shallower, the vessel could run aground.

We can't tell you the safe depth for navigating through a conversation. But in this book, we hope we have given you the ability to sound the depths and avoid hitting bottom. Whether speaking or sailing, however, to go anywhere, you need to weigh anchor and get under way.

As Mr. Twain wrote in *The Innocents Abroad*, "Broad, wholesome, charitable views of men and things cannot be acquired by vegetating in one little corner of the earth all one's lifetime."

We couldn't agree more.

Notes

Preface

1. For the claim that men and women are from different cultures, see Deborah Tannen, *You Just Don't Understand: Women and Men in Conversation* (New York: Ballantine Books, 1991); and John Gray, *Men Are from Mars, Women Are from Venus: A Practical Guide for Improving Communication and Getting What You Want in Your Relationships* (New York: HarperCollins, 1992).

2. This definition of culture was proposed in 1871 by E. B. Tylor, and appears in Heather Bowe, Kylie Martin, and Howard Manns, *Communication across Cultures: Mutual Understanding in a Global World*, 2nd ed. (Port Melbourne, Australia: Cambridge University Press), 3.

3. John Powelson, *The Institutions of Economic Growth: A Theory of Conflict Management in Developing Countries* (Princeton, NJ: Princeton University Press, 1972), 123.

1 Culture and Its Consequences

1. Researchers have long debated how language, culture, and cognition interact with one another. Issues related to linguistic relativity are not particularly relevant to the topics we will explore, however. Those interested in the controversy may want to read the following books, which lay out the claims made by the opposing camps: Guy Deutscher's

Through the Language Glass (New York: Metropolitan Books, 2010) and John H. McWhorter's *The Language Hoax* (Oxford: Oxford University Press, 2014).

2. In their model of cultural sense making, Osland and Bird also emphasized the importance of making accurate attributions. They highlighted the role of attributions in reconciling the context with appropriate cultural scripts, which are influenced by the history and the values of the culture: Joyce S. Osland, and Allan Bird, "Beyond Sophisticated Stereotyping: Cultural Sensemaking in Context," *Academy of Management Executive* 14, no. 1 (2000): 65–77. Lawrence Bouton found that nonnative speakers of English often do not make the same implicatures that native speakers do. He also reported that it takes time for nonnative speakers of English to learn how to make accurate implicatures in English. A pilot study showed that some types of common implicatures can be learned quickly when explicitly taught in the ESL classroom. Lawrence F. Bouton, "Can NNS Skill in Interpreting Implicature in American English Be Improved through Explicit Instruction? Pilot Study," *Pragmatics and Language Learning* 5 (1994): 88–109.

3. Grice laid out his argument in two book chapters, now classics in the field of pragmatics: H. Paul Grice, "Logic and Conversation," in *Syntax and Semantics*, vol. 3: *Speech Acts*, ed. Peter Cole and Jerry L. Morgan (New York: Academic Press, 1975), 41–58; H. Paul Grice, "Further notes on Logic and Conversation," in *Syntax and Semantics*, vol. 9: *Pragmatics*, ed. Peter Cole (New York: Academic Press, 183–197).

4. For an example of how another culture may show cooperation differently, see Elinor Ochs Keenan, "The Universality of Conversational Postulates," *Language in Society* 5, no. 1 (1976): 67–80.

5. The American psychologist Harold Kelley proposed a covariation model to explain the attribution process. See Howard H. Kelley, "The Process of Causal Attribution," *American Psychologist* 28, no. 2 (1973): 107–128.

6. This is the so-called fundamental attribution error, or correspondence bias. See Edward E. Jones and Victor A. Harris, "The Attribution of Attitudes," *Journal of Experimental Social Psychology* 3, no. 1 (1967): 1–24.

7. For information on the use of metacognitive strategies to promote culturally appropriate behavioral assessments that improve cross-cultural competence, see Winston R. Sieck, Jennifer L. Smith, and Louise J. Rasmussen, "Metacognitive Strategies for Making Sense of Cross-Cultural Encounters," *Journal of Cross-Cultural Psychology* 44, no. 6 (2013): 1007–1023.

8. For an example of the different ways that Britons and Germans speak, see Stephen Evan, "What Paddington Tells Us about German versus British Manners," *BBC News*, May 26, 2011, http://www.bbc .com/news/world-europe-13545386.

9. Group Chairman's Factual Report, January 18, 2000, National Transportation Safety Board, https://www.ntsb.gov/investigations/AccidentReports/ Reports/AAB0201.pdf.

10. Egyptian Civil Aviation Authority, *Report of Investigation of Accident*, October 31, 1999, https://web.archive.org/web/20110622102818/http:// www.ntsb.gov/events/ea990/docket/ecaa_report.pdf.

11. ABC News, *Transcript of Last Moments of EgyptAir Flight 990*, August 10 (year unknown), http://abcnews.go.com/International/story ?id=82910&page=1.

12. Mike Ghouse, "Islam Misunderstood: Tawakkaltu Ala-Allah, In God We Trust," *Muslim Speaker*, May 15, 2013, http://muslimspeakers .blogspot.com/2013/05/islam-misunderstood-tawakkaltu-ala.html.

13. Christopher Wren, "The Crash of EgyptAir: The Statement; Arabic Speakers Dispute Inquiry's Interpretation of Pilot's Words," *New York Times*, November 18, 1990, http://www.nytimes.com/1999/11/18/us/ crash-egyptair-statement-arabic-speakers-dispute-inquiry-s -interpretation-pilot.html.

14. "Batouty Clan Stands United," *Cairo Times*, 2004, http://web .archive.org/web/20040607134321/http://www.cairotimes.com/news/ batfam.html.

15. For a discussion of three types of empathy, see Daniel Goleman, *Three Kinds of Empathy: Cognitive, Emotional, Compassionate*, June 12, 2007,

http://www.danielgoleman.info/three-kinds-of-empathy-cognitive
-emotional-compassionate/.

16. Kevin Dutton, "Psychopaths Recognize Emotions Better Than Most Normal People," *Globe and Mail*, November 1, 2012, https://www.sott.net/article/253012-Psychopaths-recognise-emotions-better-than-most-normal-people; Daniel Goleman, *Social Intelligence: The New Science of Human Relationships* (New York: Bantam Books, 2006).

17. Uta Frith and Frederique de Vignemont, "Egocentrism, Allocentrism, and Asperger Ayndrome," *Consciousness and Cognition* 14, no. 4 (2005): 719–738.

18. Paul Ekman, "An Argument for Basic Emotions," *Cognition and Emotion* 6, no. 3–4 (1992): 169–200.

19. On December 3, 2014, Hillary Clinton made the following remark in a speech at Georgetown University entitled "Smart Power: Security through Inclusive Leadership." At the time of this speech, her tenure as Secretary of State had ended and she had yet to announce her candidacy for US President.

This is what we call Smart Power, using every possible tool … leaving no one on the sidelines, showing respect even for one's enemies, trying to understand, and insofar as is psychologically possible, empathize with their perspective and point of view, helping to define the problems [and] determine a solution, that is what we believe in the twenty-first century will change the prospect for peace.

Georgetown University, December 3, 2014, *Clinton: Including Women Essential to Peace Process*, https://www.georgetown.edu/news/hillary-clinton-security-inclusive-leadership.html.

20. Fox News Politics, "Clinton Says America Should 'Empathize' with Its Enemies," December 5, 2014, http://www.foxnews.com/politics/2014/12/05/clinton-says-america-should-empathize-with-its-enemies.html.

21. LaRay M. Barna, "Stumbling Blocks in Intercultural Communication," in *Basic Concepts of Intercultural Communication: Selected Readings*, ed. Milton J. Bennett (Boston: Intercultural Press, 1998), 173–190.

22. Eiko Tai, "Modification of the Western Approach to Intercultural Communication for the Japanese Context," master's thesis, Portland State University, Portland, OR, 1986. (Cited in Barna, "Stumbling Blocks.")

23. Dr. Seuss was the pen name of Theodore Geisel. He wrote *Horton Hears a Who* in 1953 as an allegory of the US occupation of Japan after World War II (Richard H. Minear, *Dr. Seuss Goes to War: The World War II Editorial Cartoons of Theodore Seuss Geisel* [New York: New Press, 1999]).

24. For more information about how speakers adjust their referents for their hearers, see Herbert H. Clark and Susan E. Haviland, "Comprehension and the Given-New Contract," in *Discourse Comprehension*, ed. Roy O. Freedle (Norwood, NJ: Ablex, 1977), 1–40.

25. The term "common ground" as it applies to language use was introduced by the American psychologist Herbert Clark: see Herbert H. Clark, "Language Use and Language Users," in *Handbook of Social Psychology*, 3rd ed., ed. Gardner Lindzey and Elliot Aronson (New York: Harper & Row, 1985), 179–231. For more on how shared common ground affects pragmatics, see Istvan Kecskes, *Intercultural Pragmatics* (Oxford: Oxford University Press, 2014).

26. For more on lexical entrainment, see Susan E. Brennan, "Lexical Entrainment in Spontaneous Dialog," *Proceedings of the International Symposium on Spoken Dialogue* (1996): 41–44; and Susan E. Brennan and Herbert H. Clark, "Conceptual Pacts and Lexical Choice in Conversation," *Journal of Experimental Psychology: Learning, Memory, and Cognition* 22, no. 6 (1996): 1482–1493.

27. Robert M. Krauss and Sam Glucksberg, "Social and Nonsocial Speech," *Scientific American* 236, no. 2 (1977): 100–105.

28. Howard Giles, Justine Coupland, and Nikolas Coupland, eds., *Contexts of Accommodation: Studies in Emotion and Social Interaction* (Cambridge: Cambridge University Press, 1991).

29. Howard Giles, Donald M. Taylor, and Richard Bourhis, "Toward a Theory of Interpersonal Accommodation through Language: Some

Canadian Data," *Language in Society* 2, no. 2 (1973): 177–192; Thomas M. Holtgraves, *Language as Social Action: Social Psychology and Language Use* (Mahwah, NJ: Erlbaum, 2002).

30. Richard Roberts and Roger Kreuz, *Becoming Fluent: How Cognitive Science Can Help Adults Learn a Foreign Language* (Cambridge, MA: MIT Press, 2015).

31. Alia Wong, "De-Stigmatizing Hawaii's Creole Language," *Atlantic*, November 20, 2015, http://www.theatlantic.com/education/archive/2015/11/hawaiian-pidgin-recognized/416883/.

32. See, e.g., Charles J. Bailey and Karl Maroldt, "The French Lineage of English," in *Langues en contact—Pidgins—Creoles—Languages in Contact*, ed. Jürgen M. Meisel (Tübingen: TBL-Verlag Narr, 1977), 21–53. For an opposing point of view, see Manfred Görlach, "Middle English—A Creole?" in *Linguistics across Historical and Geographical Boundaries*, vol. 1, ed. Dieter Kastovsky and Alexandr Szwedek (Berlin: Mouton de Gruyter, 1986), 329–344.

33. If you're interested in how adults can do this, check out our book *Becoming Fluent*.

34. Carmit T. Tadmor, Adam D. Galinsky, and William W. Maddux, "Getting the Most Out of Living Abroad: Biculturalism and Integrative Complexity as Key Drivers of Creative and Professional Success," *Journal of Personality and Social Psychology* 103, no. 3 (2012): 520–542, at 520.

2   Pragmatics and Its Principles

1. Philip N. Johnson-Laird and Peter C. Wason, *Thinking: Readings in Cognitive Science* (Cambridge: Cambridge University Press, 1977), 400.

2. Jacob L. Mey, *Pragmatics: An Introduction*, 2nd ed. (Oxford: Blackwell, 2001), 19.

3. Greville G. Corbett, *Gender* (Cambridge: Cambridge University Press, 1991).

4. Joseph H. Greenberg, "Some Universals of Grammar with Particular Reference to the Order of Meaningful Elements," in *Universals of Grammar*, ed. Joseph H. Greenberg (Cambridge, MA: MIT Press, 1963), 73–113. See also Robert L. Trask, *A Dictionary of Grammatical Terms in Linguistics* (London: Routledge, 1993).

5. Noam Chomsky, *Knowledge of Language: Its Nature, Origin, and Use* (Westport, CT: Praeger, 1986), 146.

6. For a review of this distinction, see Harry Triandis, "Collectivism v. Individualism: A Reconceptualisation of a Basic Concept in Cross-Cultural Social Psychology," in *Cross-Cultural Studies of Personality, Attitudes, and Cognition*, ed. Gajendra K.Verma and Christopher Bagley (New York: St. Martin's Press, 1988), 60–95.

7. Edward T. Hall, *Beyond Culture* (New York: Doubleday, 1976).

8. For differences in conflict resolution, see Elizabeth G. Chua and William B. Gudykunst, "Conflict Resolution Styles in Low- and High-Context Cultures," *Communication Research Reports* 4, no. 1 (1987): 32–37. For differences in celebrity endorsements, see Sejung M. Choi, Wei-Na Lee, and Hee-Jong Kim, "Lessons from the Rich and Famous: A Cross-Cultural Comparison of Celebrity Endorsement in Advertising," *Journal of Advertising* 34, no. 2 (2005): 85–98. For differences in the use of visual effects on web pages, see Elizabeth Würtz, "A Cross-Cultural Analysis of Websites from High-Context Cultures and Low-Context Cultures," *Journal of Computer-Mediated Communication* 11, no. 1 (2005): art. 13. For an example of research that has not supported this distinction, see Donghoon Kim, Yigang Pan, and Heung S. Park, "High- versus Low-Context Culture: A Comparison of Chinese, Korean, and American Cultures," *Psychology and Marketing* 15, no. 6 (1998): 507–521.

9. Richard D. Lewis, *When Cultures Collide: Leading across Cultures*, 3rd ed. (Boston: Nicholas Brealey, 2006).

10. Yoichi Sato, "'Kuki ga Yomenai': Situated Face-Threatening Act within Japanese Social Interaction," *Novitas-ROYAL (Research on Youth and Language)* 4, no. 2 (2010): 173–181.

11. Roger J. Kreuz, "The Use of Verbal Irony: Cues and Constraints," in *Metaphor: Implications and Applications*, ed. Jeffrey S. Mio and Albert N. Katz (Mahwah, NJ: Erlbaum, 1996), 23–38.

12. Roger J. Kreuz and Richard M. Roberts, "When Collaboration Fails: Consequences of Pragmatic Errors in Conversation," *Journal of Pragmatics* 19, no. 3 (1993): 239–252.

13. Erving Goffman, *Behavior in Public Places: Notes on the Social Organization of Gatherings* (New York: Simon & Schuster, 1963).

14. Jeremy C. Justus, "Piss Stance: Private Parts in Public Places: An Analysis of the Men's Room and Gender Control," *Studies in Popular Culture* 28, no. 3 (2006): 59–70.

15. Erving Goffman, "On Face-Work: An Analysis of Ritual Elements of Social Interaction," *Psychiatry: Journal for the Study of Interpersonal Processes* 18, no. 3 (1955): 213–231.

16. Dacher Keltner, Lisa Capps, Ann M. Kring, Randall C. Young, and Erin A. Heerey, "Just Teasing: A Conceptual Analysis and Empirical Review," *Psychological Bulletin* 127, no. 2 (2001): 229–248, at 229.

17. For an example in Japanese, see Naomi Geyer, "Teasing and Ambivalent Face in Japanese Multi-Party Discourse," *Journal of Pragmatics* 42, no. 8 (2010): 2120–2130.

18. John Oetzel, Stella Ting-Toomey, Tomoko Masumoto, Yumiko Yokochi, Xiaohui Pan, Jiro Takai, and Richard Wilcox, "Face and Facework in Conflict: A Cross-Cultural Comparison of China, Germany, Japan, and the United States," *Communication Monographs* 68, no. 3 (2001): 235–258.

19. Penelope Brown and Stephen C. Levinson, *Politeness: Some Universals in Language Usage* (Cambridge: Cambridge University Press, 1978/1987).

20. Jean B. Gleason, Rivka Y. Perlmann, and Esther B. Greif, "What's the Magic Word: Learning Language through Politeness Routines," *Discourse Processes* 7, no. 4 (1984): 493–502.

21. Herbert H. Clark and Catherine R. Marshall, "Definite Reference and Mutual Knowledge," in *Elements of Discourse Understanding*, ed. Aravind K. Joshe, Bruce H. Webber, and Ivan A. Sag (Cambridge: Cambridge University Press, 1981), 10–63.

22. Saul Zaentz (producer) and Miloš Forman (director), *Amadeus* (New York: HBO Video, 1984).

23. Kreuz, "The Use of Verbal Irony."

3   How Speech Acts

1. John R. Searle, "A Taxonomy of Illocutionary Acts," in *Language, Mind, and Knowledge*, vol. 7, ed. Keith Günderson (Minneapolis: University of Minneapolis Press, 1975), 344–369.

2. John Dore, "Holophrases, Speech Acts, and Language Universals," *Journal of Child Language* 2, no. 1 (1975): 21–40.

3. Roy G. D'Andrade and Myron Wish, "Speech Act Theory in Quantitative Research on Interpersonal Behavior," *Discourse Processes* 8, no. 2 (1985): 229–259.

4. Several rounds of refusals: Zohreh Eslami, "Invitations in Persian and English: ostensible or genuine?" *Intercultural Pragmatics* 2, no. 4 (2005): 453–480. Owner refusing to take money: Christopher De Bellaigue, "Talk Like an Iranian," *Atlantic*, September 2012, http://www.theatlantic.com/magazine/archive/2012/09/talk-like-an-iranian/309056/.

5. Ellen A. Isaacs and Herbert H. Clark, "Ostensible Invitations," *Language in Society* 19, no. 4 (1990): 493–509.

6. Kristen E. Link and Roger J. Kreuz, "The Comprehension of Ostensible Speech Acts," *Journal of Language and Social Psychology* 24, no. 3 (2005): 227–251.

7. Marsha D. Walton, "Ostensible Lies and the Negotiation of Shared Meanings," *Discourse Processes* 26, no. 1 (1998): 27–41, at 27.

8. Mehdi Dastpak and Fatemeh Mollaei, "A Comparative Study of Ostensible Invitations in English and Persian," *Higher Education of Social*

Science 1, no. 1 (2011): 33–42; Zohreh Eslami-Rasekh, "Raising the Pragmatic Awareness of Language Learners," *ELT Journal* 59, no. 3 (2005): 199–208; Istvan Kecskes, Dan E. Davidson, and Richard Brecht, "The Foreign Language Perspective," *Intercultural Pragmatics* 2, no. 4 (2005): 361–368.

9. LuMing Mao, "Invitational Discourse and Chinese Identity," *Journal of Asian Pacific Communication* 3, no. 1 (1992): 70–96; Hui Wang, "A Study on the Politeness of the Speech Act of Ostensible Refusal," *Journal of Mianyang Normal University* 33, no. 7 (1992): 95–98.

10. Herbert H. Clark, "Responding to Indirect Speech Acts," *Cognitive Psychology* 11, no. 4 (1979): 430–477.

11. Thomas M. Holtgraves and Joong-nam Yang, "Interpersonal Underpinnings of Request Strategies: General Principles and Differences due to Culture and Gender," *Journal of Personality and Social Psychology* 62, no. 2 (1992): 246–256, at 253.

12. Thomas M. Holtgraves, "Styles of Language Use: Individual and Cultural Variability in Conversational Indirectness," *Journal of Personality and Social Psychology* 73, no. 3 (1997): 624–637; Thomas M. Holtgraves, *Language as Social Action: Social Psychology and Language Use* (Mahwah, NJ: Erlbaum, 2002); Theresa Youn-ja Shim, Min-Sun Kim, and Judith N. Martin, *Changing Korea: Understanding Culture and Communication*, vol. 10 (New York: Peter Lang, 2008).

13. Criticisms: Brown and Levinson, *Politeness*. Clarify and show negative emotion: Richard M. Roberts and Roger J. Kreuz, "Why Do People Use Figurative Language?" *Psychological Science* 5, no. 3 (1994): 159–163. Relatively hostile: John S. Leggitt and Raymond W. Gibbs Jr., "Emotional Reactions to Verbal Irony," *Discourse Processes* 29, no. 1 (2000): 1–24. Claims and assertions: Irene Koshik, *Beyond Rhetorical Questions: Assertive Questions in Everyday Interaction* (Amsterdam: John Benjamins, 2005). Humorous effect: Deborah Schaffer, "Can Rhetorical Questions Function as Retorts? Is the Pope Catholic?" *Journal of Pragmatics* 37, no. 4 (2005): 433–460.

14. Increase persuasiveness: Kevin L. Blankenship and Traci Y. Craig, "Rhetorical Question Use and Resistance to Persuasion: An Attitude Strength Hypothesis," *Journal of Language and Social Psychology* 25, no. 2 (2006): 111–128. Can be distracting: David R. Roskos-Ewoldsen, "What Is the Role of Rhetorical Questions in Persuasion?" in *Communication and Emotion: Essays in Honor of Dolf Zillmann*, ed. Jennings Bryant, David Roskos-Ewoldsen, and Joanne Cantor (Mahwah, NJ: Erlbaum, 2003), 297–321.

15. Tzeltal: Brown and Levinson, *Politeness*. Tamil: Susan C. Herring, "The Grammaticalization of Rhetorical Questions in Tamil," in *Approaches to Grammaticialization*, vol. 1: *Focus on Theoretical and Methodological Issues*, ed. Elizabeth Closs Traugott and Bernd Heine (Amsterdam: John Benjamins, 1991), 253–284. Korean: Seongha Rhee, "From Discourse to Grammar: Grammaticalization and Lexicalization of Rhetorical Questions in Korean," in *LACUS Forum 30: Language, Thought and Reality*, ed. Gordon D. Fulton, William J. Sullivan, and Arle R. Lommel, 413–423 (Houston, TX: The Linguistic Association of Canada and the United States, 2004). Jordanian Arabic: Muhammad A. Badarneh, "Proverbial Rhetorical Questions in Colloquial Jordanian Arabic," *Folia Linguistica* 50, no. 1 (2016): 207–242.

16. Roger J. Kreuz, Max A. Kassler, Laurie Coppenrath, and Bonnie McLain Allen, "Tag Questions and Common Ground Effects in the Perception of Verbal Irony," *Journal of Pragmatics* 31, no. 12 (1999): 1685–1700.

17. Anna Wierzbicka, *Cross-Cultural Pragmatics: The Semantics of Human Interaction* (Berlin: Mouton de Gruyter, 2003).

18. Alex Osmand, *Academic Writing and Grammar for Students*, 2nd ed. (Thousand Oaks, CA: Sage, 2016).

19. Eli Hinkel, "Indirectness in L1 and L2 Academic Writing," *Journal of Pragmatics* 27, no. 3 (1997): 361–386.

20. Keiko Hirose, "Comparing L1 and L2 Organizational Patterns in the Argumentative Writing of Japanese EFL Students," *Journal of Second Language Writing* 12, no. 2 (2003): 181–209; Hacer H. Uysal,

"Argumentation across L1 and L2 Writing: Exploring Cultural Influences and Transfer Issues," *Vigo International Journal of Applied Linguistics* 9 (2012): 133–159.

21. Renad Abbadi, "The Construction of Arguments in English and Arabic: A Comparison of the Linguistic Strategies Employed in Editorials," *Argumentum* 10 (2014): 724–746.

22. NASA, "The Flight of Apollo-Soyuz," 2004, http://history.nasa.gov/apollo/apsoyhist.html.

23. Ben Evans, *At Home in Space: The Late Seventies into the Eighties* (New York: Springer, 2012).

24. Thomas P. Stafford and Michael Cassutt, *We Have Capture: Tom Stafford and the Space Race* (Washington, DC: Smithsonian Books, 2002).

25. "A-O.K.—but Oklahomski?" *Chicago Tribune*, July 20, 1975, http://archives.chicagotribune.com/1975/07/20/page/2/article/a-o-k-but-oklahomski.

26. P. Christopher Earley and Soon Ang, *Cultural Intelligence: Individual Interactions across Cultures* (Stanford, CA: Stanford University Press, 2003).

27. It's worth noting, however, that humor was still possible under such circumstances: at one point, Leonov rapped on the still-closed hatch that separated the two men, and Stafford called out, "Кто Будет там?" (*Kto Budet tam*, or "Who's there?"; Stafford and Cassutt, *We Have Capture*).

4   The Elements of Pragmatic Style

1. Richard Wiseman *Laughlab: The Scientific Search for the World's Funniest Joke* (New York: Random House, 2002).

2. A preliminary report from this project asserted that a joke about Sherlock Holmes, Dr. Watson, and a camping trip was the world's funniest joke. However, it was edged out by the hunter joke in the final tally.

3. Audrey Adams, "High-Context Humor," in *Encyclopedia of Humor Studies*, vol. 1, ed. Salvatore Attardo (Thousand Oaks, CA: Sage, 2014), 288–289.

4. Ofra Nevo, Baruch Nevo, and Janie Leong Siew Yin, "Singaporean Humor: A Cross-Cultural, Cross-Gender Comparison," *Journal of General Psychology* 128, no. 2 (2001): 143–156.

5. Germans and Italians: Willibald Ruch and Giovannantonio Forabosco, "A Cross-Cultural Study of Humor Appreciation: Italy and Germany," *Humor* 9, no. 1 (1996): 1–18. Egyptians, Lebanese, and Americans: Morris Kalliny, Kevin W. Cruthirds, and Michael S. Minor, "Differences between American, Egyptian and Lebanese Humor Styles," *International Journal of Cross Cultural Management* 6, no. 1 (2006): 121–134. French and Australians: Christine Béal and Kerry Mullan, "Issues in Conversational Humor from a Cross-Cultural Perspective: Comparing French and Australian Corpora," in *Cross-Culturally Speaking, Speaking Cross-Culturally*, ed. Bert Peeters, Kerry Mullan, and Christine Béal (Newcastle upon Tyne, UK: Cambridge Scholars Publishing, 2013), 107–139. Japan: Kimie Oshima, "An Examination for Styles of Japanese Humor: Japan's Funniest Story Projects 2010 to 2011," *Intercultural Studies* 22, no. 2 (2013): 91–109.

6. Michael Haugh, "Jocular Mockery, (Dis)affliation, and Face," *Journal of Pragmatics* 42, no. 8 (2010): 2106–2119; Michael Haugh and Derek Bousfield, "Mock Impoliteness, Jocular Mockery and Jocular Abuse in Australian and British English," *Journal of Pragmatics* 44, no. 9 (2012): 1099–1144.

7. Catherine Evans Davies, "How English-Learners Joke with Native Speakers: An Interactional Sociolinguistic Perspective on Humor as Collaborative Discourse across Cultures," *Journal of Pragmatics* 35, no. 9 (2003): 1361–1385.

8. Associated Press, "Cussing Canoeist Convicted in Michigan," *Los Angeles Times*, June 12, 1999, http://articles.latimes.com/1999/jun/12/news/mn-45705; Stephanie Simon, "Michigan Man Swears by His Right to Use Profanity," *Los Angeles Times*, January 25, 1999, http://articles

.latimes.com/1999/jan/25/news/mn-1502; Kari Haskell, "The People v. the Potty Mouth," *New York Times Week in Review*, April 7, 2002, http://www.nytimes.com/2002/04/07/weekinreview/the-people-v-potty-mouth.html.

9. Juliane Pepitone, "FCC Indecency Ban Struck Down," *CNN Money*, July 13, 2010, http://money.cnn.com/2010/07/13/news/economy/fcc_indecency/?iref=NS1; Melissa Mohr, *Holy Sh*t: A Brief History of Swearing* (Oxford: Oxford University Press, 2013).

10. James Vinci, "US Supreme Court Rules against FCC on Nudity and Swear Words on TV," *National Post*, June 21, 2012, http://news.nationalpost.com/news/u-s-supreme-court-rules-against-fcc-on-nudity-and-swear-words-on-tv. Zach Schonfeld, "Does the Parental Advisory Label Still Matter?" *Newsweek*, November 10, 2015, http://www.newsweek.com/does-parental-advisory-label-still-matter-tipper-gore-375607.

11. Occidental College Special Collections & College Archives, "Banned Books: Shakespeare Censored!" http://sites.oxy.edu/special-collections/bannedbooks/censoredworks.htm.

12. Magnus Ljung, *Swearing: A Cross-Cultural Linguistic Study* (New York: Palgrave Macmillan, 2011).

13. Keith Allan and Kate Burridge, *Euphemism and Dysphemism: Language Used as Shield and Weapon* (New York: Oxford University Press, 1991).

14. Karyn Stapleton, "Swearing," in *Interpersonal Pragmatics*, ed. Miriam A. Locher and Sage L. Graham (Berlin: De Gruyter Mouton, 2010), 289–305.

15. Nicola Daly, Janet Holmes, Jonathan Newton, and Maria Stubbe, "Expletives as Solidarity Signals in FTAs on the Factory Floor," *Journal of Pragmatics* 36, no. 5 (2004): 945–964.

16. Ülker Vanci-Osam, "May You Be Shot with Greasy Bullets: Curse Utterances in Turkish," *Asian Folklore Studies* 57, no. 1 (1998): 71–86.

17. Michele J. Gelfand, Jana L. Raver, Lisa Nishii, Lisa M. Leslie, Janetta Lun, Beng Chong Lim, Lili Duan, et al., "Differences between Tight and Loose Cultures: A 33-Nation Study," *Science* 332 (2011): 1100–1104.

18. C. Goddard, "'Swear Words' and 'Curse Words' in Australian (and American) English: At the Crossroads of Pragmatics, Semantics, and Sociolinguistics," *Intercultural Pragmatics* 12, no. 2 (2015): 189–218.

19. Timothy Jay and Kristen Janschewitz, "The Pragmatics of Swearing," *Journal of Politeness Research* 4, no. 2 (2008): 267–288.

20. Jean-Marc Dewaele, "The Emotional Force of Swearwords and Taboo Words in the Speech of Multilinguals," *Journal of Multilingual and Multicultural Development* 25, nos. 2–3 (2004a): 204–222; Jean-Marc Dewaele, "Blistering Barnacles! What Language Do Multilinguals Swear In?!" *Estudios de Sociolingüística* 5, no. 1 (2004a): 83–105.

21. Dacher Keltner and Brenda N. Buswell, "Embarrassment: Its Distinct Form and Appeasement Functions," *Psychological Bulletin* 122, no. 3 (1997): 250–270.

22. Hillary A. Elfenbein, Martin Beaupré, Manon Lévesque, and Ursula Hess, "Toward a Dialect Theory: Cultural Differences in the Expression and Recognition of Posed Facial Expressions," *Emotion* 7, no. 1 (2007): 131–146.

23. Ping Dong, Xun I. Huang, and Robert S. Wyer Jr., "The Illusion of Saving Face: How People Symbolically Cope with Embarrassment," *Psychological Science* 24, no. 10 (2013): 2005–2012.

24. Jennifer Goetz and Dacher Keltner, "Shifting Meanings of Self-Conscious Emotions across Cultures," in *The Self-Conscious Emotions: Theory and Research*, ed. Jessica L. Tracy, Richard W. Robins, and June P. Tangney (New York: Guilford Press, 2007), 153–173.

25. Jonathan Haidt and Darcher Keltner, "Culture and Facial Expression: Open-Ended Methods Find More Expressions and a Gradient of Recognition," *Cognition and Emotion* 13, no. 3 (1999): 225–266.

26. Karin Aronsson and Bengt Rundström, "Cats, Dogs, and Sweets in the Clinical Negotiation of Reality: On Politeness and Coherence in Pediatric Discourse," *Language in Society* 18, no. 4 (1989): 483–504.

27. Chinese terms: Jin Li, Lianqin Wang, and Kurt Fischer, "The Organization of Chinese Shame Concepts?" *Cognition and Emotion* 18, no. 6 (2004): 767–797. Confucian traditions: David Y. F. Ho, Wai Fu, and Siu Man Ng, "Guilt, Shame, and Embarrassment: Revelations of Face and Self," *Culture and Psychology* 10, no. 1 (2004): 64–84.

28. Rebecca S. Merkin, "Uncertainty Avoidance and Facework: A Test of the Hofstede Model," *International Journal of Intercultural Relations* 30, no. 2 (2006): 213–228.

29. Geert H. Hofstede, *Culture's Consequences: Comparing Values, Behaviors, Institutions, and Organizations across Nations*, 2nd ed. (Thousand Oaks, CA: Sage, 2001).

30. Tendency to resort to confrontation: Wonsun Kim, Xiaowen Guan, and Hee S. Park, "Face and Facework: A Cross-Cultural Comparison of Managing Politeness Norms in the United States and Korea," *International Journal of Communication* 6, no. 1 (2012): 1100–1118. Coping response: T. Todd Imahori and William R. Cupach, "A Cross-Cultural Comparison of the Interpretation and Management of Face: US American and Japanese Responses to Embarrassing Predicaments," *International Journal of Intercultural Relations* 18, no. 2 (1994): 193–219.

31. Allen C. Bluedorn, Carol F. Kaufman, and Paul M. Lane, "How Many Things Do You Like to Do at Once? An Introduction to Monochronic and Polychronic Time," *Executive* 6, no. 4 (1992): 17–26.

32. Bronisław Malinowsky, "The Problem of Meaning in Primitive Languages," in *The Meaning of Meaning: A Study of the Influence of Language Upon Thought and the Science of Symbolism*, ed. Charles K. Ogden and Ian A. Richards (London: Routledge, 1923), 146–152.

33. Aaron Ben-Ze'ev, "The Vindication of Gossip," in *Good Gossip*, ed. Robert F. Goodman and Aaron Ben-Ze'ev (Lawrence: University Press of Kansas, 1994), 11–24.

34. Christine Béal, "Did You Have a Good Weekend: Or Why There Is No Such Thing as a Simple Question in Cross-Cultural Encounters," *Australian Review of Applied Linguistics* 15, no. 1 (1992): 23–52.

35. Hye-Kyung Ryoo, "Achieving Friendly Interactions: A Study of Service Encounters between Korean Shopkeepers and African-American Customers," *Discourse and Society* 16, no. 1 (2005): 79–105.

36. Lewis, *When Cultures Collide*.

37. No term in German: Juliane House, "Impoliteness in Germany: Intercultural Encounters in Everyday and Institutional Talk," *Intercultural Pragmatics* 7, no. 4 (2010): 561–595. Finns and small talk: Markus Grandlund and Kari Lukka, "Toward Increasing Business Orientation: Finnish Management Accountants in a Changing Cultural Context," *Management Accounting Research* 9, no. 2 (1998): 185–211.

38. German and Greek phone calls: Theodossia-Soula Pavlidou, "Telephone conversations in Greek and German: Attending to the relationship aspect of communication," in *Culturally Speaking: Managing Rapport through Talk across Cultures*, ed. Helen Spencer-Oatley (London: Continuum, 2000), 121–140. Theodossia Pavlidou, "Contrasting German-Greek Politeness and the Consequences," *Journal of Pragmatics* 21, no. 5 (1994): 487–511.

39. Maria E. Placencia, "Pragmatic Variation in Corner Store Interactions in Quito and Madrid," *Hispania* 88, no. 3 (2005): 583–598.

40. Evangellos Deloussis, "A Cross-Cultural Comparison of Organizational Culture: Evidence from Universities in the Arab World and Japan," *Cross Cultural Management: An International Journal* 11, no. 1 (2004): 15–34.

41. Dean C. Barlund, "Communicative Styles in Two Cultures: Japan and the United States," in *Organization of Behavior in Face-to-Face Interaction*, ed. Adam Kendon, Richard M. Harris, and Mary R. Key (The Hague: Mouton, 1975), 427–456.

42. Language Realm, http://www.languagerealm.com/german/du_sie .php.

43. Birgit Görtz, "The 'du/Sie' Dilemma in German," *Deutsche Welle*, 2013, http://www.dw.de/the-du-sie-dilemma-in-german/a-16494631.

44. Michael H. Agar, *Language Shock: Understanding the Culture of Conversation* (New York: William Morrow, 1994).

45. Gaston Dorren, *Lingo: Around Europe in Sixty Languages* (New York: Atlantic Monthly Press, 2015).

46. William Peregoy, "As a Beginner in Japanese, Don't Worry about the Formality," *Fluent in 3 Months* (n.d.), http://www.fluentin3months.com/formal-japanese/.

47. Janet Holmes, *An Introduction to Sociolinguistics* (London: Routledge, 2013), 450.

48. For a discussion of the how language use in Korean is influenced by the relative age of the participants, see Kyung-Joo Yoon, "Not Just Words: Korean Social Models and the Use of Honorifics," *Intercultural Pragmatics* 1, no. 2 (2004): 189–210.

49. For more on the role of Confucianism and the family in Korea, see Insook H. Park and Lee-Jay Cho, "Confucianism and the Korean Family," *Journal of Comparative Family Studies* 26, no. 1 (1995): 117–134.

50. We only scratch the surface here in exploring the relationship between age and honorific speech in Korean. As one more example, language use also differs between those who are considered to be one's senior (선배) or one's junior (후배) based on when someone started at a school, joined the military, or began work at a company. The system also has many other subtle gradations.

51. If you'd like to calculate your Korean age, see Billy Go, "How to Find Your 'Korean Age,'" *Dramafever.com*, February 20, 2015, https://www.dramafever.com/news/how-to-find-your-korean-age/.

52. Norbert Paxton, *The Rough Guide to Korea*, 2nd ed. (London: Rough Guides, 2011).

5 The Mechanics of Cross-Cultural Communication

1. Pino Cutrone, "A Case Study Examining Backchannels in Conversations between Japanese–British Dyads," *Multilingua* 24, no. 3 (2005): 237–274.

2. Victor Yngve, "On Getting a Word in Edgewise," in *Papers from the Sixth Regional Meeting, Chicago Linguistic Society*, ed. M. A. Campbell (Chicago: Chicago Linguistic Society, 1970), 567–578.

3. Signaling disagreement: Pino Cutrone, *Assessing Pragmatic Competence in the Japanese EFL Context: Toward the Learning of Listener Responses* (Newcastle upon Tyne: Cambridge Scholars Publishing, 2013). Specific type of speech act: Marja-Leena Sorjonen, *Responding in Conversation: A Study of Response Particles in Finnish* (Amsterdam: John Benjamins, 2001).

4. Senko K. Maynard, "Conversation Management in Contrast: Listener Response in Japanese and American English," *Journal of Pragmatics* 14, no. 3 (1990): 397–412. Even larger differences: Ron White, "Back Channeling, Repair, Pausing, and Private Speech," *Applied Linguistics* 18, no. 3 (1997): 314–344.

5. Nobuko Mizutani, "The Listener's Responses in Japanese Conversation," *Sociolinguistics* 13, no. 1 (1982): 33–38.

6. Sheida White, "Backchannels across Cultures: A Study of Americans and Japanese," *Language in Society* 18, no. 1 (1989): 59–76.

7. Bettina Heinz, "Backchannel Responses as Strategic Responses in Bilingual Speakers' Conversations," *Journal of Pragmatics* 35, no. 7 (2003): 1113–1142.

8. White, "Back Channeling, Repair, Pausing."

9. Lars Fant, "Cultural Mismatch in Conversation: Spanish and Scandinavian Communicative Behavior in Negotiation Settings," *Hermes: Journal of Language and Communication in Business* 2, no. 3 (2015): 247–265.

10. Robert A. Heinlein, *Stranger in a Strange Land* (New York: Putnam, 1961).

11. George Lakoff, "Hedges: A Study in Meaning Criteria and the Logic of Fuzzy Concepts," *Journal of Philosophical Logic* 2, no. 4 (1973): 458–508.

12. Daniel Z. Kádar and Michael Haugh, *Understanding Politeness* (Cambridge: Cambridge University Press, 2013).

13. Ignacio Vázquez and Diana Giner, "Writing with Conviction: The Use of Boosters in Modeling Persuasion in Academic Discourses," *Revista Alicantina de Estudios Ingleses* 22 (2009): 219–237.

14. Robin Lakoff, *Language and Woman's Place* (New York: Harper & Row, 1975).

15. Deborah Tannen, *You Just Don't Understand*. Research has not always supported these claims: Janet Holmes, "Hedges and Boosters in Women's and Men's Speech," *Language and Communication* 10, no. 3 (1990): 185–205.

16. Raija Markkanen and Hartmut Schröder, "Hedging: A Challenge for Pragmatics and Discourse Analysis," in *Hedging and Discourse: Approaches to the Analysis of a Pragmatic Phenomenon in Academic Texts*, ed. Raija Markkanen and Hartmut Schröder (Berlin: Walter de Gruyter, 1997), 3–18.

17. Heinz Kreutz and Annette Harres, "Some Observations on the Distribution and Function of Hedging in German and English Academic Writing," in *Culture and Styles of Academic Discourse*, ed. Anna Duszak, 181–202 (Berlin: Mouton de Grutyer, 1997).

18. Ken Hyland and John Milton, "Qualification and Certainty in L1 and L2 Students' Writing," *Journal of Second Language Writing* 6, no. 2 (1997): 183–205.

19. Mahmoodreza Atai and Leyla Sadr, "A Cross-Cultural Study of Hedging Devices in Discussion Section of Applied Linguistics Research Articles," *Teaching English Language and Literature* 2 (2008): 1–22; Atefeh Rezanejad, Zahra Lari, and Zahra Mosalli, "A Cross-Cultural Analysis of

the Use of Hedging Devices in Scientific Research Articles," *Journal of Language Teaching and Research* 6, no. 6 (2008): 1384–1392.

20. Hacer H. Uysal, "A Cross-Cultural Study of Indirectness and Hedging in the Conference Proposals of English NS and NNS Scholars," in *Occupying Niches: Interculturality, Cross-Culturality and Aculturality in Academic Research*, ed. Andrzej Łyda and Krystyna Warchał (Cham, Switzerland: Springer International, 2014), 179–195.

21. Ken Hyland, "Hedges, Boosters, and Lexical Invisibility: Noticing Modifiers in Academic Texts," *Language Awareness* 9, no. 4 (2000): 179–197.

22. Alfredo Ardila, "Spanglish: An Anglicized Spanish Dialect," *Hispanic Journal of Behavioral Sciences* 27, no. 1 (2005): 60–81.

23. Alan S. Brown, *The Tip of the Tongue State* (New York: Psychology Press, 2012).

24. Leigh Swigart, "Two Codes or One? The Insiders' View and the Description of Codeswitching in Dakar," in *Codeswitching*, ed. Carol Eastman (Clevedon, UK: Multilingual Matters, 1992), 83–102.

25. Penelope Gardner-Chloros, *Code-Switching* (Cambridge: Cambridge University Press, 2009).

26. Shana Poplack, "Contrasting Patterns of Code-Switching in Two Communities," in *Aspects of Multilingualism*, ed. Erling Wande (Uppsala: Borgströms, 1987), 51–77.

27. Carol M. Scotton and William Ury, "Bilingual Strategies: The Social Functions of Code-Switching," *Linguistics: An Interdisciplinary Journal of the Language Sciences* 15, no. 193 (1977): 5–20.

28. Diana Yankova and Irena Vassileva, "Functions and Mechanisms of Code-Switching in Bulgarian Canadians," *Études Canadiennes/Canadian Studies: Revue Interdisciplinaire des Études Canadiennes en France* 74 (2013): 103–121.

29. Using the local dialect: Jan-Petter Blom and John J. Gumperz, "Social Meaning in Linguistic Structure: Code-Switching in Norway," in

The Bilingualism Reader, ed. Li Wei (New York: Routledge, 2000), 111–136. Child code switching: Elizabeth Lanza, "Can Bilingual Two-Year-Olds Code Switch?" *Journal of Child Language* 19, no. 3 (2000): 633–658.

30. Li Wei, "How Can You Tell? Toward a Common Sense Explanation of Conversational Code-Switching," *Journal of Pragmatics* 37, no. 3 (2005): 375–389.

31. Roberto R. Heredia and Jeanette Altarriba, "Bilingual Language Mixing: Why Do Bilinguals Code-Switch?" *Current Directions in Psychological Science* 10, no. 5 (2001): 164–168.

32. Michael H. Bond and Tat-Ming Lai, "Embarrassment and Code-Switching into a Second Language," *Journal of Social Psychology* 126, no. 2 (1986): 179–186.

33. Albert Costa, Alice Foucart, Sayuri Hayakawa, Melina Aparici, Jose Apesteguia, Joy Heafner, and Boaz Keysar, "Your Morals Depend on Language," *Plos One* 9, no. 4 (2014): e94842.

34. J. Normann Jørgensen, "Plurilingual Conversations among Bilingual Adolescents," *Journal of Pragmatics* 37, no. 3 (2005): 391–402.

35. Duane P. Schultz and Sydney E. Schultz, *A History of Modern Psychology,* 11th ed. (Boston: Cengage Learning, 2016), 89.

36. Was Friedline's gender a factor in the conflagration? That she was a woman seems less of an issue, since Cornell was, from its founding, committed to educating women and began admitting female graduate students in 1873. Titchener's own first graduate student, Margaret Floy Washburn, became the first woman ever to be awarded a doctorate in psychology, in 1894.

37. Agustín Gravano and Julia Hirschberg, "A Corpus-Based Study of Interruptions in Spoken Dialogue," *Interspeech* (2012): 855–858.

38. Kumiko Murata, "Intrusive or Co-operative? A Cross-Cultural Study of Interruption," *Journal of Pragmatics* 21, no. 4 (1994): 385–400.

39. Fant, "Cultural Mismatch in Conversation."

40. Han Z. Li, "Cooperative and Intrusive Interruptions in Inter- and Intracultural Dyadic Discourse," *Journal of Language and Social Psychology* 20, no. 3 (2001): 259–284.

41. Jan M. Ulijn and Xiangling Li, "Is Interrupting Impolite? Some Temporal Aspects of Turn-Taking in Chinese-Western and Other Intercultural Business Encounters," *Text* 15, no. 4 (1995): 589–627.

42. Reiko Hayashi, "Simultaneous Talk—From the Perspective of Floor Management of English and Japanese Speakers," *World Englishes* 7, no. 3 (1988): 269–288.

43. O. Mizutani, "Hanashikotoba no tokushoku [characteristics of spoken Japanese]," in *Nihongo*, ed. Y. Miyaji and O. Mizutani, 55–65 (Tokyo: NHK). As cited in Han Z. Li, Young-ok Yum, Robin Yates, Laura Aguilera, Ying Mao, and Yue Zheng, "Interruption and Involvement in Discourse: Can Intercultural Interlocutors Be Trained? *Journal of Intercultural Communication Research* 34, no. 4 (2005): 233–254.

44. Edward T. Hall, *The Hidden Dimension* (New York: Doubleday, 1966).

45. "Editorial: Barack Takes a Bow," *Washington Times*, April 7, 2009, http://www.washingtontimes.com/news/2009/apr/7/barack-takes-a-bow/.

46. Abby Ohlheiser, "A Not-so-Brief List of All the Things President Obama Has Bowed To," *Wire*, April 24, 2014, http://www.thewire.com/politics/2014/04/a-not-so-brief-list-of-all-the-things-president-obama-has-bowed-to/361160/.

47. Justin McCurry, "Obama's Critics Should Be Bowing Their Heads," *Guardian*, November 18, 2009, https://www.theguardian.com/world/blog/2009/nov/18/obama-japan-bow.

48. Raymond Firth, "Verbal and Bodily Rituals of Greeting and Parting," in *The Interpretation of Ritual: Essays in Honor of A. I. Richards*, ed. Jean S. La Fontaine (London: Routledge, 1972), 1–38.

49. Terri Morrison and Wayne A. Conaway, *Kiss, Bow, or Shake Hands*, 2nd ed. (Avon, MA: Adams Media, 2006).

50. "Some Royal Curtsey Etiquette," *Royal Post* (May 2015), http://theroyalpost.com/2015/05/16/some-royal-curtsy-etiquettc/.

51. Chris Rovzar, "Michelle Obama Partially Embraces Queen, Brits Go a Bit Mad," *New York* magazine (April 2009), http://nymag.com/daily/intelligencer/2009/04/michelle_obama_partially_embra.html.

52. Maja Bratanić, "Nonverbal Communication as a Factor in Linguistic Cultural Miscommunication," in *Fundamentals of Verbal and Nonverbal Communication and the Biometric Issue*, ed. Ana Esposito, Maja Bratanić, Eric Keller, and Maria Marinaro (Amsterdam: IOS Press, 2007), 82–91.

53. William R. Jankowiak, Shelly L. Volsche, and Justin R. Garcia, "Is the Romantic–Sexual Kiss a Near Human Universal?" *American Anthropologist* 117, no. 3 (2015): 535–539.

54. Jeanette S. Martin and Lillian H. Chaney, *Global Business Etiquette: A Guide to International Communication and Customs*, 2nd ed. (Santa Barbara, CA: Praeger, 2012).

55. Helena Bachman and Jane Omyanga-Omara, "Muslim Students Face $5K Fine if They Refuse Swiss Teachers' Handshakes," *USA Today*, May 26, 2016, http://www.usatoday.com/story/news/world/2016/05/25/swiss-authorities-overule-teacher-handshake-ban/84899900/; "Switzerland: Muslim Students Must Shake Teacher's Hand," BBC News, May 25, 2016, http://www.bbc.com/news/world-europe-36382596.

56. Takahiko Hattori, "A Study of Nonverbal Intercultural Communication between Japanese and Americans—Focusing on the Use of the Eyes," *Japan Association of Language Teachers Journal* 8 (1985): 109–118.

57. Robert S. Feldman, "Nonverbal Behavior, Race, and the Classroom Teacher," *Theory into Practice* 24, no. 1 (1985): 45–49.

58. David Matsumoto, "Culture and Nonverbal Behavior," in *The SAGE Handbook of Nonverbal Communication*, ed. Valerie Manusov and Miles L. Patterson (Thousand Oaks, CA: Sage, 2006), 219–235.

6   Pragmatics in Action

1. Andreas Knorr and Andreas Arndt, "Why Did *Wal-Mart* Fail in Germany?" in *Materialien des Wissenschaftsschwerpunktes "Globalisierung der Weltwirtschaft,"* vol. 24 (Bremen: Universität Bremen, 2003), 22.

2. For more on preparatory conditions in openings and closings see Deborah Shiffrin, "Opening Encounters," *American Sociological Review* 42, no. 5 (1977): 679–691.

3. Heinz L. Kretzenbacher, "Perceptions of National and Regional Standards of Addressing in Germany and Austria," *Pragmatics* 21, no. 1 (2011): 69–83.

4. Mahmoud A. Rababa'h and Nibal A. A. Malkawi, "The Linguistic Etiquette of Greeting and Leave-Taking in Jordanian Arabic," *European Scientific Journal* 8, no. 18 (2012): 14–28.

5. Miriam E. Ebsworth, Jean W. Bodman, and Mary Carpenter, "Cross-Cultural Realization of Greetings in American English," in *Speech Acts across Cultures: Challenges to Communication in a Second Language*, ed. Susan M. Gass and Joyce Neu (Berlin: Mouton de Gruyter, 1996), 89–108.

6. Alessandro Duranti, "Universal and Culture-Specific Properties of Greetings," *Journal of Linguistic Anthropology* 7, no. 1 (1997): 63–97.

7. Herbert H. Clark and J. Wade French, "Telephone Goodbyes," *Language in Society* 10, no. 1 (1981): 1–19.

8. Liz Coppock, *Politeness Strategies in Conversation Closings*, unpublished MS, http://citeseerx.ist.psu.edu/viewdoc/download?doi=10.1.1.121.883&rep=rep1&type=pdf.

9. Emanuel A. Schegloff and Harvey Sacks, "Opening Up Closings," *Semiotica* 8, no. 4 (1973): 289–327.

10. For more on joint projects, see Adrian Bangerter and Herbert H. Clark, "Navigating Joint Projects with Dialogue," *Cognitive Science* 27, no. 2 (2003): 195–225.

11. Beverly S. Hartford and Kathleen Bardovi-Harlig, "Closing the Conversation: Evidence from the Academic Advising Session," *Discourse Processes* 15, no. 1 (1992): 93–116.

12. Ecuadorian Spanish: Maria E. Plancencia, "Opening Up Closings—The Ecuadorian Way," *Text* 17, no. 1 (1997): 53–81. Persian speakers:

Akram Khadem and Abbas E. Rasekh, "Discourse Structure of Persian Telephone Conversation: A Description of the Closing," *International Review of the Social Sciences and Humanities* 2, no. 2 (2012): 150–161.

13. Hongyin J. Chen, *Cross-Cultural Comparison of English and Chinese Metapragmatics in Refusal*, Indiana University, 1996 (ERIC Document Reproduction Service No. ED 408 860).

14. Hamid Allami and Amin Naeimi, "A Cross-Linguistic Study of Refusals: An Analysis of Pragmatic Competence Development in Iranian EFL Learners," *Journal of Pragmatics* 43, no. 1 (2011): 385–406.

15. Sharyl Tanck, *Speech Act Sets of Refusal and Complaint: A Comparison of Native and Non-native English Speakers' Production*, unpublished MS, 2002, American University, Washington, DC, http://www.american.edu/cas/tesol/pdf/upload/WP-2004-Tanck-Speech-Act.pdf.

16. J. César Félix-Brasdefer, *Politeness in Mexico and the United States: A Contrastive Study of the Realization and Perception of Refusals* (Amsterdam: John Benjamins, 2008).

17. Anchalee Wannaruk, "Pragmatic Transfer in Thai EFL Refusals," *RELC Journal* 39, no. 3 (2008): 318–337.

18. Jihyn Kwon, "Expressing Refusals in Korean and American English," *Multilingua* 23, no. 4 (2004): 339–364, at 339.

19. Leslie M. Beebe, Tomoko Takahashi, and Robin Uliss-Weltz, "Pragmatic Transfer in ESL Refusals," in *Developing Communicative Competence in a Second Language*, ed. Robin C. Scarcella, Elaine S. Anderson, and Stephen D. Krashen (New York: Newbury, 1990, 55–73; Sachiko Kondo, "Effects on Pragmatic Development through Awareness-Raising Instruction: Refusals by Japanese EFL Learners," in *Investigating Pragmatics in Foreign Language Learning, Teaching and Testing*, ed. Eva A. Soler and Alicia Martínez-Flor (Bristol, UK: Multilingual Matters, 2008), 153–177.

20. Thi Minh Nguyen, "Cross-Cultural Pragmatics: Refusals of Requests by Australian Native Speakers of English and Vietnamese Learners of English," master's thesis, The University of Queensland, Brisbane, Australia, 2006, http://www.asian-efl-journal.com/Thesis_Phuong.pdf.

21. Explicit instruction more effective: Duan Lingli and Anchalee Wannaruk, "The Effects of Explicit and Implicit Instruction in English Refusals," *Chinese Journal of Applied Linguistics* 33, no. 3 (2010): 93–109. Role playing activities: Zohreh R. Eslami, "How to Develop Appropriate Refusal Strategies," in *Speech Act Performance: Theoretical, Empirical, and Methodological Issues*, ed. Alicia Martínze-Flor and Esther Usó-Juan (Amsterdam: John Benjamins, 2010), 217–236.

22. Agnieszka Rakowicz, "Ambiguous Invitations: The Interlanguage of Pragmatics of Polish English Language Learners," doctoral dissertation, New York University, New York, 2009.

23. Brown and Levinson, *Politeness*, 216.

24. Christian Licoppe, "Living Inside Location-Aware Mobile Social Information: The Pragmatics of Foursquare Notifications," in *Living Inside Mobile Social Information*, ed. James E. Katz (Dayton, OH: Greyden Press, 2014), 109–130.

25. J. César Félix-Brasdefer, "Perceptions of Refusals to Invitations: Exploring the Minds of Foreign Language Learners," *Language Awareness* 17, no. 3 (2008): 195–211, at 205, 208.

26. Mahmood K. M. Eshreteh, "Re-assessing Cross-Cultural Pragmatics: Insistence as a Marker of Affiliation and Connectedness," *Cross-Cultural Communication* 11, no. 1 (2015): 1–7.

27. Jie Fang, "A Study of Pragmatic Failure in Cross-Cultural Communication," *Sino-US English Teaching* 7, no. 12 (2010): 42–46.

28. Samaneh Mehdipour, Zohreh Eslami, and Hamid Allami, "A Comparative Sociopragmatic Analysis of Wedding Invitations in American and Iranian Societies and Teaching Implications," *Applied Research on English Language* 4, no. 8 (2015): 62–77.

29. Michelle R. Nelson and Cele C. Otnes, "Exploring Cross-Cultural Ambivalence: A Netnography of Intercultural Wedding Message Boards," *Journal of Business Research* 58, no. 1 (2005): 89–95.

30. Geoffrey Leech, *The Pragmatics of Politeness* (Oxford: Oxford University Press, 2014).

31. Barry R. Schlenker and Bruce W. Darby, "The Use of Apologies in Social Predicaments," *Social Psychology Quarterly* 44, no. 3 (1981): 271–278.

32. Extravagant apology: Noriko Tanaka, "An Investigation of Apology: Japanese in Comparison with Australian," *Meikai Journal* 4 (1991): 35–53. Overly polite apologies: Maria Shardakova, "Intercultural Pragmatics in the Speech of American L2 Learners of Russian: Apologies Offered by Americans in Russian," *Intercultural Pragmatics* 2, no. 4 (2005): 423–451.

33. Legal redress: R. Zimmerman, "Doctors' New Tool to Fight Lawsuits: Saying 'I'm Sorry,'" *Wall Street Journal*, May 28, 2004, http://www.wsj .com/articles/SB108482777884713711. Used against physician in a lawsuit: Batya S. Yasgur, "Malpractice: Should You Say 'I'm Sorry'?" *Medscape Business of Medicine*, September 4, 2013, http://www.medscape .com/viewarticle/809560.

34. Naomi Sugimoto, "A Japanese–US Comparison of Apology Styles," *Communication Research* 24, no. 4 (1997): 349–369.

35. Ann Borkin and Susan M. Reinhart, "Excuse Me and I'm Sorry," *TESOL Quarterly* 12, no. 1 (1978): 57–69.

36. Brown and Levinson, *Politeness*.

37. Laura Hartley, "A Sociolinguistic Analysis of Face-Threat and Face-Management in Potential Complaint Situations," doctoral dissertation, Department of Linguistics, Michigan State University, East Lansing, MI, 1998, 78–79.

38. Beth Murphy and Joyce Neu, "My Grade's Too Low: The Speech Act Set of Complaining," in *Speech Acts across Cultures: Challenges to Communication in a Second Language*, ed. Susan M. Gass and Joyce Neu (Berlin: Mouton de Gruyter, 1995), 191–216.

39. Mahboube Nakhle, Mohammad Naghavi, and Abdullah Razavi, "Complaint Behaviors among Native Speakers of Canadian English, Iranian EFL Learners, and Native Speakers of Persian (Contrastive

Pragmatic Study)," *Procedia—Social and Behavioral Sciences* 98 (2014): 1316–1324.

40. Diana Boxer, "A Descriptive Analysis of Indirect Complaint Sequences among Speakers of American English," doctoral dissertation, University of Pennsylvania, Philadelphia, 1991.

41. Diana Boxer, "Complaints as Positive Strategies: What the Learner Needs to Know," *TESOL Quarterly* 27, no. 2 (1993): 277–299, at 290, 292.

42. Robert K. Herbert, "The Ethnography of English Compliments and Compliment Responses: A Contrastive Sketch," in *Contrastive Pragmatics*, ed. Wieslaw Oleksy (Amsterdam: John Benjamins, 1989), 3–35.

43. Roos Vonk, "Self-Serving Interpretations of Flattery: Why Ingratiation Works," *Journal of Personality and Social Psychology* 82, no. 4 (2002): 515–526.

44. Minimize self-praise: Geoffrey N. Leech, *Principles of Pragmatics* (London: Longman, 1983). Agree with the speaker: Anita Pomerantz, "Compliment Responses: Notes on the Co-operation of Multiple Constraints," in *Studies in the Organization of Conversational Interaction*, ed. Jim Schenkein (New York: Academic Press, 1978), 79–112.

45. Men praising other men: Janet Holmes, "Politeness Strategies in New Zealand Women's Speech," In *New Zealand Ways of Speaking English*, ed. Allan Bell and Janet Homes (Clevedon, UK: Multilingual Matters, 1990), 252–276. Positive affect toward other men: Janet Holmes, *Women, Men, and Politeness* (London: Routledge, 1999).

46. Janet Holmes, "Paying Compliments: A Sex Preferential Politeness Strategy," *Journal of Pragmatics* 12, no. 4 (1988): 445–465.

47. Candis Lee, "*Cute yaw haiya—nah!* Hawai'i Creole English Compliments and Their Responses: Implications for Cross-Cultural Failure," *University of Hawai'i Working Papers in ESL* 9, no. 1 (1990): 115–160.

48. Chen-Hsin Tang and Grace Qiao Zhang, "A Contrastive Study of Compliment Responses among Australian English and Mandarin Chinese Speakers," *Journal of Pragmatics* 41, no. 2 (2009): 325–345.

49. Rong Chen and Dafu Yang, "Responding to Compliments in Chinese: Has It Changed?" *Journal of Pragmatics* 42, no. 7 (2010): 1951–1963.

50. Accept compliments in their responses: Andrea Golato, "German Compliment Responses," *Journal of Pragmatics* 34, no. 5 (2002): 547–571. Rather than its social functions: Heidi Byrnes, "Interactional Style in German and American Conversations," *Text* 6, no. 2 (1986): 189–206.

51. Nuria Lorenzo-Dus, "Compliment Responses among British and Spanish University Students: A Contrastive Study," *Journal of Pragmatics* 33, no. 1 (2001): 107–127.

52. Dawn Archer, "Slurs, Insults, (Backhanded) Compliments and Other Strategic Facework Moves," *Language Sciences* 52 (2015): 82–97.

53. Jonathan D. Brown, Shelly D. Farnham, and Kathleen E. Cook, "Emotional Responses to Changing Feedback: Is It Better to Have Won and Lost Than Never to Have Won at All?" *Journal of Personality* 70, no. 1 (2002): 127–141; Simon Moss and Ronald Francis, *The Science of Management: Fighting Fads and Fallacies with Evidence-based Practice* (Samford Valley, Queensland: Australian Academic Press, 2007).

7   Pragmatics in a Changing World

1. Yanrong Chang, "You Think I Am Stupid? Face Needs in Intercultural Conflicts," *Journal of Intercultural Communication* 25 (2011).

2. Justin Kruger, Nicholas Epley, Jason Parker, and Zhi-Wen Ng, "Egocentrism Over E-mail: Can We Communicate as Well as We Think?" *Journal of Personality and Social Psychology* 89, no. 6 (2005): 925–936; Monica A. Riordan and Lauren A. Trichtinger, "Overconfidence at the Keyboard: Confidence and Accuracy in Interpreting Affect in E-mail Exchanges," *Human Communication Research* 43, no. 1 (2017): 1–24.

3. Kirk W. Duthler, "The Politeness of Requests Made via Email and Voicemail: Support for the Hyperpersonal Model," *Journal of Computer-Mediated Communication* 11, no. 2 (2006): 500–521.

4. Maria Economidou-Kogetsidis, "'Please Answer Me as Soon as Possible': Pragmatic Failure in Nonnative Speakers' E-mail Requests to Faculty," *Journal of Pragmatics* 43, no. 13 (2011): 3193–3215.

5. Margaret Murphy and Mike Levy, "Politeness in Intercultural Email Communication: Australian and Korean Perspectives," *Journal of Intercultural Communication* 12 (2006).

6. Scott E. Fahlman, "Smiley Lore :-)," http://www.cs.cmu.edu/~sef/sefSmiley.htm.

7. Morton A. Gernsbacher, "Internet-Based Communication," *Discourse Processes* 51, nos. 5–6 (2014): 359–373.

8. Alexis C. Madrigal, "The first emoticon may have appeared in … 1648," *Atlantic*, April 2014, http://www.theatlantic.com/technology/archive/2014/04/the-first-emoticon-may-have-appeared-in-1648/360622/.

9. Fred Benenson, ed., *Emoji Dick; or The Whale*, 2010, http://www.czyborra.com/unicode/emojidick.pdf.

10. Katy Waldman, "This Year's Word of the Year Isn't Even a Word," *Slate*, November 16, 2015, http://www.slate.com/blogs/lexicon_valley/2015/11/16/the_face_with_tears_of_joy_emoji_is_the_word_of_the_year_says_oxford_dictionaries.html.

11. Matt Alt, "Why Japan Got Over Emojis," *Slate*, December 2015, http://www.slate.com/articles/technology/technology/2015/12/emojis_are_no_longer_cool_in_japan.2.html.

12. Joseph B. Walther and Kyle P. D'Addario, "The Impacts of Emoticons on Message Interpretation in Computer-Mediated Communication," *Social Science Computer Review* 19, no. 3 (2001): 324–347.

13. Zuzana Komrsková, "The Use of Emoticons in Polite Phrases of Greeting and Thanks," *World Academy of Science, Engineering, and Technology: International Journal of Social, Behavioral, Educational, Economic, and Management Engineering* 9, no. 4 (2015): 1313–1316.

14. Taku Sugimoto and James A. Levin, "Multiple Literacies and Multimedia: A Comparison of Japanese and American Uses of the Internet," in *Global Literacies and the World-Wide Web*, ed. Gail E. Hawisher and Cynthia L. Self (London: Routledge, 2000), 133–153.

15. Hyisung C. Hwang and David Matsumoto, "Nonverbal Behaviors and Cross-Cultural Communication in the New Era," in *Language and Intercultural Communication in the New Era*, ed. Farzad Sharifan and Maryam Jamarini (New York: Routledge, 2013), 116–137.

16. Jaram Park, Vladimir Barash, Clay Fink, and Cha Meeyoung Cha, "Emoticon Style: Interpreting Differences in Emoticons across Cultures," in *Proceedings of the Seventh International AAAI Conference on Weblogs and Social Media* (Palo Alto, CA: AAAI Press, 2013), 466–475.

17. Whitney Phillips, *This Is Why We Can't Have Nice Things: Mapping the Relationship between Online Trolling and Mainstream Culture* (Cambridge, MA: MIT Press, 2015).

18. Claire Hardaker, "Trolling in Asynchronous Computer-Mediated Communication: From User Discussions to Academic Definitions," *Journal of Politeness Research* 6 (2010): 215–242, at 224.

19. Susan Herring, Kirk Job-Sluder, Rebecca Scheckler, and Sasha Barab, "Searching for Safety Online: Managing 'Trolling' in a Feminist Forum," *Information Society* 18, no. 5 (2002): 371–384; Tammara Combs Turner, Marc A. Smith, Danyel Fisher, and Howard T. Welser, "Picturing Usenet: Mapping Computer-Mediated Collective Action," *Journal of Computer-Mediated Communication* 10, no. 4 (2005).

20. Jonathan Bishop, "Representations of 'Trolls' in Mass Media Communication: A Review of Media-Texts and Moral Panics Relating to 'Internet Trolling.'" *International Journal of Web Based Communities* 10, no. 1 (2014): 7–24.

21. Daniel D. Turner, "Comments Gone Wild: Trolls, Flames, and the Crisis at Online Newspapers" (2010), http://static1.squarespace.com/static/5133ffdde4b0c6fb04ddab8f/t/5217da16e4b000bbb34b75d2/1377294870640/CrisisInCommenting.pdf.

22. Fruzsina Eördögh, "Gamergate and the New Horde of Digital Saboteurs," *Christian Science Monitor*, November 25, 2014, http://www .csmonitor.com/Technology/Tech-Culture/2014/1125/Gamergate-and -the-new-horde-of-digital-saboteurs.

23. Richard R. Jurin, Donny Roush, and Jeff Danter, *Environmental Communication: Skills and Principles for Natural Resource Managers, Scientists, and Engineers*, 2nd ed. (Dordrecht: Springer, 2010).

24. Kirk St. Amant, "When Cultures and Computers Collide: Rethinking Computer-Mediated Communication According to International and Intercultural Communication Expectations," *Journal of Business and Technical Communication* 16, no. 2 (2002): 196–214.

25. For more information on this incident, see Alexandra Topping, "Sign Language Interpreter at Mandela Memorial Accused of Being a Fake," *Guardian*, December 11, 2013, https://www.theguardian.com/ society/2013/dec/11/mandela-memorial-sign-language-interpreter -making-it-up-fake. For Loening's comments, see Euronews, "Mandela Memorial Sign Language Interpreter a 'Fraud,'" http://www.euronews .com/2013/12/11/mandela-memorial-sign-language-interpreter-a-fraud. See also Nicholas Kulish, John Eligon, and Alan Cowell, "Interpreter at Mandela Service Says He Is Schizophrenic and Saw Angels Descend," *New York Times*, December 12, 2013, http://www.nytimes.com/2013/12/ 13/world/africa/mandela-memorial-interpreter.html.

26. Kulish, Eligon, and Cowell, "Interpreter at Mandela Service Says He Is Schizophrenic."

27. For more on this story from a blog that describes itself as "focus[ing] on the full range of the deaf experience, publishing blogs by Deaf people across the UK and the world, laying eggs every weekday morning," see Charlie Swinbourne, "Exclusive: 'Fake' Sign Language Interpreter Mars Nelson Mandela Service for Deaf People Worldwide," *Limping Chicken*, December 10, 2013, http://limpingchicken.com/2013/ 12/10/fake-interpreter-mandela/.

28. The word "Deaf," with a capital *D*, refers to the culture, value systems, and sense of unity and purpose of those in Deaf communities.

The word "deaf," with a lowercase *d*, refers to the condition in which an individual partially or completely lacks the ability to hear. It is therefore possible to be deaf without being Deaf. Likewise, "Sign language," with a capital *S*, refers to languages that are used by Deaf communities to communicate. But "sign language," with a lowercase *s*, refers to any system that uses signs. American Sign Language (ASL) is a Sign language; underwater sign language, although actually based on ASL, is a sign language. It's similar to the difference between Romance languages and romance languages: the former, with a capital *R*, is a noun; the latter, with a lowercase *r*, is an adjective. World Federation of the Deaf, n.d., "Deaf Culture," https://wfdeaf.org/our-work/focus-areas/deaf-culture.

29. For the complete list of all 271 systems, see Gallaudet University Library, "Sign Language: Sign Languages of the World by Name," http://libguides.gallaudet.edu/content.php?pid=114804&sid=991940.

30. Other Sign languages are used by Deaf communities in Canada and the United States. In Quebec, the Sign language is Quebec Sign Language (La Langue des Signes Quebecoise, or LSQ); Inuit Sign Language (IUR, or Inuit Uukturausingit) is used in Nunavut; and in the Maritime Provinces the language is Maritimes Sign Language (MSL). In the United States, in addition to ASL there is Black American Sign Language, Hawaii Pidgin Sign Language, and Puerto Rican Sign Language (Gallaudet University Library, "Sign Language: Americas," http://libguides.gallaudet.edu/content.php?pid=114804&sid=997859). For more on the now obsolete Martha's Vineyard Sign Language, see Nora E. Groce, *Everyone Here Spoke Sign Language* (Cambridge, MA: Harvard University Press, 1985); and Cari Romm, "The Life and Death of Martha's Vineyard Sign Language," *Atlantic*, September 25, 2015, http://www.theatlantic.com/health/archive/2015/09/marthas-vineyard-sign-language-asl/407191/.

31. For a discussion of the relationships among Sign Languages, see Benice Woll, Rachel Sutton-Spence, and Frances Elton, "Multilingualism: The Global Approach to Sign Languages," in *The Sociolinguistics of Sign Languages*, ed. Ceil Lucas (Cambridge: Cambridge University Press, 2004), 8–32.

32. ASL is not the only language native to the United States that counts as a foreign language at some universities. Navajo and Cherokee are just two additional examples. For this reason, some schools are dropping the term "foreign language" in favor of "second language." For example, the University of Hawai'i refers to its language requirements as "Hawaiian or second language" requirements.

33. To read the complete argument, see Sherman Wilcox, "ASL as a Foreign Language Fact Sheet" (1991), http://www.unm.edu/~wilcox/UNM/facts.html.

34. For a review of the literature on shared signing communities and the need for more study on this issue, see Annelies Kusters, "Deaf Utopias? Reviewing the Sociocultural Literature on the World's 'Martha's Vineyard Situations,'" *Journal of Deaf Studies and Deaf Education* 15, no. 1 (2010): 3–16.

35. For a discussion of the ways in which the Japanese gay argot *onee kotoba* mixes both feminine and masculine speech styles, see Wim Lunsing and Claire Maree, "Shifting Speakers," in *Japanese Language, Gender, and Ideology: Cultural Models and Real People*, ed. Shigeko Okamoto and Janet S. Shibamoto Smith (New York: Oxford University Press, 2004), 92–109. See also Claire Maree, "Grrrl-Queens: One-Kotoba and the Negotiation of Heterosexist Gender Language Norms and Lesbo (Homo) Phobic Stereotypes in Japan," in *AsiaPacifiQUEER: Rethinking Genders and Sexualities*, ed. Fran Martin, Peter A. Jackson, Mark McLelland, and Audrey Yue (Champaign: University of Illinois Press, 2008), 67–84.

36. Michael A. K. Halliday, "Anti-Languages," *American Anthropologist* 78, no. 3 (1976): 570–584.

37. For more on isiNgqumo, see Stephanie Rudwick, "'Gay and Zulu, We Speak IsiNgqumo': Ethnolinguistic Identity Constructions," *Transformation: Critical Perspectives on Southern Africa* 74, no. 1 (2010): 112–134. See also Stephanie Rudwick and Mduduzi Ntuli, "IsiNgqumo— Introducing a Gay Black South African Linguistic Variety," *Southern African Linguistics and Applied Language Studies* 26, no. 4 (2008): 445–456.

38. Ken Cage, *Gayle: The Language of Kinks and Queens: A History and Dictionary of Gay Language in South Africa* (Houghton, South Africa: Jacana Media, 2003).

39. Paul Baker argues that Polari is more appropriately considered an antilanguage rather than an argot or other linguistic grouping. See Paul Baker, *Polari: The Lost Language of Gay Men* (London: Routledge, 2003).

40. For a discussion, see Tom Boellstorff, "'Authentic, of course!': Gay Language in Indonesia and Cultures of Belonging," in *Speaking in Queer Tongues: Globalization and Gay Language*, ed. William Leap and Tom Boellstorff (Champaign: University of Illinois Press, 2004), 181–201; and Tom Boellstorff, "*Gay* Language and Indonesia: Registering Belonging," *Journal of Linguistic Anthropology* 14, no. 2 (2004): 248–268.

41. Donn Hart and Harriett Hart, "Visayan Swardspeak: The Language of a Gay Community in the Philippines," *Crossroads: An Interdisciplinary Journal of Southeast Asian Studies* 5, no. 2 (1990): 27–49.

42. DelliSwararao Konduru, "Hijra's and Their Social Life in South Asia," *Imperial Journal of Interdisciplinary Research* 2, no. 4 (2016): 515–521.

43. William L. Leap, "Studying Lesbian and Gay Languages: Vocabulary, Text-Making, and Beyond," in *Out in Theory: The Emergence of Lesbian and Gay Anthropology*, ed. Ellen Lewin and William L. Leap (Champaign: University of Illinois Press, 2002), 128–154. For more on the language choices of LGBTQ people in Thailand, Israel, New Zealand, Germany, and the United States, see Leap Boellstorff, *Speaking in Queer Tongues*. For a discussion of gay men's English in the United States, see William L. Leap, *Word's Out: Gay Men's English* (Minneapolis: University of Minnesota Press, 1996).

44. For more on the historical connection between Polari and Elizabethan thieves' cant, see Baker, *Polari*. See also Heather Taylor, "Polari: A Sociohistorical Study of the Life and Decline of a Secret Language," doctoral dissertation, University of Manchester, 2007, as well as Paul Baker, "Polari: A Vibrant Language Born Out of Prejudice," *Guardian*, May 24, 2010, https://www.theguardian.com/commentisfree/2010/may/24/

polari-language-origins. For an article that discusses the idea that Elizabethan thieves' cant was more of a literary invention than an actual argot, see Linda Woodbridge, "Jest Books, the Literature of Roguery, and the Vagrant Poor in Renaissance England," *English Literary Renaissance* 33, no. 2 (2003): 201–210.

45. For an analysis of Martian use among youth, see Jie Dong, Caixia Du, Kasper Juffermans, Jinling Li, Piia Varis, and Xuan Wang, "Chinese in a Superdiverse World," in *Papers of the Anéla 2012 Applied Linguistics Conference*, ed. Nel de Jong, Kasper Juffermans, Merel Keijzer, and Laurent Rasier (Delft: Uitgeverij Eburon, 2012), 349–366. For a discussion of the use of Martian as a tool to avoid censorship, see Audrey M. Wozniak, "River-Crabbed Shitizens and Missing Knives: A Sociolinguistic Analysis of Trends in Chinese Language Use Online as a Result of Censorship," *Applied Linguistics Review* 6, no. 1 (2015): 97–120.

46. A bear is a large, usually hairy, man; a cub is a younger version of a bear; an otter is a thin version of a bear, also usually hairy; and pandas are—you guessed it—Asian bears.

47. Baker, *Polari*, 3.

48. Vladimir Žegarac and Martha C. Pennington, "Pragmatic Transfer in Intercultural Communication," in *Culturally Speaking: Managing Rapport through Talk across Cultures*, ed. Helen Spencer-Oatey (London: Continuum, 2004), 165–190.

49. Yule has used the term "pragmatic accent" to refer more generally to "aspects of our talk that indicate what we assume is communicated without being said." George Yule, *Pragmatics* (Oxford: Oxford University Press, 1996), 88.

50. Andrea deCapua, "An Analysis of Pragmatic Transfer in the Speech Acts of Complaints as Produced by Native Speakers of German in English," doctoral dissertation, Teachers College, Columbia University, New York, 1989.

51. In *Cultural Intelligence*, Earley and Ang point out that one pitfall in speaking a foreign language well is that native speakers may be less forgiving of mistakes. To avoid having this happen, they recommend

doing things to let native speakers know you may not be able to speak the language perfectly.

52. Gila A. Schauer, "Pragmatic Awareness in ESL and EFL Contexts: Contrast and Development," *Language Learning* 56, no. 2 (2006): 269–318.

53. Hidetoshi Saito and Masako Beecken, "An Approach to Instruction of Pragmatic Aspects: Implications of Pragmatic Transfer by American Learners of Japanese," *Modern Language Journal* 81, no. 3 (1997): 363–377.

54. Mark Snyder, "Self-Monitoring of Expressive Behavior," *Journal of Personality and Social Psychology* 30, no. 4 (1974): 526–537.

55. You can discover for yourself where you fall on the Self-Monitoring Scale by visiting the website of the Psychometrics Center at the University of Cambridge at http://discovermyprofile.com/selfmonitoring/introduction.html.

56. Hartmut Blank, René Ziegler, and Jessica de Bloom, "Self-Monitoring and Linguistic Adaptation," *Social Psychology* 43, no. 2 (2012): 67–80.

References

Abbadi, Renad. 2014. The construction of arguments in English and Arabic: A comparison of the linguistic strategies employed in editorials. *Argumentum* 10:724–746.

ABC News. n.d. Transcript of last moments of EgyptAir Flight 990. http://abcnews.go.com/International/story?id=82910&page=1.

Adams, Audrey. 2014. High-context humor. In *Encyclopedia of Humor Studies*, vol. 1, ed. Salvatore Attardo, 288–289. Thousand Oaks, CA: Sage.

Agar, Michael H. 1994. *Language Shock: Understanding the Culture of Conversation*. New York: William Morrow.

Allami, Hamid, and Amin Naeimi. 2011. A cross-linguistic study of refusals: An analysis of pragmatic competence development in Iranian EFL learners. *Journal of Pragmatics* 43 (1): 385–406.

Allan, Keith, and Kate Burridge. 1991. *Euphemism and Dysphemism: Language Used as Shield and Weapon*. New York: Oxford University Press.

Alt, Matt. 2015. Why Japan got over emojis. *Slate*. http://www.slate.com/articles/technology/technology/2015/12/emojis_are_no_longer_cool_in_japan.2.html.

Archer, Dawn. 2015. Slurs, insults, (backhanded) compliments, and other strategic facework moves. *Language Sciences* 52:82–97.

Ardila, Alfredo. 2005. Spanglish: An anglicized Spanish dialect. *Hispanic Journal of Behavioral Sciences* 27 (1): 60–81.

Aronsson, Karin, and Bengt Rundström. 1989. Cats, dogs, and sweets in the clinical negotiation of reality: On politeness and coherence in pediatric discourse. *Language in Society* 18 (4): 483–504.

Associated Press. 1999. Cussing canoeist convicted in Michigan. *Los Angeles Times*, June 12. http://articles.latimes.com/1999/jun/12/news/mn-45705.

Atai, Mahmoodreza, and Leyla Sadr. 2008. A cross-cultural study of hedging devices in discussion section of applied linguistics research articles. *Teaching English Language and Literature* 2:1–22.

Bachman, Helena, and Jane Omyanga-Omara. 2016. Muslim students face $5K fine if they refuse Swiss teachers' handshakes. *USA Today*, May 26. http://www.usatoday.com/story/news/world/2016/05/25/swiss-authorities-overule-teacher-handshake-ban/84899900.

Badarneh, Muhammad A. 2016. Proverbial rhetorical questions in colloquial Jordanian Arabic. *Folia Linguistica* 50 (1): 207–242.

Bailey, Charles J., and Karl Maroldt. 1977. The French lineage of English. In *Langues en contact—Pidgins—Creoles—Languages in Contact*, ed. Jürgen M. Meisel, 21–53. Tübingen: TBL-Verlag Narr.

Baker, Paul. 2003. *Polari: The Lost Language of Gay Men*. London: Routledge.

Baker, Paul. 2010. Polari, a vibrant language born out of prejudice. *Guardian*, May 24. https://www.theguardian.com/commentisfree/2010/may/24/polari-language-origins.

Bangerter, Adrian, and Herbert H. Clark. 2003. Navigating joint projects with dialogue. *Cognitive Science* 27 (2): 195–225.

Barlund, Dean C. 1975. Communicative styles in two cultures: Japan and the United States. In *Organization of Behavior in Face-to-Face Interaction*, ed. Adam Kendon, Richard M. Harris, and Mary R. Key, 427–456. The Hague: Mouton.

Barna, LaRay M. 1998. Stumbling blocks in intercultural communication. In *Basic Concepts of Intercultural Communication: Selected Readings*, ed. Milton J. Bennett, 173–190. Boston: Intercultural Press.

BBC News. 2016. Switzerland: Muslim students must shake teacher's hand. May 25. http://www.bbc.com/news/world-europe-36382596.

Béal, Christine. 1992. Did you have a good weekend: Or why there is no such thing as a simple question in cross-cultural encounters. *Australian Review of Applied Linguistics* 15 (1): 23–52.

Béal, Christine, and Kerry Mullan. 2013. Issues in conversational humour from a cross-cultural perspective: Comparing French and Australian corpora. In *Cross-Culturally Speaking, Speaking Cross-Culturally*, ed. Bert Peeters, Kerry Mullan, and Christine Béal, 107–139. Newcastle upon Tyne, UK: Cambridge Scholars Publishing.

Beebe, Leslie M., Tomoko Takahashi, and Robin Uliss-Weltz. 1990. Pragmatic transfer in ESL refusals. In *Developing Communicative Competence in a Second Language*, ed. Robin C. Scarcella, Elaine S. Anderson, and Stephen D. Krashen, 55–73. New York: Newbury.

Benenson, Fred, ed. 2010. *Emoji Dick; or, The Whale*. http://www.czyborra.com/unicode/emojidick.pdf.

Ben-Ze'ev, Aaron. 1994. The vindication of gossip. In *Good Gossip*, ed. Robert F. Goodman and Aaron Ben-Ze'ev, 11–24. Lawrence: University Press of Kansas.

Bishop, Jonathan. 2014. Representations of "trolls" in mass media communication: A review of media-texts and moral panics relating to "Internet trolling." *International Journal of Web Based Communities* 10 (1): 7–24.

Blank, Hartmut, René Ziegler, and Jessica de Bloom. 2012. Self-monitoring and linguistic adaptation. *Social Psychology* 43 (2): 67–80.

Blankenship, Kevin L., and Traci Y. Craig. 2006. Rhetorical question use and resistance to persuasion: An attitude strength hypothesis. *Journal of Language and Social Psychology* 25 (2): 111–128.

Blom, Jan-Petter, and John J. Gumperz. 2000. Social meaning in linguistic structure: Code-switching in Norway. In *The Bilingualism Reader*, ed. Li Wei, 111–136. New York: Routledge.

Bluedorn, Allen C., Carol F. Kaufman, and Paul M. Lane. 1992. How many things do you like to do at once? An introduction to monochronic and polychronic time. *Executive* 6 (4): 17–26.

Boellstorff, Tom. 2004a. "Authentic, of course!": Gay language in Indonesia and cultures of belonging. In *Speaking in Queer Tongues: Globalization and Gay Language*, ed. William Leap and Tom Boellstorff, 181–201. Champaign: University of Illinois Press.

Boellstorff, Tom. 2004b. Gay language and Indonesia: Registering belonging. *Journal of Linguistic Anthropology* 14 (2): 248–268.

Bond, Michael H., and Tat-Ming Lai. 1986. Embarrassment and code-switching into a second language. *Journal of Social Psychology* 126 (2): 179–186.

Borkin, Ann, and Susan M. Reinhart. 1978. Excuse me and I'm sorry. *TESOL Quarterly* 12 (1): 57–69.

Bouton, Lawrence F. 1994. Can NNS skill in interpreting implicature in American English be improved through explicit instruction? Pilot study. *Pragmatics and Language Learning* 5:88–109.

Bowe, Heather, Kylie Martin, and Howard Manns. 2014. *Communication across Cultures: Mutual Understanding in a Global World*. 2nd ed. Port Melbourne, Australia: Cambridge University Press.

Boxer, Diana. 1991. A descriptive analysis of indirect complaint sequences among speakers of American English. Doctoral diss., University of Pennsylvania, Philadelphia.

Boxer, Diana. 1993. Complaints as positive strategies: What the learner needs to know. *TESOL Quarterly* 27 (2): 277–299.

Bratanić, Maja. 2007. Nonverbal communication as a factor in linguistic cultural miscommunication. In *Fundamentals of Verbal and Nonverbal*

Communication and the Biometric Issue, ed. Ana Esposito, Maja Bratanić, Eric Keller, and Maria Marinaro, 82–91. Amsterdam: IOS Press.

Brennan, Susan E. 1996. Lexical entrainment in spontaneous dialog. In *Proceedings of the International Symposium on Spoken Dialogue*, 41–44. Philadelphia, PA: Acoustical Society of Japan.

Brennan, Susan E., and Herbert H. Clark. 1996. Conceptual pacts and lexical choice in conversation. *Journal of Experimental Psychology: Learning, Memory, and Cognition* 22 (6): 1482–1493.

Brown, Alan S. 2012. *The Tip of the Tongue State*. New York: Psychology Press.

Brown, Jonathan D., Shelly D. Farnham, and Kathleen E. Cook. 2002. Emotional responses to changing feedback: Is it better to have won and lost than never to have won at all? *Journal of Personality* 70 (1): 127–141.

Brown, Penelope, and Stephen C. Levinson. 1978/1987. *Politeness: Some Universals in Language Usage*. Cambridge: Cambridge University Press.

Byrnes, Heidi. 1986. Interactional style in German and American conversations. *Text* 6 (2): 189–206.

Cage, Ken. 2003. *Gayle: The Language of Kinks and Queens: A History and Dictionary of Gay Language in South Africa*. Houghton, South Africa: Jacana Media.

Cairo Times. 2004. Batouty clan stands united. http://web.archive.org/web/20040607134321/http://www.cairotimes.com/news/batfam.html.

Chang, Yanrong. 2011. You think I am stupid? Face needs in intercultural conflicts. *Journal of Intercultural Communication* 25.

Chen, Hongyin J. 1996. Cross-cultural comparison of English and Chinese metapragmatics in refusal. Indiana University. ERIC Document Reproduction Service No. ED 408 860.

Chen, Rong, and Dafu Yang. 2010. Responding to compliments in Chinese: Has it changed? *Journal of Pragmatics* 42 (7): 1951–1963.

Chicago Tribune. 1975. A-O.K.—but Oklahomski? *Chicago Tribune*, July 20. http://archives.chicagotribune.com/1975/07/20/page/2/article/a-o-k-but-oklahomski.

Choi, Sejung M., Wei-Na Lee, and Hee-Jung Kim. 2005. Lessons from the rich and famous: A cross-cultural comparison of celebrity endorsement in advertising. *Journal of Advertising* 34 (2): 85–98.

Chomsky, Noam. 1986. *Knowledge of Language: Its Nature, Origin, and Use*. Westport, CT: Praeger.

Chua, Elizabeth G., and William B. Gudykunst. 1987. Conflict resolution styles in low- and high-context cultures. *Communication Research Reports* 4 (1): 32–37.

Clark, Herbert H. 1979. Responding to indirect speech acts. *Cognitive Psychology* 11 (4): 430–477.

Clark, Herbert H. 1985. Language use and language users. In *Handbook of Social Psychology*, 3rd ed., ed. Gardner Lindzey and Elliot Aronson, 179–231. New York: Harper & Row.

Clark, Herbert H., and J. W. French. 1981. Telephone goodbyes. *Language in Society* 10 (1): 1–19.

Clark, Herbert H., and Susan E. Haviland. 1977. Comprehension and the given-new contract. In *Discourse Comprehension*, ed. Roy O. Freedle, 1–40. Norwood, NJ: Ablex.

Clark, Herbert H., and Catherine R. Marshall. 1981. Definite reference and mutual knowledge. In *Elements of Discourse Understanding*, ed. Aravind K. Joshe, Bruce H. Webber, and Ivan A. Sag, 10–63. Cambridge: Cambridge University Press.

Coppock, Liz. 2005. Politeness strategies in conversation closings. Unpublished MS. http://citeseerx.ist.psu.edu/viewdoc/download?doi=10.1.1.121.883&rep=rep1&type=pdf.

Corbett, Greville G. 1991. *Gender*. Cambridge: Cambridge University Press.

Costa, Albert, Alice Foucart, Sayuri Hayakawa, Melina Aparici, Jose Apesteguia, Joy Heafner, and Boaz Keysar. 2014. Your morals depend on language. *PLoS One* 9 (4): e94842.

Cutrone, Pino. 2005. A case study examining backchannels in conversations between Japanese–British dyads. *Multilingua* 24 (3): 237–274.

Cutrone, Pino. 2013. *Assessing Pragmatic Competence in the Japanese EFL Context: Towards the Learning of Listener Responses*. Newcastle upon Tyne, UK: Cambridge Scholars Publishing.

Daly, Nicola, Janet Holmes, Jonathan Newton, and Maria Stubbe. 2004. Expletives as solidarity signals in FTAs on the factory floor. *Journal of Pragmatics* 36 (5): 945–964.

D'Andrade, Roy G., and Myron Wish. 1985. Speech act theory in quantitative research on interpersonal behavior. *Discourse Processes* 8 (2): 229–259.

Dastpak, Mehdi, and Fatemeh Mollaei. 2011. A comparative study of ostensible invitations in English and Persian. *Higher Education of Social Science* 1 (1): 33–42.

Davies, Catherine Evans. 2003. How English-learners joke with native speakers: An interactional sociolinguistic perspective on humor as collaborative discourse across cultures. *Journal of Pragmatics* 35 (9): 1361–1385.

De Bellaigue, Christopher. 2012. Talk like an Iranian. *Atlantic*, September. http://www.theatlantic.com/magazine/archive/2012/09/talk-like-an-iranian/309056/.

deCapua, Andrea. 1989. An analysis of pragmatic transfer in the speech acts of complaints as produced by native speakers of German in English. Doctoral diss., Teachers College, Columbia University, New York.

Deloussis, Evangelllos. 2004. A cross-cultural comparison of organizational culture: Evidence from universities in the Arab world and Japan. *Cross Cultural Management* 11 (1): 15–34.

Deutscher, Guy. 2010. *Through the Language Glass: Why the World Looks Different in Other Languages*. New York: Metropolitan Books.

Dewaele, Jean-Marc. 2004a. The emotional force of swearwords and taboo words in the speech of multilinguals. *Journal of Multilingual and Multicultural Development* 25 (2–3): 204–222.

Dewaele, Jean-Marc. 2004b. Blistering barnacles! What language do multilinguals swear in?! *Estudios de Sociolingüística* 5 (1): 83–105.

Dong, Jie, Caixia Du, Kasper Juffermans, Jinling Li, Piia Varis, and Xuan Wang. 2012. Chinese in a superdiverse world. In *Papers of the Anéla 2012 Applied Linguistics Conference*, ed. Nel de Jong, Kasper Juffermans, Merel Keijzer, and Laurent Rasier, 349–366. Delft: Uitgeverij Eburon.

Dong, Ping, Xun I. Huang, and Robert S. Wyer Jr. 2013. The illusion of saving face: How people symbolically cope with embarrassment. *Psychological Science* 24 (10): 2005–2012.

Dore, John. 1975. Holophrases, speech acts and language universals. *Journal of Child Language* 2 (1): 21–40.

Dorren, Gaston. 2015. *Lingo: Around Europe in Sixty Languages*. New York: Atlantic Monthly Press.

Duthler, Kirk W. 2006. The politeness of requests made via email and voicemail: Support for the hyperpersonal model. *Journal of Computer-Mediated Communication* 11 (2): 500–521.

Dutton, Kevin. 2012. Psychopaths recognize emotions better than most normal people. *Globe and Mail*, November 1. https://www.sott.net/article/253012-Psychopaths-recognise-emotions-better-than-most-normal-people.

Duranti, Alessandro. 1997. Universal and culture-specific properties of greetings. *Journal of Linguistic Anthropology* 7 (1): 63–97.

Earley, P. Christopher, and Soon Ang. 2003. *Cultural Intelligence: Individual Interactions across Cultures*. Stanford, CA: Stanford University Press.

Ebsworth, Miriam E., Jean W. Bodman, and Mary Carpenter. 1996. Cross-cultural realization of greetings in American English. In *Speech*

Acts across Cultures: Challenges to Communication in a Second Language, ed. Susan M. Gass and Joyce Neu, 89–108. Berlin: Mouton de Gruyter.

Economidou-Kogetsidis, Maria. 2011. "Please answer me as soon as possible": Pragmatic failure in nonnative speakers' e-mail requests to faculty. *Journal of Pragmatics* 43 (13): 3193–3215.

Egyptian Civil Aviation Authority. 1999. *Report of Investigation of Accident.* October 31. https://web.archive.org/web/20110622102818/http://www.ntsb.gov/events/ea990/docket/ecaa_report.pdf.

Ekman, Paul. 1992. An argument for basic emotions. *Cognition and Emotion* 6 (3–4): 169–200.

Elfenbein, Hillary A., Martin Beaupré, Manon Lévesque, and Ursula Hess. 2007. Toward a dialect theory: Cultural differences in the expression and recognition of posed facial expressions. *Emotion* 7 (1): 131–146.

Eördögh, Fruzsina. 2014. Gamergate and the new horde of digital saboteurs. *Christian Science Monitor,* November 25. http://www.csmonitor.com/Technology/Tech-Culture/2014/1125/Gamergate-and-the-new-horde-of-digital-saboteurs.

Eshreteh, Mahmood K. M. 2015. Re-assessing cross-cultural pragmatics: Insistence as a marker of affiliation and connectedness. *Cross-Cultural Communication* 11 (1): 1–7.

Eslami, Zohreh R. 2005. Invitations in Persian and English: Ostensible or genuine? *Intercultural Pragmatics* 2 (4): 453–480.

Eslami, Zohreh R. 2010. How to develop appropriate refusal strategies. In *Speech Act Performance: Theoretical, Empirical, and Methodological Issues,* ed. Alicia Martínze-Flor and Esther Usó-Juan, 217–236. Amsterdam: John Benjamins.

Eslami-Rasekh, Zohreh. 2005. Raising the pragmatic awareness of language learners. *ELT Journal* 59 (3): 199–208.

Euronews. 2013. Mandela memorial sign language interpreter a "fraud." http://www.euronews.com/2013/12/11/mandela-memorial-sign-language-interpreter-a-fraud.

Evan, Stephen. 2011. What Paddington tells us about German versus British Manners. *BBC News*, May 26. http://www.bbc.com/news/world-europe-13545386.

Evans, Ben. 2012. *At Home in Space: The Late Seventies into the Eighties*. New York: Springer.

Fahlman, Scott E. n.d. Smiley Lore :-). http://www.cs.cmu.edu/~sef/sefSmiley.htm.

Fang, Jie. 2010. A study of pragmatic failure in cross-cultural communication. *Sino-U.S. English Teaching* 7 (12): 42–46.

Fant, Lars. 2015. Cultural mismatch in conversation: Spanish and Scandinavian communicative behaviour in negotiation settings. *Hermes: Journal of Language and Communication in Business* 2 (3): 247–265.

Feldman, Robert S. 1985. Nonverbal behavior, race, and the classroom teacher. *Theory into Practice* 24 (1): 45–49.

Félix-Brasdefer, J. César. 2008a. *Politeness in Mexico and the United States: A Contrastive Study of the Realization and Perception of Refusals*. Amsterdam: John Benjamins.

Félix-Brasdefer, J. César. 2008b. Perceptions of refusals to invitations: Exploring the minds of foreign language learners. *Language Awareness* 17 (3): 195–211.

Firth, Raymond. 1972. Verbal and bodily rituals of greeting and parting. In *The Interpretation of Ritual: Essays in Honour of A. I. Richards*, ed. Jean S. La Fontaine, 1–38. London: Routledge.

Fox News Politics. December 5, 2014. Clinton says America should "empathize" with its enemies. http://www.foxnews.com/politics/2014/12/05/clinton-says-america-should-empathize-with-its-enemies.html.

Frith, Uta, and Frederique de Vignemont. 2005. Egocentrism, allocentrism, and Asperger syndrome. *Consciousness and Cognition* 14 (4): 719–738.

Gallaudet University Library. n.d. Sign language: Americas. http://libguides.gallaudet.edu/content.php?pid=114804&sid=997859.

Gallaudet University Library. n.d. Sign language: Sign languages of the world by name. http://libguides.gallaudet.edu/content.php?pid=114804 &sid=991940.

Gardner-Chloros, Penelope. 2009. *Code-Switching*. Cambridge: Cambridge University Press.

Gelfand, Michele J., Jana L. Raver, Lisa Nishii, Lisa M. Leslie, Janetta Lun, Beng Chong Lim, Lili Duan, et al. 2011. Differences between tight and loose cultures: A 33-nation study. *Science* 332:1100–1104.

Georgetown University. December 3, 2014. *Clinton: Including Women Essential to Peace Process*. https://www.georgetown.edu/news/hillary -clinton-security-inclusive-leadership.html.

Gernsbacher, Morton A. 2014. Internet-based communication. *Discourse Processes* 51 (5–6): 359–373.

Geyer, Naomi. 2010. Teasing and ambivalent face in Japanese multi-party discourse. *Journal of Pragmatics* 42 (8): 2120–2130.

Ghouse, Mike. 2013. Islam misunderstood: *Tawakkaltu ala-Allah*, In God we trust. *Muslim Speaker*, May 15. http://muslimspeakers.blogspot .com/2013/05/islam-misunderstood-tawakkaltu-ala.html.

Giles, Howard, Justine Coupland, and Nikolas Coupland, eds. 1991. *Contexts of Accommodation: Studies in Emotion and Social Interaction*. Cambridge: Cambridge University Press.

Giles, Howard, Donald M. Taylor, and Richard Bourhis. 1973. Towards a theory of interpersonal accommodation through language: Some Canadian data. *Language in Society* 2 (2): 177–192.

Gleason, Jean B., Rivka Y. Perlmann, and Esther B. Greif. 1984. What's the magic word: Learning language through politeness routines. *Discourse Processes* 7 (4): 493–502.

Go, Billy. 2015. How to find your "Korean age." February 20. https:// www.dramafever.com/news/how-to-find-your-korean-age/

Goddard, C. 2015. "Swear words" and "curse words" in Australian (and American) English: At the crossroads of pragmatics, semantics and soci-olinguistics. *Intercultural Pragmatics* 12 (2): 189–218.

Goetz, Jennifer, and Dacher Keltner. 2007. Shifting meanings of self-conscious emotions across cultures. In *The Self-Conscious Emotions: Theory and Research*, ed. Jessica L. Tracy, Richard W. Robins, and June P. Tangney, 153–173. New York: Guilford Press.

Goffman, Erving. 1955/1967. On face-work: An analysis of ritual elements of social interaction. *Psychiatry* 18 (3): 213–231.

Goffman, Erving. 1963. *Behavior in Public Places: Notes on the Social Organization of Gatherings*. New York: Simon & Schuster.

Golato, Andrea. 2002. German compliment responses. *Journal of Pragmatics* 34 (5): 547–571.

Goleman, Daniel. 2006. *Social Intelligence: The New Science of Human Relationships*. New York: Bantam Books.

Goleman, Daniel. 2007. Three kinds of empathy: Cognitive, emotional, compassionate. Danielgoleman.info, June 12. http://www.danielgoleman.info/three-kinds-of-empathy-cognitive-emotional-compassionate.

Görlach, Manfred. 1986. Middle English—a creole? In *Linguistics across Historical and Geographical Boundaries*, vol. 1, ed. Dieter Kastovsky and Alexandr Szwedek, 329–344. Berlin: Mouton de Gruyter.

Görtz, Birgit. 2013. The "Du/Sie" dilemma in German. *Deutsche Welle*, May 1. http://www.dw.de/the-du-sie-dilemma-in-german/a-16494631.

Grandlund, Markus, and Kari Lukka. 1998. Towards increasing business orientation: Finnish management accountants in a changing cultural context. *Management Accounting Research* 9 (2): 185–211.

Gravano, Agustín, and Julia Hirschberg. 2012. A corpus-based study of interruptions in spoken dialogue. *Interspeech* 2012:855–858.

Gray, John. 1992. *Men Are from Mars, Women Are from Venus: A Practical Guide for Improving Communication and Getting What You Want in Your Relationships*. New York: Harper Collins.

Greenberg, Joseph H. 1963. Some universals of grammar with particular reference to the order of meaningful elements. In *Universals of Grammar*, ed. Joseph H. Greenberg, 73–113. Cambridge, MA: MIT Press.

Grice, H. Paul. 1975. Logic and conversation. In *Syntax and Semantics, vol. 3: Speech Acts*, ed. Peter Cole and Jerry L. Morgan, 41–58. New York: Academic Press.

Grice, H. Paul. 1978. Further notes on logic and conversation. In *Syntax and Semantics*, vol. 9: *Pragmatics*, ed. Peter Cole, 183–197. New York: Academic Press.

Groce, Nora E. 1985. *Everyone Here Spoke Sign Language.* Cambridge, MA: Harvard University Press.

Haidt, Jonathan, and Darcher Keltner. 1999. Culture and facial expression: Open-ended methods find more expressions and a gradient of recognition. *Cognition and Emotion* 13 (3): 225–266.

Hall, Edward T. 1966. *The Hidden Dimension.* New York: Doubleday.

Hall, Edward T. 1976. *Beyond Culture.* New York: Doubleday.

Halliday, Michael A. K. 1976. Anti-languages. *American Anthropologist* 78 (3): 570–584.

Hardaker, Claire. 2010. Trolling in asynchronous computer-mediated communication: From user discussions to academic definitions. *Journal of Politeness Research* 6:215–242.

Hart, Donn, and Harriet Hart. 1990. Visayan Swardspeak: The language of a gay community in the Philippines. *Crossroads: An Interdisciplinary Journal of Southeast Asian Studies* 5 (2): 27–49.

Hartford, Beverly S., and Kathleen Bardovi-Harlig. 1992. Closing the conversation: Evidence from the academic advising session. *Discourse Processes* 15 (1): 93–116.

Hartley, Laura. 1998. A sociolinguistic analysis of face-threat and face-management in potential complaint situations. Doctoral diss., Department of Linguistics, Michigan State University, East Lansing.

Haskell, Kari. 2002. The people v. the potty mouth. *New York Times Week in Review*, April 7. http://www.nytimes.com/2002/04/07/weekinreview/the-people-v-potty-mouth.html.

Hattori, Takahiko. 1985. A study of nonverbal intercultural communication between Japanese and Americans—focusing on the use of the eyes. *Japan Association of Language Teachers Journal* 8:109–118.

Haugh, Michael. 2010. Jocular mockery, (dis)affliation, and face. *Journal of Pragmatics* 42 (8): 2106–2119.

Haugh, Michael, and Derek Bousfield. 2012. Mock impoliteness, jocular mockery and jocular abuse in Australian and British English. *Journal of Pragmatics* 44 (9): 1099–1144.

Hayashi, Reiko. 1988. Simultaneous talk—from the perspective of floor management of English and Japanese speakers. *World Englishes* 7 (3): 269–288.

Heinlein, Robert A. 1961. *Stranger in a Strange Land*. New York: Putnam.

Heinz, Bettina. 2003. Backchannel responses as strategic responses in bilingual speakers' conversations. *Journal of Pragmatics* 35 (7): 1113–1142.

Herbert, Robert K. 1989. The ethnography of English compliments and compliment responses: A contrastive sketch. In *Contrastive Pragmatics*, ed. Wieslaw Oleksy, 3–35. Amsterdam: John Benjamins.

Heredia, Roberto R., and Jeanette Altarriba. 2001. Bilingual language mixing: Why do bilinguals code-switch? *Current Directions in Psychological Science* 10 (5): 164–168.

Herring, Susan C. 1991. The grammaticalization of rhetorical questions in Tamil. In *Approaches to Grammaticalization*, vol. 1: *Focus on Theoretical and Methodological Issues*, ed. Elizabeth Closs Traugott and Bernd Heine, 253–284. Amsterdam: John Benjamins.

Herring, Susan, Kirk Job-Sluder, Rebecca Scheckler, and Sasha Barab. 2002. Searching for safety online: Managing "trolling" in a feminist forum. *Information Society* 18 (5): 371–384.

Hinkel, Eli. 1997. Indirectness in L1 and L2 academic writing. *Journal of Pragmatics* 27 (3): 361–386.

Hirose, Keiko. 2003. Comparing L1 and L2 organizational patterns in the argumentative writing of Japanese EFL students. *Journal of Second Language Writing* 12 (2): 181–209.

Ho, David Y. F., Wai Fu, and Siu Man Ng. 2004. Guilt, shame, and embarrassment: Revelations of face and self. *Culture and Psychology* 10 (1): 64–84.

Hofstede, Geert H. 2001. *Culture's Consequences: Comparing Values, Behaviors, Institutions, and Organizations across Nations.* 2nd ed. Thousand Oaks, CA: Sage.

Holmes, Janet. 1988. Paying compliments: A sex preferential politeness strategy. *Journal of Pragmatics* 12 (4): 445–465.

Holmes, Janet. 1990a. Hedges and boosters in women's and men's speech. *Language and Communication* 10 (3): 185–205.

Holmes, Janet. 1990b. Politeness strategies in New Zealand women's speech. In *New Zealand Ways of Speaking English*, ed. Allan Bell and Janet Homes, 252–276. Clevendon, UK: Multilingual Matters.

Holmes, Janet. 1999. *Women, Men, and Politeness.* London: Routledge.

Holmes, Janet. 2013. *An Introduction to Sociolinguistics.* London: Routledge.

Holtgraves, Thomas M. 1997. Styles of language use: Individual and cultural variability in conversational indirectness. *Journal of Personality and Social Psychology* 73 (3): 624–637.

Holtgraves, Thomas M. 2002. *Language as Social Action: Social Psychology and Language Use.* Mahwah, NJ: Erlbaum.

Holtgraves, Thomas M., and Yang Joong-nam. 1992. Interpersonal underpinnings of request strategies: General principles and differences due to culture and gender. *Journal of Personality and Social Psychology* 62 (2): 246–256.

House, Juliane. 2010. Impoliteness in Germany: Intercultural encounters in everyday and institutional talk. *Intercultural Pragmatics* 7 (4): 561–595.

Hwang, Hyisung C., and David Matsumoto. 2013. Nonverbal behaviors and cross-cultural communication in the new era. In *Language and Intercultural Communication in the New Era*, ed. Farzad Sharifan and Maryam Jamarini, 116–137. New York: Routledge.

Hyland, Ken. 2000. Hedges, boosters, and lexical invisibility: Noticing modifiers in academic texts. *Language Awareness* 9 (4): 179–197.

Hyland, Ken, and John Milton. 1997. Qualification and certainty in L1 and L2 students' writing. *Journal of Second Language Writing* 6 (2): 183–205.

Imahori, T. Todd, and William R. Cupach. 1994. A cross-cultural comparison of the interpretation and management of face: US American and Japanese responses to embarrassing predicaments. *International Journal of Intercultural Relations* 18 (2): 193–219.

Isaacs, Ellen A., and Herbert H. Clark. 1990. Ostensible invitations. *Language in Society* 19 (4): 493–509.

Jankowiak, William R., Shelly L. Volsche, and Justin R. Garcia. 2015. Is the romantic–sexual kiss a near human universal? *American Anthropologist* 117 (3): 535–539.

Jay, Timothy, and Kristen Janschewitz. 2008. The pragmatics of swearing. *Journal of Politeness Research* 4 (2): 267–288.

Johnson-Laird, Philip N., and Peter C. Wason. 1977. *Thinking: Readings in Cognitive Science*. Cambridge: Cambridge University Press.

Jones, Edward E., and Victor A. Harris. 1967. The attribution of attitudes. *Journal of Experimental Social Psychology* 3 (1): 1–24.

Jørgensen, J. Normann. 2005. Plurilingual conversations among bilingual adolescents. *Journal of Pragmatics* 37 (3): 391–402.

Jurin, Richard R., Donny Roush, and Jeff Danter. 2010. *Environmental Communication: Skills and Principles for Natural Resource Managers, Scientists, and Engineers*. 2nd ed. Dordrecht: Springer.

Justus, Jeremy C. 2006. Piss stance: Private parts in public places; An analysis of the men's room and gender control. *Studies in Popular Culture* 28 (3): 59–70.

Kádar, Daniel Z., and Michael Haugh. 2013. *Understanding Politeness*. Cambridge: Cambridge University Press.

Kalliny, Morris, Kevin W. Cruthirds, and Michael S. Minor. 2006. Differences between American, Egyptian and Lebanese humor styles. *International Journal of Cross Cultural Management* 6 (1): 121–134.

Kecskes, Istvan. 2014. *Intercultural Pragmatics*. Oxford: Oxford University Press.

Kecskes, Istvan, Dan E. Davidson, and Richard Brecht. 2005. The foreign language perspective. *Intercultural Pragmatics* 2 (4): 361–368.

Keenan, Elinor Ochs. 1976. The universality of conversational postulates. *Language in Society* 5 (1): 67–80.

Kelley, Harold H. 1973. The process of causal attribution. *American Psychologist* 28 (2): 107–128.

Keltner, Dacher, and Brenda N. Buswell. 1997. Embarrassment: Its distinct form and appeasement functions. *Psychological Bulletin* 122 (3): 250–270.

Keltner, Dacher, Lisa Capps, Ann M. Kring, Randall C. Young, and Erin A. Heerey. 2001. Just teasing: A conceptual analysis and empirical review. *Psychological Bulletin* 127 (2): 229–248.

Khadem, Akram, and Abbas E. Rasekh. 2012. Discourse structure of Persian telephone conversation: A description of the closing. *International Review of the Social Sciences and Humanities* 2 (2): 150–161.

Kim, Donghoon, Yigang Pan, and Heung S. Park. 1998. High- versus low-context culture: A comparison of Chinese, Korean, and American cultures. *Psychology and Marketing* 15 (6): 507–521.

Kim, Wonsun, Xiaowen Guan, and Hee S. Park. 2012. Face and face-work: A cross-cultural comparison of managing politeness norms in the

United States and Korea. *International Journal of Communication* 6 (1): 1100–1118.

Knorr, Andreas, and Andreas Arndt. 2003. *Why did Wal-Mart fail in Germany?* Materialien des Wissenschaftsschwerpunktes "Globalisierung der Weltwirtschaft," 24. Bremen: Universität Bremen.

Komrsková, Zuzana. 2015. The use of emoticons in polite phrases of greeting and thanks. *International Journal of Social, Behavioral, Educational, Economic, Business, and Industrial Engineering* 9 (4): 1313–1316.

Kondo, Sachiko. 2008. Effects on pragmatic development through awareness-raising instruction: Refusals by Japanese EFL learners. In *Investigating Pragmatics in Foreign Language Learning, Teaching and Testing*, ed. Eva A. Soler and Alicia Martínez-Flor, 153–177. Bristol, UK: Multilingual Matters.

Konduru, Delliswararao. 2016. Hijra's and their social life in South Asia. *Imperial Journal of Interdisciplinary Research* 2 (4): 515–521.

Koshik, Irene. 2005. *Beyond Rhetorical Questions: Assertive Questions in Everyday Interaction*. Amsterdam: John Benjamins.

Krauss, Robert M., and Sam Glucksberg. 1977. Social and nonsocial speech. *Scientific American* 236 (2): 100–105.

Kretzenbacher, Heinz L. 2011. Perceptions of national and regional standards of addressing in Germany and Austria. *Pragmatics* 21 (1): 69–83.

Kreutz, Heinz, and Annette Harres. 1997. Some observations on the distribution and function of hedging in German and English academic writing. In *Culture and Styles of Academic Discourse*, ed. Anna Duszak, 181–202. Berlin: Mouton de Grutyer.

Kreuz, Roger J. 1996. The use of verbal irony: Cues and constraints. In *Metaphor: Implications and Applications*, ed. Jeffrey S. Mio and Albert N. Katz, 23–38. Mahwah, NJ: Erlbaum.

Kreuz, Roger J., Max A. Kassler, Laurie Coppenrath, and Bonnie McLain Allen. 1999. Tag questions and common ground effects in the perception of verbal irony. *Journal of Pragmatics* 31 (12): 1685–1700.

Kreuz, Roger J., and Richard M. Roberts. 1993. When collaboration fails: Consequences of pragmatic errors in conversation. *Journal of Pragmatics* 19 (3): 239–252.

Kruger, Justin, Nicholas Epley, Jason Parker, and Zhi-Wen Ng. 2005. Egocentrism over e-mail: Can we communicate as well as we think? *Journal of Personality and Social Psychology* 89 (6): 925–936.

Kulish, Nicholas, John Eligon, and Alan Cowell. 2013. Interpreter at Mandela service says he is schizophrenic and saw angels descend. *New York Times*, December 12. http://www.nytimes.com/2013/12/13/world/africa/mandela-memorial-interpreter.html.

Kusters, Annelies. 2010. Deaf utopias? Reviewing the sociocultural literature on the world's "Martha's Vineyard situations." *Journal of Deaf Studies and Deaf Education* 15 (1): 3–16.

Kwon, Jihyn. 2004. Expressing refusals in Korean and American English. *Multilingua* 23 (4): 339–364.

Lakoff, George. 1973. Hedges: A study in meaning criteria and the logic of fuzzy concepts. *Journal of Philosophical Logic* 2 (4): 458–508.

Lakoff, Robin. 1975. *Language and Woman's Place*. New York: Harper and Row.

Language Realm. n.d. Du and Sie. http://www.languagerealm.com/german/du_sie.php.

Lanza, Elizabeth. 1992. Can bilingual two-year-olds code switch? *Journal of Child Language* 19 (3): 633–658.

Leap, William L. 1996. *Word's Out: Gay Men's English*. Minneapolis: University of Minnesota Press.

Leap, William L. 2002. Studying lesbian and gay languages: Vocabulary, text-making, and beyond. In *Out in Theory: The Emergence of Lesbian and Gay Anthropology*, ed. Ellen Lewin and William L. Leap, 128–154. Champaign: University of Illinois Press.

Leap, William L., and Tom Boellstorff. 2004. *Speaking in Queer Tongues: Globalization and Gay Language*. Champaign: University of Illinois Press.

Lee, Candis. 1990. *Cute yaw haiya—nah!* Hawai'i Creole English compliments and their responses: Implications for cross-cultural failure. *University of Hawai'i Working Papers in ESL* 9 (1): 115–160.

Leech, Geoffrey N. 1983. *Principles of Pragmatics*. London: Longman.

Leech, Geoffrey. 2014. *The Pragmatics of Politeness*. Oxford: Oxford University Press.

Leggitt, John S., and Raymond W. Gibbs Jr. 2000. Emotional reactions to verbal irony. *Discourse Processes* 29 (1): 1–24.

Lewis, Richard D. 2006. *When Cultures Collide: Leading across Cultures*. 3rd ed. Boston, MA: Nicholas Brealey.

Li, Han Z. 2001. Cooperative and intrusive interruptions in inter- and intracultural dyadic discourse. *Journal of Language and Social Psychology* 20 (3): 259–284.

Li, Han Z., Yum Young-ok, Robin Yates, Laura Aguilera, Ying Mao, and Yue Zheng. 2005. Interruption and involvement in discourse: Can intercultural interlocutors be trained? *Journal of Intercultural Communication Research* 34 (4): 233–254.

Li, Jin, Lianqin Wang, and Kurt Fischer. 2004. The organisation of Chinese shame concepts? *Cognition and Emotion* 18 (6): 767–797.

Licoppe, Christian. 2014. Living inside location-aware mobile social information: The pragmatics of Foursquare notifications. In *Living inside Mobile Social Information*, ed. James E. Katz, 109–130. Dayton, OH: Greyden Press.

Lingli, Duan, and Anchalee Wannaruk. 2010. The effects of explicit and implicit instruction in English refusals. *Chinese Journal of Applied Linguistics* 33 (3): 93–109.

Link, Kristen E., and Roger J. Kreuz. 2005. The comprehension of ostensible speech acts. *Journal of Language and Social Psychology* 24 (3): 227–251.

Ljung, Magnus. 2011. *Swearing: A Cross-Cultural Linguistic Study*. New York: Palgrave Macmillan.

Lorenzo-Dus, Nuria. 2001. Compliment responses among British and Spanish university students: A contrastive study. *Journal of Pragmatics* 33 (1): 107–127.

Lunsing, Wim, and Claire Maree. 2004. Shifting speakers. In *Japanese Language, Gender, and Ideology: Cultural Models and Real People*, ed. Shigeko Okamoto and Janet S. Shibamoto Smith, 92–109. New York: Oxford University Press.

Madrigal, Alexis C. 2014. The first emoticon may have appeared in ... 1648. *Atlantic*, April. http://www.theatlantic.com/technology/archive/2014/04/the-first-emoticon-may-have-appeared-in-1648/360622.

Malinowsky, Bronisław. 1923. The problem of meaning in primitive languages. In *The Meaning of Meaning: A Study of the Influence of Language upon Thought and the Science of Symbolism*, ed. Charles K. Ogden and Ian A. Richards, 146–152. London: Routledge.

Mao, LuMing. 1992. Invitational discourse and Chinese identity. *Journal of Asian Pacific Communication* 3 (1): 70–96.

Maree, Claire. 2008. Grrrl-queens: One-kotoba and the negotiation of heterosexist gender language norms and lesbo (homo) phobic stereotypes in Japan. In *AsiaPacifiQUEER: Rethinking Genders and Sexualities*, ed. Fran Martin, Peter A. Jackson, Mark McLelland, and Audrey Yue, 67–84. Champaign: University of Illinois Press.

Markkanen, Raija, and Hartmut Schröder. 1997. Hedging: A challenge for pragmatics and discourse analysis. In *Hedging and Discourse: Approaches to the Analysis of a Pragmatic Phenomenon in Academic Texts*, ed. Raija Markkanen and Hartmut Schröder, 3–18. Berlin: Walter de Gruyter.

Martin, Jeanette S., and Lillian H. Chaney. 2012. *Global Business Etiquette: A Guide to International Communication and Customs*. 2nd ed. Santa Barbara, CA: Praeger.

Matsumoto, David. 2006. Culture and nonverbal behavior. In *The Sage Handbook of Nonverbal Communication*, ed. Valerie Manusov and Miles L. Patterson, 219–235. Thousand Oaks, CA: Sage.

Maynard, Senko K. 1990. Conversation management in contrast: Listener response in Japanese and American English. *Journal of Pragmatics* 14 (3): 397–412.

McCurry, Justin. 2009. Obama's critics should be bowing their heads. *Guardian*, November 18. https://www.theguardian.com/world/blog/2009/nov/18/obama-japan-bow.

McWhorter, John H. 2014. *The Language Hoax: Why the World Looks the Same in Any Language*. Oxford: Oxford University Press.

Mehdipour, Samaneh, Zohreh Eslami, and Hamid Allami. 2015. A comparative sociopragmatic analysis of wedding invitations in American and Iranian societies and teaching implications. *Applied Research on English Language* 4 (8): 62–77.

Merkin, Rebecca S. 2006. Uncertainty avoidance and facework: A test of the Hofstede model. *International Journal of Intercultural Relations* 30 (2): 213–228.

Mey, Jacob L. 2001. *Pragmatics: An Introduction*. 2nd ed. Oxford: Blackwell.

Minear, Richard H. 1999. *Dr. Seuss Goes to War: The World War II Editorial Cartoons of Theodore Seuss Geisel*. New York: New Press.

Mizutani, Nobuko. 1982. The listener's responses in Japanese conversation. *Sociolinguistics* 13 (1): 33–38.

Mohr, Melissa. 2013. *Holy Sh*t: A Brief History of Swearing*. Oxford: Oxford University Press.

Morrison, Terri, and Wayne A. Conaway. 2006. *Kiss, Bow or Shake Hands*. 2nd ed. Avon, MA: Adams Media.

Moss, Simon, and Ronald Francis. 2007. *The Science of Management: Fighting Fads and Fallacies with Evidence-Based Practice*. Samford Valley, Queensland: Australian Academic Press.

Murata, Kumiko. 1994. Intrusive or co-operative? A cross-cultural study of interruption. *Journal of Pragmatics* 21 (4): 385–400.

Murphy, Beth, and Joyce Neu. 1995. My grade's too low: The speech act set of complaining. In *Speech Acts across Cultures: Challenges to Communication in a Second Language*, ed. Susan M. Gass and Joyce Neu, 191–216. Berlin: Mouton de Gruyter.

Murphy, Margaret, and Mike Levy. 2006. Politeness in intercultural email communication: Australian and Korean perspectives. *Journal of Intercultural Communication* 12.

Nakhle, Mahboube, Mohammad Naghavi, and Abdullah Razavi. 2014. Complaint behaviors among native speakers of Canadian English, Iranian EFL learners, and native speakers of Persian (contrastive pragmatic study). *Procedia: Social and Behavioral Sciences* 98:1316–1324.

NASA. 2004. *The Flight of Apollo-Soyuz.* http://history.nasa.gov/apollo/apsoyhist.html.

National Transportation Safety Board. 2000. Group Chairman's Factual Report, January 18. https://www.ntsb.gov/investigations/AccidentReports/Reports/AAB0201.pdf.

Nelson, Michelle R., and Cele C. Otnes. 2005. Exploring cross-cultural ambivalence: A netnography of intercultural wedding message boards. *Journal of Business Research* 58 (1): 89–95.

Nevo, Ofra, Baruch Nevo, and Janie Leong Siew Yin. 2001. Singaporean humor: A cross-cultural, cross-gender comparison. *Journal of General Psychology* 128 (2): 143–156.

Nguyen, Thi Minh. 2006. Cross-cultural pragmatics: Refusals of requests by Australian native speakers of English and Vietnamese learners of English. Master's thesis, University of Queensland, Brisbane, Australia.

Occidental College. 2013. Banned books: Shakespeare censored! Occidental College Special Collections and College Archives. http://sites.oxy.edu/special-collections/bannedbooks/censoredworks.htm.

Oetzel, John, Stella Ting-Toomey, Tomoko Masumoto, Yumiko Yokochi, Xiaohui Pan, Jiro Takai, and Richard Wilcox. 2001. Face and facework in conflict: A cross-cultural comparison of China, Germany, Japan, and the United States. *Communication Monographs* 68 (3): 235–258.

Ohlheiser, Abby. 2014. A not-so-brief list of all the things President Obama has bowed to. *Wire*, April 24. http://www.thewire.com/politics/2014/04/a-not-so-brief-list-of-all-the-things-president-obama-has-bowed-to/361160.

Oshima, Kimie. 2013. An examination for styles of Japanese humor: Japan's funniest story projects, 2010 to 2011. *Intercultural Studies* 22 (2): 91–109.

Osland, Joyce S., and Allan Bird. 2000. Beyond sophisticated stereotyping: Cultural sensemaking in context. *Academy of Management Executive* 14 (1): 65–77.

Osmand, Alex. 2016. *Academic Writing and Grammar for Students*. 2nd ed. Thousand Oaks, CA: Sage.

Park, Insook H., and Lee-Jay Cho. 1995. Confucianism and the Korean Family. *Journal of Comparative Family Studies* 26 (1): 117–134.

Park, Jaram, Vladimir Barash, Clay Fink, and Cha Meeyoung Cha. 2013. Emoticon style: Interpreting differences in emoticons across cultures. In *Proceedings of the Seventh International AAAI Conference on Weblogs and Social Media*, 466–475. Palo Alto, CA: AAAI Press.

Pavlidou, Theodossia. 1994. Contrasting German-Greek politeness and the consequences. *Journal of Pragmatics* 21 (5): 487–511.

Pavlidou, Theodossia-Soula. 2000. Telephone conversations in Greek and German: Attending to the relationship aspect of communication. In *Culturally Speaking: Managing Rapport through Talk across Cultures*, ed. Helen Spencer-Oatley, 121–140. London: Continuum.

Paxton, Norbert. 2011. *The Rough Guide to Korea*. 2nd ed. London: Rough Guides.

Pepitone, Juliane. 2010. FCC indecency ban struck down. *CNN Money*, July 13. http://money.cnn.com/2010/07/13/news/economy/fcc_indecency/?iref=NS1.

Peregoy, William. n.d. As a beginner in Japanese, don't worry about the formality. *Fluent in 3 Months*. http://www.fluentin3months.com/formal-japanese.

Phillips, Whitney. 2015. *This Is Why We Can't Have Nice Things: Mapping the Relationship between Online Trolling and Mainstream Culture*. Cambridge, MA: MIT Press.

Plancencia, María E. 1997. Opening up closings—the Ecuadorian way. *Text* 17 (1): 53–81.

Placencia, María E. 2005. Pragmatic variation in corner store interactions in Quito and Madrid. *Hispania* 88 (3): 583–598.

Pomerantz, Anita. 1978. Compliment responses: Notes on the cooperation of multiple constraints. In *Studies in the Organization of Conversational Interaction*, ed. Jim Schenkein, 79–112. New York: Academic Press.

Poplack, Shana. 1987. Contrasting patterns of code-switching in two communities. In *Aspects of Multilingualism*, ed. Erling Wande, 51–77. Uppsala: Borgströms.

Powelson, John P. 1972. *The Institutions of Economic Growth: A Theory of Conflict Management in Developing Countries*. Princeton, NJ: Princeton University Press.

Rababa'h, Mahmoud A., and Nibal A. A. Malkawi. 2012. The linguistic etiquette of greeting and leave-taking in Jordanian Arabic. *European Scientific Journal* 8 (18): 14–28.

Rakowicz, Agnieszka. 2009. Ambiguous invitations: The interlanguage of pragmatics of Polish English language learners. Doctoral diss., New York University, New York.

Rezanejad, Atefeh, Zahra Lari, and Zahra Mosalli. 2015. A cross-cultural analysis of the use of hedging devices in scientific research articles. *Journal of Language Teaching and Research* 6 (6): 1384–1392.

Rhee, Seongha. 2004. From discourse to grammar: Grammaticalization and lexicalization of rhetorical questions in Korean. In *LACUS Forum 30:*

Language, Thought and Reality, ed. Gordon D. Fulton, William J. Sullivan, and Arle R. Lommel, 413–423. Houston, TX: Linguistic Association of Canada and the United States.

Riordan, Monica A., and Lauren A. Trichtinger. 2017. Overconfidence at the keyboard: Confidence and accuracy in interpreting affect in e-mail exchanges. *Human Communication Research* 43 (1): 1–24.

Roberts, Richard M., and Roger J. Kreuz. 1994. Why do people use figurative language? *Psychological Science* 5 (3): 159–163.

Roberts, Richard, and Roger Kreuz. 2015. *Becoming Fluent: How Cognitive Science Can Help Adults Learn a Foreign Language*. Cambridge, MA: MIT Press.

Romm, Cari. 2015. The life and death of Martha's Vineyard sign language. *Atlantic*, September 25. http://www.theatlantic.com/health/archive/2015/09/marthas-vineyard-sign-language-asl/407191.

Roskos-Ewoldsen, David R. 2003. What is the role of rhetorical questions in persuasion? In *Communication and Emotion: Essays in Honor of Dolf Zillmann*, ed. Jennings Bryant, David Roskos-Ewoldsen, and Joanne Cantor, 297–321. Mahwah, NJ: Erlbaum.

Rovzar, Chris April. 2009. Michelle Obama partially embraces Queen, Brits go a bit mad. *New York Magazine*. http://nymag.com/daily/intelligencer/2009/04/michelle_obama_partially_embra.html.

Royal Post. 2015. Some royal curtsey etiquette. May 16. http://theroyalpost.com/2015/05/16/some-royal-curtsy-etiquette.

Ruch, Willibald, and Giovannantonio Forabosco. 1996. A cross-cultural study of humor appreciation: Italy and Germany. *Humor: International Journal of Humor Research* 9 (1): 1–18.

Rudwick, Stephanie. 2010. "Gay and Zulu, we speak isiNgqumo": Ethnolinguistic identity constructions. *Transformation: Critical Perspectives on Southern Africa* 74 (1): 112–134.

Rudwick, Stephanie, and Mduduzi Ntuli. 2008. IsiNgqumo: Introducing a gay black South African linguistic variety. *Southern African Linguistics and Applied Language Studies* 26 (4): 445–456.

Ryoo, Hye-Kyung. 2005. Achieving friendly interactions: A study of service encounters between Korean shopkeepers and African-American customers. *Discourse and Society* 16 (1): 79–105.

Saito, Hidetoshi, and Masako Beecken. 1997. An approach to instruction of pragmatic aspects: Implications of pragmatic transfer by American learners of Japanese. *Modern Language Journal* 81 (3): 363–377.

Sato, Yoichi. 2010. "Kuki ga Yomenai": Situated face-threatening act within Japanese social interaction. *Novitas-ROYAL (Research on Youth and Language)* 4 (2): 173–181.

Schaffer, Deborah. 2005. Can rhetorical questions function as retorts? Is the Pope Catholic? *Journal of Pragmatics* 37 (4): 433–460.

Schauer, Gila A. 2006. Pragmatic awareness in ESL and EFL contexts: Contrast and development. *Language Learning* 56 (2): 269–318.

Schegloff, Emanuel A., and Harvey Sacks. 1973. Opening up closings. *Semiotica* 8 (4): 289–327.

Schlenker, Barry R., and Bruce W. Darby. 1981. The use of apologies in social predicaments. *Social Psychology Quarterly* 44 (3): 271–278.

Schonfeld, Zach. 2015. Does the parental advisory label still matter? *Newsweek*, November 10. http://www.newsweek.com/does-parental -advisory-label-still-matter-tipper-gore-375607.

Schultz, Duane P., and Sydney E. Schultz. 2016. *A History of Modern Psychology*. 11th ed. Boston: Cengage Learning.

Scotton, Carol M., and William Ury. 1977. Bilingual strategies: The social functions of code-switching. *Linguistics: An Interdisciplinary Journal of the Language Sciences* 15 (193): 5–20.

Searle, John R. 1975. A taxonomy of illocutionary acts. In *Language, Mind, and Knowledge*, vol. 7, ed. Keith Günderson, 344–369. Minneapolis: University of Minnesota Press.

Shardakova, Maria. 2005. Intercultural pragmatics in the speech of American L2 learners of Russian: Apologies offered by Americans in Russian. *Intercultural Pragmatics* 2 (4): 423–451.

Shiffrin, Deborah. 1977. Opening encounters. *American Sociological Review* 42 (5): 679–691.

Shim, Theresa Youn-ja, Min-Sun Kim, and Judith N. Martin. 2008. *Changing Korea: Understanding Culture and Communication*, vol. 10. New York: Peter Lang.

Sieck, Winston R., Jennifer L. Smith, and Louise J. Rasmussen. 2013. Metacognitive strategies for making sense of cross-cultural encounters. *Journal of Cross-Cultural Psychology* 44 (6): 1007–1023.

Simon, Stephanie. 1999. Michigan man swears by his right to use profanity. *Los Angeles Times*, January 25. http://articles.latimes.com/1999/jan/25/news/mn-1502.

Snyder, Mark. 1974. Self-monitoring of expressive behavior. *Journal of Personality and Social Psychology* 30 (4): 526–537.

Sorjonen, Marja-Leena. 2001. *Responding in Conversation: A Study of Response Particles in Finnish*. Amsterdam: John Benjamins.

St. Amant, Kirk. 2002. When cultures and computers collide: Rethinking computer-mediated communication according to international and intercultural communication expectations. *Journal of Business and Technical Communication* 16 (2): 196–214.

Stafford, Thomas P., and Michael Cassutt. 2002. *We Have Capture: Tom Stafford and the Space Race*. Washington, DC: Smithsonian Books.

Stapleton, Karyn. 2010. Swearing. In *Interpersonal Pragmatics*, ed. Miriam A. Locher and Sage L. Graham, 289–305. Berlin: Mouton De Gruyter.

Sugimoto, Naomi. 1997. A Japanese–U.S. comparison of apology styles. *Communication Research* 24 (4): 349–369.

Sugimoto, Taku, and James A. Levin. 2000. Multiple literacies and multimedia: A comparison of Japanese and American uses of the Internet.

In *Global Literacies and the World-Wide Web*, ed. Gail E. Hawisher and Cynthia L. Self, 133–153. London: Routledge.

Swigart, Leigh. 1992. Two codes or one? The insiders' view and the description of codeswitching in Dakar. In *Codeswitching*, ed. Carol Eastman, 83–102. Clevedon, UK: Multilingual Matters.

Swinbourne, Charlie. 2013. Exclusive: "Fake" sign language interpreter mars Nelson Mandela service for Deaf people worldwide. *Limping Chicken*, December 10. http://limpingchicken.com/2013/12/10/fake-interpreter-mandela.

Tadmor, Carmit T., Adam D. Galinsky, and William W. Maddux. 2012. Getting the most out of living abroad: Biculturalism and integrative complexity as key drivers of creative and professional success. *Journal of Personality and Social Psychology* 103 (3): 520–542.

Tai, Eiko. 1986. Modification of the Western approach to intercultural communication for the Japanese context. Master's thesis, Portland State University, Portland, OR.

Tanaka, Noriko. 1991. An investigation of apology: Japanese in comparison with Australian. *Meikai Journal* 4:35–53.

Tanck, Sharyl. 2002. Speech act sets of refusal and complaint: A comparison of native and non-native English speakers' production. Unpublished MS, American University, Washington, DC.

Tang, Chen-Hsin, and Grace Qiao Zhang. 2009. A contrastive study of compliment responses among Australian English and Mandarin Chinese speakers. *Journal of Pragmatics* 41 (2): 325–345.

Tannen, Deborah. 1991. *You Just Don't Understand: Women and Men in Conversation*. New York: Ballantine Books.

Taylor, Heather. 2007. Polari: A sociohistorical study of the life and decline of a secret language. Doctoral diss., University of Manchester.

Topping, Alexandra. 2013. Sign language interpreter at Mandela memorial accused of being a fake. *Guardian*, December 11. https://www

.theguardian.com/society/2013/dec/11/mandela-memorial-sign -language-interpreter-making-it-up-fake.

Trask, Robert L. 1993. *A Dictionary of Grammatical Terms in Linguistics*. London: Routledge.

Triandis, Harry. 1988. Collectivism v. individualism: A reconceptualisation of a basic concept in cross-cultural social psychology. In *Cross-Cultural Studies of Personality, Attitudes and Cognition*, ed. Gajendra K. Verma and Christopher Bagley, 60–95. New York: St. Martin's Press.

Turner, Daniel D. 2010. Comments gone wild: Trolls, flames, and the crisis at online newspapers. http://static1.squarespace.com/static/ 5133ffdde4b0c6fb04ddab8f/t/5217da16e4b000bbb34b75d2/ 1377294870640/CrisisInCommenting.pdf.

Turner, Tammara Combs, Marc A. Smith, Danyel Fisher, and Howard T. Welser. 2005. Picturing Usenet: Mapping computer-mediated collective action. *Journal of Computer-Mediated Communication* 10 (4).

Ulijn, Jan M., and Xiangling Li. 1995. Is interrupting impolite? Some temporal aspects of turn-taking in Chinese-Western and other intercultural business encounters. *Text* 15 (4): 589–627.

Uysal, Hacer H. 2012. Argumentation across L1 and L2 writing: Exploring cultural influences and transfer issues. *Vigo International Journal of Applied Linguistics* 9:133–159.

Uysal, Hacer H. 2014. A cross-cultural study of indirectness and hedging in the conference proposals of English NS and NNS Scholars. In *Occupying Niches: Interculturality, Cross-Culturality and Aculturality in Academic Research*, ed. Andrzej Łyda and Krystyna Warchał, 179–195. Cham, Switzerland: Springer International.

Vanci-Osam, Ülker. 1998. May you be shot with greasy bullets: Curse utterances in Turkish. *Asian Folklore Studies* 57 (1): 71–86.

Vázquez, Ignacio, and Diana Giner. 2009. Writing with conviction: The use of boosters in modelling persuasion in academic discourses. *Revista Alicantina de Estudios Ingleses* 22:219–237.

Vinci, James. 2012. U.S. Supreme Court rules against FCC on nudity and swear words on TV. *National Post*, June 21. http://news.nationalpost .com/news/u-s-supreme-court-rules-against-fcc-on-nudity-and-swear -words-on-tv.

Vonk, Roos. 2002. Self-serving interpretations of flattery: Why ingratiation works. *Journal of Personality and Social Psychology* 82 (4): 515–526.

Waldman, Katy. 2015. This year's word of the year isn't even a word. http://www.slate.com/blogs/lexicon_valley/2015/11/16/the_face_with _tears_of_joy_emoji_is_the_word_of_the_year_says_oxford_dictionaries .html.

Walther, Joseph B., and Kyle P. D'Addario. 2001. The impacts of emoticons on message interpretation in computer-mediated communication. *Social Science Computer Review* 19 (3): 324–347.

Walton, Marsha D. 1998. Ostensible lies and the negotiation of shared meanings. *Discourse Processes* 26 (1): 27–41.

Wang, Hui. 2014. A study on the politeness of the speech act of ostensible refusal. *Journal of Mianyang Normal University* 33 (7): 95–98.

Wannaruk, Anchalee. 2008. Pragmatic transfer in Thai EFL refusals. *RELC Journal* 39 (3): 318–337.

Washington Times. 2009. Barack takes a bow. April 7. http://www .washingtontimes.com/news/2009/apr/7/barack-takes-a-bow.

Wei, Li. 2005. How can you tell? Toward a common sense explanation of conversational code-switching. *Journal of Pragmatics* 37 (3): 375–389.

White, Ron. 1997. Back channeling, repair, pausing, and private speech. *Applied Linguistics* 18 (3): 314–344.

White, Sheida. 1989. Backchannels across cultures: A study of Americans and Japanese. *Language in Society* 18 (1): 59–76.

Wierzbicka, Anna. 2003. *Cross-Cultural Pragmatics: The Semantics of Human Interaction*. Berlin: Mouton de Gruyter.

Wilcox, Sherman. 1991. ASL as a foreign language fact sheet. http://www.unm.edu/~wilcox/UNM/facts.html.

Wiseman, Richard. 2002. *Laughlab: The Scientific Search for the World's Funniest Joke*. New York: Random House.

Woll, Benice, Rachel Sutton-Spence, and Frances Elton. 2004. Multilingualism: The global approach to sign languages. In *The Sociolinguistics of Sign Languages*, ed. Ceil Lucas, 8–32. Cambridge: Cambridge University Press.

Wong, Alia. 2015. De-stigmatizing Hawaii's Creole language. *Atlantic*, November 20. http://www.theatlantic.com/education/archive/2015/11/hawaiian-pidgin-recognized/416883.

Woodbridge, Linda. 2003. Jest books, the literature of roguery, and the vagrant poor in Renaissance England. *English Literary Renaissance* 33 (2): 201–210.

World Federation of the Deaf. n.d. Deaf culture. https://wfdeaf.org/our-work/focus-areas/deaf-culture.

Wozniak, Audrey M. 2015. River-crabbed shitizens and missing knives: A sociolinguistic analysis of trends in Chinese language use online as a result of censorship. *Applied Linguistics Review* 6 (1): 97–120.

Wren, Christopher. 1990. The crash of EgyptAir: The statement; Arabic speakers dispute inquiry's interpretation of pilot's words. *New York Times*, November 18. http://www.nytimes.com/1999/11/18/us/crash-egyptair-statement-arabic-speakers-dispute-inquiry-s-interpretation-pilot.html.

Würtz, Elizabeth. 2005. A cross-cultural analysis of websites from high-context cultures and low-context cultures. *Journal of Computer-Mediated Communication* 11 (1): 13.

Yankova, Diana, and Irena Vassileva. 2013. Functions and mechanisms of code-switching in Bulgarian Canadians . *Études Canadiennes/Canadian Studies: Revue Interdisciplinaire des Études Canadiennes en France* 74: 103–121.

Yasgur, Batya S. 2013. Malpractice: Should you say "I'm sorry"? Medscape Business of Medicine, September 4. http://www.medscape.com/viewarticle/809560.

Yngve, Victor. 1970. On getting a word in edgewise. In *Papers from the Sixth Regional Meeting, Chicago Linguistic Society*, ed. M. A. Campbell, 567–578. Chicago: Chicago Linguistic Society.

Yoon, Kyung-Joo. 2004. Not just words: Korean social models and the use of honorifics. *Intercultural Pragmatics* 1 (2): 189–210.

Yule, George. 1996. *Pragmatics*. Oxford: Oxford University Press.

Zaentz, Saul (producer), and Miloš Forman (director). 1984. *Amadeus*. New York: HBO Video.

Žegarac, Vladimir, and Martha C. Pennington. 2004. Pragmatic transfer in intercultural communication. In *Culturally Speaking: Managing Rapport through Talk across Cultures*, ed. Helen Spencer-Oatey, 165–190. London: Continuum.

Zimmerman, R. 2004. Doctors' new tool to fight lawsuits: Saying "I'm sorry." *Wall Street Journal*, May 18. http://www.wsj.com/articles/SB108482777884713711.

Index